Richard Hurd

An Introduction to the Study of the Prophecies Concerning the Christian Church

Richard Hurd

An Introduction to the Study of the Prophecies Concerning the Christian Church

ISBN/EAN: 9783337104702

Printed in Europe, USA, Canada, Australia, Japan

Cover: Foto ©Lupo / pixelio.de

More available books at **www.hansebooks.com**

AN

INTRODUCTION

TO THE STUDY OF THE

PROPHECIES

Concerning the CHRISTIAN CHURCH;

AND, IN PARTICULAR,

Concerning the Church of PAPAL ROME:

IN TWELVE SERMONS,

PREACHED IN LINCOLN'S-INN-CHAPEL,

AT THE LECTURE OF

The Right Reverend WILLIAM WARBURTON
Lord Biſhop of GLOUCESTER.

By RICHARD HURD, D.D.
Preacher to the Honourable Society of LINCOLN's-INN.

Ita, ſi potuero, ſtylo moderabor meo, ut nec ea, quæ ſuper-
ſint, dicam, nec ea, quæ ſatis ſint, prætermittam.
Auguſtin. C. D. l. xvii. c. 1.

LONDON,
PRINTED BY W. BOWYER AND J. NICHOLS:
FOR T. CADELL, IN THE STRAND.
MDCCLXXII.

TO THE RIGHT HONOURABLE

WILLIAM, LORD MANSFIELD,

LORD CHIEF JUSTICE OF ENGLAND,

AND

TO THE RIGHT HONOURABLE

SIR JOHN EARDLY WILMOT, KNT.

LATE LORD CHIEF JUSTICE OF THE

COMMON PLEAS,

TRUSTEES FOR THIS LECTURE,

THE FOLLOWING SERMONS

ARE MOST HUMBLY INSCRIBED

BY THE AUTHOR,

R. HURD.

LINCOLN'S-INN,
MARCH 2, 1772.

EXTRACT from the Deed of Truft for founding this Lecture.

AN Indenture, bearing date July 21, 1768, fets forth, " That the right
" reverend WILLIAM Lord Bifhop of
" Gloucefter has transferred the fum of
" 500 l. *Bank four per cent. annuities confoli-*
" *dated,* to the right honourable WILLIAM
" LORD MANSFIELD, Lord Chief Juftice
" of his Majefty's Court of King's Bench,
" the right honourable SIR JOHN EARDLY
" WILMOT, Lord Chief Juftice of his
" Majefty's Court of Common Pleas, and

A 4   " the

Extract from the DEED *of* TRUST,

" the honourable CHARLES YORKE[a], of
" Lincoln's-Inn, in the county of Middle-
" fex, UPON TRUST, for the purpofe of
" founding a *Lecture*, in the form of a
" Sermon, *To prove the truth of revealed*
" *Religion, in general, and of the Chriftian*
" *in particular, from the completion of the*
" *prophecies in the Old and New Teftament,*
" *which relate to the Chriftian church, efpe-*
" *cially to the apoftacy of Papal Rome :* That,
" in cafe of any vacancy in this truft by
" the deceafe of any one or more of the
" above-mentioned Truftees, *the place or*
" *places fhall be filled up, from time to time*

---

[a] This noble and eminent perfon was the fecond fon
of the Lord Chancellor Hardwicke. He had been, for
many years, in the firft reputation at the Bar; and,
having paffed through the offices of Sollicitor and
Attorney General, was, himfelf, made Lord Chancellor
in January 1770, but died foon after his appointment
to that high dignity—*Luctuofum hoc fuis; acerbum pa-
triæ; grave bonis omnibus.* CIC.

" *and*

" *and as occasion may require, by the surviv-*
" *ing Trustees, or Trustee, or by the Executors*
" *of the survivor of them:* That the
" Trustees *shall appoint the Preacher of*
" *Lincoln's-Inn for the time being, or some*
" *other able Divine of the Church of*
" *England,* to preach this Lecture: That
" the Lecture shall be preached every year
" *in the Chapel of Lincoln's-Inn (if the society*
" *give leave* [b]*) and on the following days, viz.*
" *the first Sunday after Michaelmas Term,*
" *the Sunday next before and the Sunday next*
" *after Hilary Term:* That the Lecturer
" shall not preach the said Lecture longer
" than *for the term of* FOUR YEARS, *and shall*
" *not again be nominated to preach the same:*
" And, when the term of four years is
" expired, that the said Lecturer shall *print*

---

[b] The Society *have* given leave that this Lecture be
preached in their Chapel, and on the days specified.

" *and*

Extract from the DEED of TRUST, &c.

" and publish, or cause to be printed and pub-
" lished, all the Sermons or Lectures, that
" shall have been so preached by him."

CON-

CONTENTS.

SER-

SER-

CONTENTS.

SER-

SER-

S E R M O N XII.

Rev. xxii. 7.

Behold, I come quickly: bleſſed is he that keepeth the ſayings of the prophecy of this book.   p. 404—437.

S E R-

SERMON I.

Falſe Ideas of PROPHECY.

2 PETER, i. 21.

Prophecy came not in old time by the will of man: but holy men of God ſpake, as they were moved by the Spirit of God.

THE argument from prophecy, in ſupport of the Chriſtian revelation, would be thought more concluſive, at leaſt would be more diſtinctly apprehended, if men could be kept from mixing their own prejudices and preconceptions with it.

The general queſtion may be expreſſed thus—" Whether the predictions in the " Old and New Teſtament do not appear " to have been ſo far, and in ſuch ſenſe,

B " fulfilled,

—— " fulfilled, as to afford a reaſonable con-
" viction, that they *came not*, as the text
" ſpeaks, *by the will of man, but from the*
" *Spirit of God.*"

In examining this queſtion, the predictions themſelves cannot be too diligently
ſtudied, or too cautiouſly applied: But,
while this work is carrying on, we are ſtill
to ſuppoſe, and ſhould not for a moment
forget, that they *may* be, what they mani-
feſtly claim to be, of divine ſuggeſtion; I
mean, we are to admit, not the truth indeed, but the poſſibility, of ſuch ſuggeſtion, till we can fairly make it appear that
they are of human contrivance, only.

It will not be denied, that the tenour of
Scripture, as well as the text, clearly aſſerts
the divine original and direction of the prophecies. A juſt reaſoner on the ſubject
will, therefore, proceed on this ſuppoſition, and only try whether it be well founded. He will conſider, whether the conſtruction of the prophecies, and the application of them, be ſuch, as may accord

to

to thoſe pretenſions; and will not argue
againſt them on other principles, which
they do not admit, or ſuppoſe. All this
is plainly nothing more than what may be
expected from a fair inquirer, and what the
rules of good reaſoning exact from him.

The uſe of this conduct would be, To
prevent, or ſet aſide, all thoſe fancies and
imaginations which too frequently miſlead
inquirers into the evidence of prophecy;
which fill their minds with needleſs perplexities, and diſgrace their books with
frivolous and impertinent diſquiſitions.
And, becauſe I take it to be of principal
moment, that this *uſe* be perfectly ſeen and
underſtood, I ſhall, *firſt*, apply myſelf to
juſtify and explain it.

It is true that *prophecy*, in the very idea
of that term, at leaſt in the ſcriptural idea
of it, implies the divine agency; and that,
exerted not merely in giving the faculty
itſelf, but in directing all its operations.

Yet I know not how it is that, when
men addreſs themſelves to the ſtudy of the

prophetic

prophetic ſcriptures, they are apt to let this ſo neceſſary idea ſlip out of their minds; and to diſcourſe upon them juſt as they would or might do, on the ſuppoſition that the prophet was left at liberty to diſpenſe this gift in all reſpects, as he ſhould think proper. No wonder then, that they ſhould miſconceive of its character, and entertain very different notions about the exerciſe of this power from what the Scriptures give them of it. Nay it is no wonder that they ſhould even treat the ſubject with ſome ſcorn, while they judge of it by the rule of human prudence, and not of divine wiſdom: for, though they would readily own themſelves incapable of pronouncing on the ſecret counſels of God, if prophecy, in its whole adminiſtration, be regarded as proceeding merely from him; yet, from their knowledge of human nature, they would think, and with ſome reaſon, they were well able to conceive how the ſpirit of prophecy would be adminiſtered, if man had the diſpoſal of this ſpirit committed to him.

Now

Now it happens, as I ſaid, (by an inex-
cuſable perverſeneſs, or inattention, indeed,
yet in fact it ſo happens) that, to the conſideration of the argument from prophecy,
as applied to the proof of the Chriſtian religion, many inquirers bring with them
this ſtrange and fatal prejudice; and then
their reaſonings, or rather conjectures, on
the SUBJECT, the END, and the DISPEN-
SATION of prophecy, are only ſuch, as
this prejudice may be expected to inſpire.

I. Judging for ourſelves, and by the
light of human inveſtigation only, there
might be ſome ground for ſuppoſing, that,
if it ſhould pleaſe God at any time to con-
fer the gift of prophecy on his favoured
ſervants, they would be ſolely or chiefly
commiſſioned to unfold the future fortunes
of the moſt conſpicuous ſtates and kingdoms in the world : that ſo divine a power
would embrace, as its peculiar object, the
counſels and enterprizes, the ſucceſſes and
triumphs of the moſt illuſtrious nations;
thoſe eſpecially, which ſhould riſe to the

ſummit

SERM.
I.
_____

ſummit of empire by generous plans of policy, and by the efforts of public virtue; of *free ſtates,* in a word, ſuch as we know to have flouriſhed in the happier ages of Greece, and ſuch as we ſtill contemplate with admiration in the vaſt and awful fabric of Conſular Rome. This we might think a fit object for the prophetic ſpirit to preſent to us; as correſponding in ſome degree to the ſublime character of a prophet; and as moſt worthy, in our conceptions, of the divine attention and regard.

But how are we ſurprized to find that this aſtoniſhing power, the moſt ſignal gift of heaven to mankind, hath, in its immediate application at leaſt, reſpected, many times, obſcure individuals, whoſe names and memory are only preſerved in one barbarous chronicle, hath been chiefly employed, and, as we are ready to expreſs it, thrown away on one ſingle ſtate, or rather family; inconſiderable in the extent of its power or territory; ſequeſtered from the reſt of the nations, and hardly known

among

among them[a]; with ſome mention, perhaps, of greater things, but incidentally
touched, as it may ſeem, and as they
chanced to have ſome connection with the
intereſts of this ſordid people!

Was this a ſtage, on which it might be
expected that the God of heaven would
condeſcend to diſplay the wonders of his
preſcience; when He kept aloof, as it were,
from more auguſt theatres, and would
ſcarcely vouchſafe to have the ſkirts of his
glory ſeen by the nobler and more dif-
tinguiſhed nations of the world?

---

[a] Thus Celſus repreſents the Jews—μηδὲν πώποτε
ἀξιόλογον πράξανίας, ὔτ᾽ ἐν λόγῳ, ὔθ᾽ ἐν ἀριθμῷ αὐτὸς ποτε
γεγενημένες. ORIG. contra CELS. *l.* iv. *p.* 181. *ed. Spenc.*
Cantab. 1677. And in *p.* 175, he repreſents it as the
higheſt abſurdity in ſuch *reptiles* to pretend that their
inſignificant concerns were the objects of divine prediction, and that the ſupreme Governor of the world,
who had ſo many greater things upon his hands, ſhould
be only ſolicitous, as it were, to keep up a perpetual
intercourſe with them. See the whole paſſage, which
the philoſopher ſeems to have taken a pleaſure to work
up with much oratorical amplification.—Julian, too,
was much pleaſed with this fooliſh objection,

B 4   Such

SERM.
I.

Such queſtions as theſe are ſometimes aſked. But they are ſurely aſked by thoſe, who conſider the prophets, as acting wholly on human views and motives; and not as over-ruled in all their predictions by *the ſpirit of God.* For it is natural enough for vain man, if left to himſelf in the exerciſe of the prophetic power, to turn his view towards ſuch objects as appear to him great, in preference to others; and to eſtimate that greatneſs by the luſtre of fame, in which they ſhine out to the obſervation of mankind. But a moment's reflection may ſhew the probability, the poſſibility at leaſt, that *God's thoughts are not as our thoughts;* and that, if the prophet's foreſight be under the divine influence, there may be reaſon enough to direct it towards ſuch ſcenes and objects, as we might be apt to under-value or overlook. It is even very conceivable, that, if God be the diſpenſer of prophecy, and not man, all that ſeems great and illuſtrious in human affairs may to his all-judging eye appear ſmall and ✗ contempt-

With Him no high, no low, no great, no ſmall

Pope.

contemptible[b]; and, on the other hand, what we account as nothing, may, for infinite reafons, unknown to us, but fo far as he is pleafed to difcover them, be of that importance as to merit the attention of all his prophets from the foundation of the world.

It is evident, then, that to reafon in this manner on the fubject of divine prophecy, is to fuffer ourfelves to be mifled by a poor and vulgar prejudice; and to forget, what we fhould ever have prefent to us, the claim of God's prophets to fpeak, not as themfelves *will*, but as they are *moved by his Spirit.*

II. The END, or ultimate purpofe of prophetic illumination, is another point, on which many perfons are apt to entertain ftrange fancies, and to frame unwarrantable conclufions, when they give themfelves leave to argue on the low fuppofition, before mentioned.

---

[b] *Behold, the nations are as a drop of a bucket, and are counted as the duft of the balance.* Ifaiah xl. 15.

I. It

1. It is then haſtily ſurmized that the ſcriptural prophecies, if any ſuch be acknowledged, could only be deſigned, like the Pagan oracles, to ſooth the impatient mind under its anxiety about future events; to ſignify beforehand to ſtates or individuals, engaged in high or hazardous undertakings, what the iſſue of them would be, that ſo they might ſuit their conduct to the information of the prophet, and either purſue their purpoſe with vigour, or expect their impending fate with reſignation. For, what other or worthier end, will ſome ſay, can heaven propoſe to itſelf by theſe extraordinary communications, than to prepare and qualify ſuch events as it decrees to bring to paſs; to animate deſponding virtue, on the one hand, or to relieve predeſtined miſery, on the other; to adapt itſelf, in ſhort, to our neceſſities by a clear diſcovery of its will in thoſe many intricate ſituations, which perplex human prudence, elude human foreſight, and, but for this previous admonition, would bear

too

too hard on the natural force, or infirmi-ty of the human mind? Some ſuch idea, as this, was plainly entertained by thoſe of the Pagan philoſophers who concluded, *from the exiſtence of a divine power, that there muſt needs be ſuch a thing as divination* [c]. They thought the attributes of their gods, if any ſuch there were, concerned in giv-ing ſome notice of futurity to mankind.

2. Others, again, encouraged in this conjectural ingenuity by partial views of ſcripture, come to perſuade themſelves that prophecy is an act of *ſpecial grace and favour*, not to this or that ſtate, or indivi-duals, indiſcriminately, as either may ſeem to ſtand in need of it; but to one peculiar and choſen people, who, on ſome account or other, had merited this extraordinary diſtinction.

Self-love ſeems to have ſuggeſted this idea to the antient and modern Jews; and many others, I doubt, are ready enough to ſuppoſe with them, that prophecy,

[c] Si dii ſunt, eſt divinatio.

under

under the Moſaic diſpenſation, had no other
reaſonable uſe, or end.

3. Laſtly, there are thoſe who erect their
thoughts to nobler contemplations, and
conclude that this intercourſe between
heaven and earth can only be carried on
with the ſublime view of preſerving an
awful ſenſe of providence in an impious
and careleſs world.

Vanity, or ſuperſtition, may they ſay,
has ſuggeſted to particular men, or to ſo-
cieties of men, that their perſonal or civil
concerns are of moment enough to be the
ſubject of divine prophecies, vouchſafed
merely for their own proper relief or ſatisfaction. But nothing leſs than the main-
tenance of God's ſupreme authority over
his moral creation could be an object worthy of his interpoſing in the affairs of men,
in ſo remarkable a manner. To keep alive
in their minds a prevailing ſenſe of their
dependance upon him, is, then, the ultimate end of prophecy: and what more
ſuitable (will they perhaps add, when
                                    warmed

warmed with this moral enthuſiaſm,) to the beſt ideas we can form of divine wiſdom, than that this celeſtial light ſhould be afforded to ſuch ages or nations as are moſt in want of that great and ſalutary principle?

There is reaſon to believe, that many of the antient ſpeculatiſts reaſoned thus on the ſubject of divination. For, as they argued *from the exiſtence of their gods, to the neceſſity of divination*; ſo, again, they turned the argument the other way, *and from the reality of divination, inferred the exiſtence and providence of their gods*[d]. In drawing the *former* concluſion, they ſhewed themſelves to be in the ſyſtem of thoſe who maintain, that the end of prophecy is *the inſtruction of men in their civil or perſonal concerns:* when they drew the *latter*, they ſeemed to eſpouſe the more enlarged ſentiments of ſuch as make the end of prophecy to be, *The inſtruction of men in the general concerns of religion.*

[d] Si divinatio ſit, dii ſunt,

I omit

I omit other inftances, that might be given; and concern myfelf no further with thefe, than juft to obferve from them; That the foundation of all fuch fyftems is laid in the prejudices of their refpective patrons; conjecturing rather what *ufe* might be made of this faculty, and to what purpofe men, according to their different views or capacities, would probably apply it, than regarding it, with due reverence, as directed by the fpirit of God. For then they would fee, that not one of thofe ends, nor any other of human conjecture, could be fafely relied upon, as being that of prophetic infpiration. Not that all thefe ends need be rejected as manifeftly unworthy of the divine intention; perhaps, each of them, in a certain fenfe, and with fome proper limitation, might without impiety be conceived to enter into it. But neither could it be prefumed, if none of thofe ends could have been pointed out, that therefore there was no reafonable end of divine prophecy; nor could it with modefty be

affirmed

affirmed that the nobleft of thefe ends was
certainly that, which the wifdom of God
propofed chiefly and ultimately to accomplifh by it, unlefs the information had
been given by himfelf.

III. But this folly of commenting on
prophecy by the falfe lights of the imagination is never more confpicuous, than
when the DISPENSATION of this gift, I
mean the *mode* of its conveyance, comes to
exercife the curiofity of prefumptuous men.

" If it be true, will fome fay, that the Supreme Being hath at any time condefcended to enlighten human ignorance by a difcovery of future events, thefe divine notices, whatever the *end* or *fubject* of them
might be, muft have been given in terms
fo precife, and fo clearly predictive of the
events to which they are applied, that no
doubt could remain either about the interpretation or completion of them.

On the contrary, thefe pretended prophecies are exprefled fo ambiguoufly or
obfcurely,

obfcurely, are fo involved in metaphor and darkened by hieroglyphics, that no clear and certain fenfe can be affixed to them, and the fagacity of a fecond prophet feems wanting to explain the meaning of the firft.

Then, again, when we come to verify thefe predictions by the light of hiftory, the correfpondence is fo flight many times, and fo indeterminate, that none but an eafy faith can affure itfelf, that they have, in a proper fenfe, been fulfilled. At the leaft, there is always room for fome degree of fufpenfe and hefitation : either the ac-complifhment fails in fome particulars, or other events might be pointed out, to which the prophecy equally correfponds : fo that the refult is, a want of that entire and perfect conviction, which prophecy, no doubt, was intended to give, and, when fulfilled, muft fupply ᵉ.

ᵉ Thefe objections were long fince urged by Celfus, who fpeaks of the Jewifh and Chriftian oracles, as *fa-natical, uncertain, and obfcure, l.* vii. *p.* 338—ἄγνωϛα, ϗ πάροιϛρα, ϗ πάνϳη ἄδηλα, ὧν τὸ μὲν γνῶμα ἐδεὶς ἂν

Indeed

Indeed, continue theſe inquirers, if our prophecies had been derived from no higher an original, than that of Pagan oracles, we might well enough have ſuppoſed them to be of this ſtamp. When men had nothing to truſt to, in their predictions, but their own ingenuity, they did well to deal in equivocal or enigmatic expreſſion, and might leave it to chance, or to the paſſions of their votaries, to find an application for their random conjectures. But when the prophet is, what he aſſumes to be, an interpreter of heaven, he may ſurely afford to ſpeak plainly, and to deliver nothing to us but what ſhall appear, with the fulleſt evidence, to be accompliſhed in the event."

ἔχων νῦν εὑρεῖν δύναιlo, ἀσαφῆ γὰρ κ̀ τὸ μηδέν. as *applicable to other ſubjects beſides thoſe to which they were referred*—τὰς εἰς τὰ περὶ τῦτῦ ἀναφερομένας προφηλίας δύναθαι κ̀ ἄλλοις ἐφαρμόζειν πράγμασι. *l. i. p.* 39.— nay, *as much more applicable to others, than to Jeſus*— μυρίοις ἄλλοις ἐφαρμοθῆναι δύναθαι πολὺ πιθανώτερον τὰ προς̀ηλικὰ ἢ τῷ Ἰησῦ. *l.* ii. *p.* 78.

C   The

The invidious comparifon, here made, between Scriptural prophecies and Pagan oracles, will be confidered in its place. To the general principle, affumed by thefe inquirers, *That divine prophecy muft be delivered with the utmoft clearnefs and perfpicuity, and fulfilled with irrefiftible evidence,* it may be fufficient to reply, as before, That, though thefe inquirers ufe the words, *divine prophecy,* they manifeftly argue on the fuppofition of its human original, or at leaft application. In this latter cafe, indeed, it is likely enough that the prophet, for his own credit, or for what he might fancy to be the fole end of prophecy, might chufe, if he were entrufted with the knowledge of future events, to predict them with all poffible clearnefs, and in fuch fort that obftinacy itfelf muft fee and admit the completion of them: but then, on the *former* fuppofition, that the prophet was only the minifter and inftrument of the divine counfels, in the high office committed to him,

they

they will do well to anſwer, at their leiſure, the following queſtions.

" How do they know in what manner, and with what circumſtances, it was fit for divine wiſdom to diſpenſe a knowledge of futurity to mankind? How can they pre-viouſly determine the degree of evidence with which a prediction muſt be either given or fulfilled? What aſſurance have they, that no reaſonable ends could be ſerv-ed by prophecies, expreſſed with ſome ob-ſcurity, and accompliſhed in a ſenſe much below what may ſeem neceſſary to un-avoidable conviction? Can they even pre-tend, on any clear principles of reaſon, that very important ends, perhaps the moſt important, may not be anſwered by that mode of conveyance, which appears to them ſo exceptionable? Can they, in a word, determine before-hand, I do not ſay with certainty, but with any colour of pro-bability; what *muſt* be the character of di-vine prophecy, when they know not the reaſon, moſt undoubtedly not *all* the rea-

C 2   ſons,

ſons, why it is given, and have even no
right to demand, that it ſhould be given
at all?"

Till theſe, and other queſtions of the
like ſort, be pertinently anſwered, it muſt
be in vain to cenſure the ways of providence, as not correſponding to our imperfect and ſhort-ſighted views.

So much for that *capital* prejudice taken
from the ſuppoſed obſcurity of the ſcriptural
prophecies. Of *ſmaller* ſcruples and difficulties on this head, there is no end.

Men may aſk, for inſtance, why the in-
ſtruments employed in conveying theſe celeſtial notices to mankind, are frequently
ſo mean and inconſiderable? The ſubject
of a prediction is the downfall of ſome
mighty ſtate, or the fortune of its gover-
nours. Why then is this important revelation intruſted to an obſcure prieſt, or
ſordid peaſant, in preference to the great
perſons, more immediately concerned in it'?

f Utrum tandem, per deos atque homines, magis
veriſimile eſt, *veſanum remigem*, aut aliquem noſtrûm,

Again ;

Again; fome momentous events have S E R M.
been fignified in dreams: why, not to per- I.
fons awake, and in the full poffeffion of
their beft faculties [g]?

And then, of thofe dreams, why are they
fometimes fent to one man, and the interpretation of them referved for another[h]?

Why—But I have done with thefe frivolous interrogatories; which, though preffed with all the advantage of Cicero's rhetoric, have really no force againft *Pagan
divination*; and therefore furely none,
againft *Scriptural prophecy*; I mean, in the
opinion of thofe who refpect it leaft.

In truth, they who put thefe queftions,
(arguing, as they muft do, on the fuppofition that prophecy is divinely infpired)

qui ibi tum eramus, *me, Catonem, Varronem, Coponium*
ipfum, concilia deorum immortalium perfpicere po-
tuiffe? *Cic. Div. l.* ii. *c.* 55.

[g] Illud etiam requiro, cur, fi deus ifta vifa nobis
providendi caufà dat, non *vigilantibus* potius dat quàm
dormientibus? l. ii. *c.* 61.

[h] Jam verò quid opus eft *circuitione et amfractu*, ut
fit utendum interpretibus fomniorum, potius quàm
directo? Ibid.

C 3   cannot

cannot excufe their presumption, even to
themfelves : and they, to whom fuch queftions are propofed, will not, if they be
wife, fo much as attempt to refolve them.
For they have the nature of arguments addreffed not only to the *ignorance*, as we fay,
of the difputant, but to an ignorance clearly
invincible by all the powers of human reafon.
Now to arguments of this fort—*I know not*
—is the anfwer of good fenfe, as well as of
modefty, and, to a juft reafoner, more fatisfactory by far, than any folution whatever of the difficulty propofed[1].

Not that reafon is to be wholly filenced
on the argument of prophecy : for then
every fpecies of impofture would be ready
to flow in upon us. The *ufe*, we fhould

---

[1] Quod eft enim criminis genus, aut rei effe alicujus
ignarum, aut ipfum, quod nefcias, fine aliquâ profiteri
diffimulatione nefcire? aut uter magis videtur irrifione
effe digniffimus vobis, qui fibi fcientiam nullam tene-
brofæ rei alicujus affumit, an ille, qui retur fe ex fe
apertiffimè fcire id, quod humanam tranfiliat notionem,
et quod fit cæcis obfcuritatibus involutum ?
                              Arnobius, adv. Gen. l. ii.

                                        make

make both of that faculty, and of theſe SERM.
I.
preliminary conſiderations on the *ſubjeƈt*,

the *end*, and the *diſpenſation* of prophecy is, briefly, this, To inquire, whether *any* prophecies have been given—in what ſenſe they are reaſonably to be interpreted—and how far, and whether in any proper ſenſe, they have been fulfilled: to examine them, in a word, by their own claims, and on the footing of their own pre-tenſions; that is, to argue on the ſup-poſition that they *may* be divine, till they can be evidently ſhewn to be other-wiſe.

This is clearly to aƈt ſuitably to our own faculties; to keep within the ſphere of our duty; and to reap the proper be-nefit, whatever it be, of a ſober inquiry into the authority, and charaƈter, and accompliſhment of the prophetic ſcrip-tures.

All the reſt is idle cavil, and miſera-ble preſumption; equally repugnant to

C 4   the

SERM. the cleareſt dictates of right reaſon, and
I. to that reſpect which every ſerious man
will think due to the ſubject, and to himſelf.

SERMON II.

The true Idea of PROPHECY.

REV. xix. 10.

The testimony of Jesus is the Spirit of Prophecy.

IT is very clear in what manner common sense instructs us to prosecute all inquiries into the divine conduct. Wise men *collect*, from what they see done in the system of nature, so far as they are able to collect it, the intention of its author. They will conclude, in like manner, from what they find delivered in the system of revelation, what the views and purposes of the revealer were.

Prophecy,

Prophecy, which makes fo confiderable a part of that fyftem, muft, therefore, be its own interpreter. My meaning is, that, fetting afide all prefumptuous imaginations of our own, we are to take our ideas of what prophecy *fhould* be, from what, in fact, we find it to have been. If it be true (as the Apoftle fays, and as the thing itfelf fpeaks) that *the things of God knoweth no man but the fpirit of God* [a], there cannot poffibly be any way of acquiring right notions of prophecy, but by attending to what the fpirit of prophecy hath revealed of itfelf. They, who admit the divine original of thofe fcriptures, which atteft the reality, and alone, as they fuppofe, contain the records, of this extraordinary difpenfation, are more than abfurd, are impious, if they defert this principle. And they, who reject or controvert their claim to fuch original, cannot, on any other principle, argue pertinently againft that difpenfation.

[a] I Cor. ii. 11.

In

In short, believers and unbelievers, whether they would support, or overturn, the system of prophecy, must be equally governed by the representation given of it in scripture. The *former* must not presume, on any other grounds, to assert the wisdom and fitness of that system: and the *latter* will then take a reasonable method of discrediting, if by such means they can discredit, the pretensions of it. For, as to vindicate prophecy on any principles but its own, can do it no honour; so, to oppose it on any other, can neither prejudice the cause itself, nor serve any reasonable end of the opposer.

To scripture then we must go for all the information we would have concerning the *use* and *intent* of prophecy: and the text, to look no farther, will clearly reveal this great secret to us.

But, before we proceed to reason from the text, in which, as it is pretended, this discovery is made, it will be necessary to explain its true meaning.

St.

St. John, in this chapter of the Revelations, from which the text is taken, had
been fhewn the downfall of Babylon, and
the confequent exaltation of the church,
in its clofeft union with Chrift, prefigured
under the Jewifh idea of a *marriage.* To
fo delightful a vifion, the Angel, in whofe
prefence, and by whofe miniftry, this fcene
of glory had been difclofed, fubjoins this
triumphant admonition—*Write,* fays he;
*Bleffed are they which are called to the mar-
riage of the Lamb. Thefe are the true fay-
ings of God.*

The Apoftle, ftruck with this emphatic
addrefs, and contemplating with grateful
admiration fo joyful a ftate of things, and
the divinity of that fore-fight by which it
was predicted, *falls down at the angel's feet
to worfhip him. But he faid unto me, See,
thou do it not; I am thy fellow-fervant,
and of thy brethren that have the teftimony
of Jefus: worfhip God: for the teftimony of
Jefus is the fpirit of prophecy.*

The

The fenfe is plainly this: Direct thy acknowledgment for this important difcovery, and that religious adoration, which it infpires, to God only who revealed it, and not to *me*, who am but thy fellow-fervant in this office of bearing teftimony to Jefus: I faid *in bearing teftimony to Jefus*; for know, that *the fpirit of prophecy*, with which I am endowed, and by which I am enabled to foretell thefe great things, is but in other words, *the teftimony of Jefus*; it has no other ufe or end, but to do honour to him; the prophet, whether he be angel or man, is only the minifter of God to bear witnefs to his Son; and his commiffion is ultimately directed to this one purpofe of manifefting the glories of his kingdom. In difcharging this prophetic office, which thou admireft fo much, I am then but the witnefs of Jefus, and fo to be confidered by thee in no other light than that of thy fellow-fervant.

It is evident from the expreffion, that the text was intended to give fome *fpecial*

inftruction

instruction to the Apostle, whose mis-
guided worship afforded the occasion of it.
For, if the design had merely been to enforce the general conclusion—*worship God*
—the premises need only have been—*I am
the servant of God, as well as thou*—for
from these premises it had followed, that
therefore God, and not the Angel, was to
be worshiped.   But the premises are not
simply, *I am thy fellow-servant,* but *I am
the fellow-servant of those who have the testimony of Jesus:* which clause indeed infers
the same conclusion, as the former; but,
as not being necessary to infer it (for the
conclusion had been just and complete
without it) was clearly added to convey a
precise idea of prophecy itself, as being
wholly subservient to Christ, and having
no other use or destination, under its various forms and in all the diversities of its
administration, but to bear testimony to
him.   Therefore the Angel says emphatically, in explanation of that latter clause,
                                        —*For*

—*For the teſtimony of Jeſus is the ſpirit of prophecy*—or, as the ſentence, in our tranſlation, ſhould have run, the order of its parts being inverted, *For the ſpirit of prophecy is the teſtimony of Jeſus.*

It may not be pretended that no more was meant by the text, than that *the particular* prophecy, here delivered, was in atteſtation of Jeſus : for then it would have been expreſſed with that limitation. The terms, on the other hand, are abſolute and indefinite—*the ſpirit of prophecy*—whence we cannot but conclude that prophecy, in general, is the ſubject of the propoſition.

We have here, then, a remarkable piece of intelligence conveyed to us (incidentally indeed conveyed, but not therefore the leſs remarkable) concerning the nature and genius of prophecy. The text is properly a key put into our hands, to open to us the myſteries of that diſpenſation ; which had in view ultimately the perſon of Chriſt and the various revolutions

of

SERM. of his kingdom—*The spirit of prophecy is,*
II.
———— universally, *the testimony of Jesus* [b].

[b] Μαρ]υρία τᾶ 'Ιησᾶ—*the testimony of,* or *concerning
Jesus,* not—*the testimony given by Jesus.*

The *former* appears to be the sense, for the following
reasons.

1. The point asserted, is, " That the Angel, who
had delivered this illustrious prophecy, was *the fellow-
servant of John,* and not of John only, but *of those who
have the testimony of Jesus.*" The proof is—*for the spirit of prophecy is the testimony of Jesus*—i. e. the end of
prophecy is to bear testimony, or, to do honour, to
Jesus; therefore, I, says the Angel, who am endowed
with this prophetic spirit, am but employed, as thou
art; who, in thy character of Apostle or Evangelist,
hast received the same general commission, namely, to
bear testimony, or to do honour, to Jesus. See *Acts*
x. 42. We are, therefore, *fellow-servants,* or joint
labourers in the same cause. All this is clear and well-
reasoned. But, now, take the words—*the testimony of
Jesus*—in the sense of—*the testimony given by Jesus*—and
how does the Angel's having *the spirit of prophecy,* prove
him to be *a fellow-servant of John?* for the reason
assigned will then stand thus—*for the spirit of prophecy is
the testimony which Jesus gives of himself.* The inference
is, that the Angel was a true prophet. Again: how
is the Angel proved, in this way, to be *the fellow-servant
of those who have the testimony of Jesus?* Why, thus; the
Angel had the spirit of prophecy, and prophecy was the
gift of Christ; therefore he was the fellow-servant of

The

The expreſſion, as I have ſhewn, is ſo ᴳᴱᴿᴹ.
precife as to leave no reaſonable doubt of

thofe, who had the ſame gift, i. e. who were prophets.
Without doubt. But why ſo ſtrange a way of prov-
ing ſo plain a point? It had been enough to ſay—*I
am a prophet, as others are.* Still, what was this to St.
John? who, in this place, is not ſuſtaining the character of a prophet; for the worſhip he was inclined to
pay the Angel was on account of the Angel's being,
what himſelf was not, *a prophet.*

Turn it which way you will, the reaſoning is frivolous, or inconſequent. I conclude therefore, that
not *this*, but the *other* interpretation gives the true ſenſe
of—*the teſtimony of Jeſus.*

2. To ſpeak of *prophecy* under the idea of *a teſtimony
to, or concerning Jeſus*, is conforming to the true ſcriptural idea of that gift. Thus we are told that—*to him
[i. e. to Jeſus] give all the prophets witneſs*—τᾱΐῳ πάνῐἐς
προφῆται μαρ͗υρᾶσιν, *Acts* x. 43. *Prophecy*, therefore,
being the thing here ſpoken of, is rightly called the
teſtimony, or witneſs to, or concerning Jeſus.

3. Laſtly, the conſtruction is fully juſtified, 1. by
obſerving, that the genitive caſe [as here Ἰησᾶ] is frequently uſed in ſcripture, not actively, but paſſively.
See a variety of inſtances in Mede, *p.* 626, where he
explains διδασκαλίαι δαιμονίων: And 2. by referring the
reader to the following paſſage of St. Paul, where the
very expreſſion of the text is ſo uſed—μὴ ἂν ἐπαιϱχυιθῇς τὸ
μαρ͗ύριον τᾶ Κυρίᾱ ἡμῶν—clearly, *be not aſhamed of bearing teſtimony to our Lord,* 2 *Tim.* i. 8.—and to *Rev.* i. 9.

D　　　　its

its meaning. Yet it may further ferve to juftify this interpretation, if we reflect, how exactly it agrees with all that the Jewifh prophets were underftood to intend, and what Jefus himfelf and his apoftles affert was intended, by their predictions.

where the Apoftle tells us, he was in the ifle of Patmos —διὰ τὸν λόγον τῦ Θεῦ, ϗ διὰ τὴν μαρτυρίαν Ἰησῦ Χρισῦ —*on account of his having been faithful in preaching the word of God, and in bearing teftimony to Jefus Chrift*— and ftill more plainly, if poffible, and indubitably, by referring him to *Rev.* xii. 17. where, fpeaking of the Dragon, he fays, he went in wrath to make war on thofe, *which keep the commandments of God, and have the teftimony of Jefus Chrift*—τῶν τηρύντων τὰς ἐντολὰς τῦ Θεῦ, ϗ ἐχόντων τὴν μαρτυρίαν τῦ Ἰησῦ Χρισῦ: for thefe objects of the Dragon's fury are properly, THE WITNESSES, thofe faithful fervants of truth, who fuffered for the courageous and perfevering *teftimony*, they gave, in evil times, to Jefus Chrift, and to his pure religion.

On the whole, there cannot be the leaft doubt of the interpretation, here given of this famous text. The *expreffion* fairly admits this interpretation; and (what the true critic will regard moft) the *fcope* of the place, or pertinence of the reafoning, addreffed to St. John, admits no other.

It

It were endlefs to enumerate all the prophecies of the Old Teftament, which have
been fuppofed to point at Jefus: and the controverfy concerning the application of *fome*
prophecies to him may be thought difficult.   But it is very certain that the Jews,
before the coming of Chrift, gave this conftruction to their fcriptures : they even
looked beyond the letter of their facred
books, and conceived *the teftimony* of the
Meffiah to be the foul and end of the commandment. *The fpirit of prophecy* was fo
firmly believed to intend that *teftimony,*
that the expectation was general of fome
fuch perfon, as Jefus, to appear among
them, and at the very time in which he
made his appearance.   This, I fay, is an
undoubted *fact*, what account foever may
be given of it ; and fo far evinces that the
principle, delivered in the text, correfponds
entirely to the idea which the fathers entertained of the prophetic fpirit.

Next, Jefus himfelf appeals to the *fpirit
of prophecy,* as bearing witnefs to his per-

fon

son and difpenfation. *Search the Scriptures,* says he to the Jews, *for in them ye think ye have eternal life, and they are they which teftify of* ME [c]. Two things are obfervable in thefe words. 1. If the Jews thought they had *eternal life* in their fcriptures, they muft needs have underftood them in a fpiritual fenfe; for the *letter* of them taught no fuch thing: and I know not what *other* fpiritual fenfe, that fhould lead them to the expectation of *eternal life,* they could put on their fcriptures, but that prophetic, or typical fenfe, which refpected the Meffiah. 2. Jefus here expreffly afferts, that their fcriptures *teftified of him.* How generally they did fo, he explained at large in that remarkable converfation with two of his difciples, after his refurrection, when, *beginning at Mofes and* ALL *the prophets, he expounded unto them in* ALL *the fcriptures the things concerning himfelf* [d].

[c] John v. 39.
[d] Luke xxiv. 27.

The

The *Apostles* of Jesus are frequent and large in the fame appeal to the fpirit of prophecy. *Thofe things,* fays St. Peter to the Jews, *which God had fhewed by the mouth of* ALL *his prophets, that Chrift fhould fuffer, he hath fo fullfilled*[e]. And, again, after quoting the authority of Mofes, *Yea, and* ALL *the prophets from Samuel, and thofe that follow after, as many as have fpoken, have likewife foretold of thefe days*[f].

St Paul feems to have compofed fome entire epiftles[g], with the view of fhewing that Chrift was prefigured in the Law itfelf, and that He was, in truth, the fubftance of the whole Jewifh difpenfation. So thoroughly, according to him, did *the fpirit of prophecy* pervade that fyftem, and fo clearly did it bear teftimony to Jefus! Whence, in his apology before Agrippa, we find him afferting of the whole Chrif- tian doctrine, *that he faid none other things*

[e] Acts iii. 18.

[f] Acts iii. 24. See alfo Acts x. 43. 1 Pet. i. 10.

[g] See efpecially the Epiftles to the *Hebrews,* and *Galatians.*

D 3 *than*

than thofe which the prophets. and Mofes did fay fhould come [h].

More citations cannot be neceffary on fo plain a point. And I bring thefe to fhew, not the truth of the principle itfelf (which is not now under confideration) but the certainty of the interpretation, here given to the text. For I make it fay no more (though it fays it indeed more precifely) than the fcriptures themfelves were *under-ftood* by the Jews to fay, and are repre-fented by Jefus and his Apoftles, as *actu-ally* faying, when I affirm its fenfe to be, " That the fcope and end of prophecy was the teftimony of Jefus."

On this principle, then, we are to regu-late all our reafonings on the fubject of prophecy. They who maintain, and they who would confute, its pretenfions, muft equally go on this fuppofition. If the fyf-tem of prophecy can be juftified, or fo far as it can be juftified, on thefe grounds, the

[h] Acts xxvi. 22. See farther, Acts xxviii. 23. Rom. iii. 21. Eph. ii. 19, &c.

defence

defence muft be thought folid and fatisfactory; becaufe thofe grounds are not arbi-
trarily aſſumed, but are fuch as that fyftem
itſelf acknowledges.   On the contrary,
whatever advantage may be fairly taken
of thofe grounds to difcredit prophecy,
muft needs be allowed, for the fame
reafon.

Again: On the believer's fcheme, that
prophecy is of divine infpiration, there can
be no *prefumption* in arguing from the
grounds, here fuppofed, in favour of prophecy.   Becaufe, though all conclufions
from a principle of human invention, muft
be hazardous and raſh, yet from a principle of divine authority, many fober and
juft inferences may be drawn.   For it is
one thing, to difcover a principle, and
another, to argue juftly and cogently from
it.

On the other hand, the unbeliever,
who regards the whole fyftem of prophecy
as of human invention, muft yet be allowed to argue pertinently from the fame

D 4   grounds,

grounds, becaufe they are the proper grounds of that fyftem: his arguments may be rightly formed, though the principle, from which he argues, appear to him of no authority. The rules of logic will indeed oblige him to argue on that principle; for, otherwife, he combats, not his adverfary's pofition, but a phantom of his own raifing.

Having premifed thus much concerning the right interpretation of the text, and the important relation it bears to the prefent fubject, I fhould now proceed to inquire what conclufions naturally and fairly refult from it. For from this affumption, that *Jefus is the end of prophecy,* it will, I think, follow very evidently, that the greater part of thofe objections which make fo much noife, and are fo confidently urged, on the fubject of prophecy, have no force at all in them.

But, before we enter on that tafk, it may be ufeful to confider more particularly what the ASSUMED PRINCIPLE itfelf is, and to

paufe

paufe a while in contemplation of this idea.

The text, as here interpreted, and in full confonance with the tenor of the facred writings, implies this fact—that *Prophecy* in general (that is, all the prophecies of the Old and New Teftament) hath its ultimate accomplifhment in the hiftory and difpenfa-tion of Jefus.

But now, if we look into thofe writings, we find, 1. That prophecy is of a prodigi-ous extent ; that it commenced from the lapfe of man, and reaches to the confum-mation of all things : that, for many ages, it was delivered darkly, to few perfons, and with large intervals from the date of one prophecy to that of another; but, at length, became more clear, more fre-quent, and was uniformly carried on in the line of one people, feparated from the reft of the world, among other reafons affigned, for this principally, to be the repofitory of the divine oracles : that, with fome intermiffion,

miffion, the fpirit of prophecy fubfifted among that people, to the coming of Chrift: that He himfelf and his Apoftles exercifed this power in the moft confpicuous manner; and left behind them many predictions, recorded in the books of the New Teftament, which profefs to refpect very diftant events, and even run out to the end of time, or, in St. John's expreffion, to that period, *when the myftery of God fhall be perfected* [i].

2, Further, befides the extent of this prophetic fcheme, the dignity of the *Perfon,* whom it concerns, deferves our confideration. He is defcribed in terms, which excite the moft auguft and magnificent ideas. He is fpoken of, indeed, fometimes as being *the feed of the woman,* and as *the fon of man;* yet fo as being at the fame time of more than mortal extraction. He is even reprefented to us, as being fuperior to men and angels; as far above all principality and power, above all that is ac-

[i] Rev. x. 7.

counted

counted great, whether in heaven or in
earth ; as the word and wisdom of God ;
as the eternal Son of the Father ; as the
heir of all things, by whom he made the
worlds ; as the brightnefs of his glory, and
the exprefs image of his perfon.

We have no words to denote greater
ideas, than thefe: the mind of man cannot
elevate itfelf to nobler conceptions. Of
fuch tranfcendent worth and excellence is
that Jefus faid to be, to whom all the
prophets bear witnefs !

3. Laftly, the declared *purpofe*, for which
the Meffiah, prefigured by fo long a train
of prophecy, came into the world, correfponds to all the reft of the reprefentation. It was not to deliver an oppreffed
nation from civil tyranny, or to erect a
great civil empire, that is, to atchieve one
of thofe acts, which hiftory accounts moft
heroic. No: it was not a mighty ftate, a
victor people—

" *Non res Romanæ perituraque regna*—"
                   that

SERM.
II.
that was worthy to enter into the contemplation of this divine perfon. It was
another and far fublimer purpofe, which
HE came to accomplifh; a purpofe, in comparifon of which, all our policies are poor
and little, and all the performances of man
as nothing. It was to deliver a world
from ruin; to abolifh fin and death; to
purify and immortalize human nature;
and thus, in the moft exalted fenfe of the
words, to be the Saviour of all men, and
the bleffing of all nations.

There is no exaggeration in this account.
I deliver the undoubted fenfe, if not always
the very words of fcripture.

Confider then to what this reprefentation
amounts. Let us unite the feveral parts
of it, and bring them to a point. A fpirit
of prophecy pervading all time—character-
izing one perfon, of the higheft dignity—
and proclaiming the accomplifhment of one
purpofe, the moft beneficent, the moft divine, that imagination itfelf can project—
Such is the fcriptural delineation, whether

we

we will receive it or no, of that œconomy,
which we call Prophetic!

And now then (if we muſt be reaſoning from our ideas of *fit and right,* to the rectitude of the divine conduct) let me aſk, in one word, whether, on the ſuppoſition that it ſhould ever pleaſe the moral Governor of the world to reveal himſelf by prophecy at all, we can conceive him to do it, in a *manner,* or for *ends,* more worthy of him? Does not the *extent* of the ſcheme correſpond to our beſt ideas of that infinite Being, to whom all duration is but a point, and to whoſe view all time is equally preſent? Is not the *object* of this ſcheme, the Lamb of God that was ſlain from the foundation of the world, worthy, in our conceptions, of all the honour that can be reflected upon him by ſo vaſt and ſplendid an œconomy? Is not the *end* of this ſcheme ſuch as we ſhould think moſt fit for ſuch a ſcheme of prophecy to predict, and for ſo divine a perſon to accompliſh?

You

——————   You fee, every thing here is of a piece:
all the parts of this difpenfation are aftonifh-
ingly great, and perfectly harmonize with
each other.

We, who admit the divinity of thofe
records, which reprefent to us this ftate of
things, cannot but be infinitely affected
with it : fince, in that cafe, we only contemplate an undoubted fact, in this reprefentation.   And it fhould further feem
that even thofe, who queftion that authority of fcripture, muft, if they be ingenuous, confefs themfelves *ftruck* by a reprefentation at once fo fublime and confiftent.
They require, on all occafions, to have
reafons of what they call *fitnefs*, in the divine conduct, pointed out to them : Can
they overlook them here, where they are
fo obvious and fo convincing ? At leaft,
the credibility of fuch a fcheme, as that of
prophecy is in Scripture reprefented to be,
appears not, fo far as we have hitherto
confidered it, to be oppofed or leffened in
any degree by our *natural* prejudices; by
the

'the beft notions, I mean, which we can
'frame on this fubject; but is, indeed, much
ftrengthened and confirmed by them.

On the idea of fuch a fcheme, as is here
prefented to us, I enlarge no farther, at
prefent, than juft to make ONE general
obfervation. It is this: That the argument from prophecy is not to be formed
from the confideration of fingle prophecies, but from all the prophecies taken
together, and confidered as making one
fyftem; in which, from the mutual dependance and connection of its parts, preceding prophecies prepare and illuftrate
thofe which follow, and thefe, again, reflect light on the foregoing: juft as, in
any philofophical fyftem, that which fhews
the folidity of it, is the harmony and correfpondence of the whole, not the application of it, in particular inftances.

Hence, though the evidence be but fmall,
from the completion of any one prophecy,
taken feparately, yet, that evidence being
always fomething, the amount of the whole
evidence,

SERM.
II.
evidence, refulting from a great number of prophecies, all relative to the fame defign, may be confiderable; like many fcattered rays, which, though each be weak in itfelf, yet, concentred into one point, fhall form a ftrong light, and ftrike the fenfe very powerfully. Still more: this evidence is not fimply a growing evidence, but is indeed multiplied upon us, from the number of reflected lights, which the feveral component parts of fuch a fyftem reciprocally throw upon each: till, at length, the conviction rife into a high degree of moral certainty.

It hath been faid indeed, of this fcheme, or way of confidering prophecy, *that it is an imaginary fcheme, of which there is not the leaft trace in any of the four Gofpels; and that it even contradicts the whole evidence of prophecy, as it was underftood and applied by the Apoftles and Evangelifts* [k].

[k] DR. MIDDLETON's *Works,* vol. III. p. 137. London, 1752, 4to.

But

But what, is there no trace of this
fcheme in the Gofpel, when Jefus himfelf
began at Mofes and the prophets, and ex-
pounded [to his difciples] *in* ALL *the fcriptures
the things concerning himfelf?* Is this fcheme
contradictory to the evidence of prophecy,
as underftood by the Apoftles, when St.
Peter argued with the Jews *from what God
had fpoken by the mouth of* ALL *his prophets,
fince the world began?*

Is not here a feries of prophecies, expreffly referred to, as running up not only
to the times of Mofes [i], but to the begin-
ing of the world? And is not this feries
argued from, as conftituting one entire
fyftem of prophecy, and as affording an
evidence diftinct from that which arifes
from the confideration of each prophecy,
taken fingly and by itfelf?

---

[i] Though by *Mofes*, is here meant, not the prophecies of Mofes only, but the *books* of Mofes, containing
thofe former prophecies, which, as St. Peter fays, had
been delivered, *fince the world began*.

E

But

But Jefus and his Apoftles, ufually, *applied the prophecies fingly and independently on each other, as fo many different arguments for the general truth of the Gofpel* [m].

Could they do *otherwife*, when the occafions offered, in the courfe of their miniftry, to which thofe prophecies were to be applied? Or, could they do *better*, in their difcourfes to the people, to whom the argument from fingle prophecies would be more familiar, than that complicated one, arifing from a whole fyftem? Does it follow, becaufe the prophecies were applied fingly, that therefore they might not with good reafon be applied fyftematically, or that they may not now be fo applied, when we have to do with thofe, who are capable of entering into this fort of argumentation? Will it be faid that, becaufe the moral precepts of the Gofpel are delivered fingly, there is therefore no fuch thing as a fyftem of morality, or that the fubject may not be treated with

[m] DR. MIDDLETON, *p.* 139.

propriety,

propriety, and with advantage too, in that form?

On the whole, the prophecies of the Old and New Testament, having clearly all the *qualities* of what we call a system, that is, consisting of many particulars, dependent on each other, and intimately connected by their reference to a common end, there is no reason why they may not be considered in this light; and there is great reason why they should be so considered, since otherwise, on many occasions, we shall not do justice to the argument itself.

To return then to the text (which implies the existence and use of such a system) and to conclude with it. *The spirit of prophecy is the testimony of Jesus.* This angelic information presents, at first sight, an idea stupendous indeed, but, on such a subject, suitable enough to our expectations. It offers no violence to the natural sense of the human mind; but, on the contrary,

E 2 hath

hath every thing in it to engage our belief and veneration.

Such is the *idea* of Prophecy, contemplated in itfelf. What *conclufions* (of importance, as we fuppofe, to the right apprehenfion and further vindication of prophecy) may be drawn from that idea, will be next confidered.

SERMON III.

Conclusions from the true Idea of PROPHECY.

REV. xix. 10.

The testimony of Jesus is the Spirit of Prophecy.

WE have seen how precarious all our reasonings on divine prophecy must be, when built on no better grounds than those of human fancy and conjecture. The text supplies us with a principle, as *we* believe, of divine authority; as *all* must confess, of scriptural authority; that is, of the same authority as that on which prophecy itself stands.

SERM.
III.

E 3

This

This principle has been explained at large. It affirms that *Jesus*, whose person and character and history are sufficiently known from the books of scripture, *is the end and object of the prophetic system*, contained in those books.

We are now at liberty to reason from this principle. Whatever conclusions are fairly drawn from it, must to the believer appear, as certain truths; must to the unbeliever appear, as very proper illustrations of that principle.

In general, if difficulties can be removed by pursuing and applying scriptural principles, they are fairly removed: and the removal of every such difficulty, on these grounds, must be a presumption in favour of that system, whether we call it of *Prophecy*, or *Revelation*, which is thus found to carry its own vindication with it.

From the principle of the text may, I think, be deduced, among others, the following conclusions; all of them tending to clear the subject of prophecy, and

to

to obviate fome or other of thofe objections, which prejudiced or hafty reafoners have been difpofed to make to it.

I. My firft conclufion is, " That, on the idea of fuch a fcheme of prophecy, as the text fuppofes, a confiderable degree of obfcurity may be reafonably expected to attend the *delivery* of the divine predictions."

There are general reafons which fhew that prophecy, as fuch, will moft probably be thus delivered. For inftance, it has been obferved, that, as the completion of prophecy is left, for the moft part, to the inftrumentality of free agents, if the circumftances of the event were predicted with the utmoft precifion, either human liberty muft be reftrained; or human obftinacy *might* be tempted to form, the abfurd indeed, but criminal purpofe, of counteracting the prediction. On the contrary, by throwing fome part of the predicted event into fhade, the moral faculties of the agent have their proper play, and

E 4   the

the guilt of an intended oppofition to the will of heaven is avoided. This reafon feems to have its weight: and many others might ftill be mentioned. But I argue, at prefent, from the *particular* principle, under confideration.

An immenfe fcheme of prophecy was ultimately defigned to bear teftimony to the perfon and fortunes of Jefus. But Jefus was not himfelf to come, till what is called the *laft age* of the world, nor all the purpofes of his coming to be fully accomplifhed, till the *end* of that age.

Now, whatever reafons might make it fit, in the view of infinite wifdom, to defer the execution of this fcheme to fo diftant a period, may probably be conceived to make it fit, that the *delivery* of it fhould be proportionably dark and obfcure. A certain degree of light, we will fay, was to be communicated from the date of the prophecy: but it is very conceivable that the ages nearer the completion of it, might be

more

more immediately concerned in the event predicted; and that, till such time approached, it might be convenient to leave the prediction in a good degree of obscurity.

The fact answers to this presumption. Prophecies of very remote events, remote, I mean, from the date of the prediction, are universally the most obscure. As the season advanced for their accomplishment, they are rendered more clear: either fresh prophecies are given, to point out the time, and other circumstances, more determinately; or the completion of some prophecies affords new light for the interpretation of others, that are unfulfilled. Yet neither are we to conceive that those *fresh prophecies*, or this *new light* removes all obscurity: enough is still left to prevent or disappoint the efforts of presumption; and only so much additional clearness is bestowed on the prophecy, as the revealer saw fit to indulge to those who lived nearer the time of its completion.

But

But this is not all : By looking into that plan of providence, which refpects Jefus, and the ends to be accomplifhed by him, as it is drawn out in the facred writings, we find a *diftinct* reafon for the obfcurity of the prophecies, relative to that fubject.

We there find it to have been in the order of the divine councils, that, between the firft dawnings of revelation and the fuller light of the Gofpel, an intermediate and very fingular œconomy, yet ftill preparatory to that of Jefus, fhould be inftituted. This œconomy (for reafons, which it is not to our prefent purpofe to deduce, and for fome, no doubt, which we fhould in vain attempt to difcover) was to continue for many ages, and *while* it continued, was to be had in honour among that people, for whom it was more immediately defigned. But now the genius of thofe two difpenfations, the Jewifh, I mean, and the Chriftian, being wholly different ; the one, carnal, and enforced by temporal fanctions only, the other, fpiritual, and eftablifhed

on

on better promises; the prophets, who lived under the former of these dispensations (and the greater part of those, who prophesied of Jesus, lived under it) were of course so to predict the future œconomy, as not to disgrace the present. They were to respect the *Law,* even while they announced the *Gospel,* which was, in due time, to supersede it*.

So much, we will say, was to be discovered as might erect the thoughts of men towards some better scheme of things, hereafter to be introduced; certainly so much, as might sufficiently evince the divine intention in that scheme, when it should actually take place; but not enough to indispose them towards that state of discipline, under the yoke of which they were then held. From this double purpose, would clearly result that character, in the prophecies concerning the new dispensation, which we find impressed upon them; and which St. Peter well describes, when he

* D. L. Vol. v. p. 288. Lond. 1765.

speaks

speaks of them, as difpenfing a light indeed, but *a light fhining in a dark place.*

Upon the whole, the delivery of prophecy feems well fuited to that difpenfation which it was given to atteft.   If the
object in view had been one fingle event,
to be accomplifhed all at once, it might
perhaps be·expected that the prophecies
concerning it would have been clear and
precife.   But, if the fcheme of Chriftianity be what the fcriptures reprefent it to
be, a fcheme, commencing from the foundation of the world, and unfolding itfelf by
juft degrees through a long fucceffion of
ages, and to be fully accomplifhed only at
the confummation of all things, *prophecy,*
which was given to attend on that fcheme,
and to furnifh a fuitable atteftation to it,
muft needs be fuppofed to adapt itfelf to
the nature of the difpenfation; that is, to
have different degrees of clearnefs or obfcurity according to its place in the general
fyftem; and not to difclofe more of it, or
in clearer terms, at any one period, than
                                    might

might confift with the various ends of S E R M.
wifdom which were to be ferved by the III.
gradual opening of fo vaft and intricate a
fcene.

ANOTHER circumftance, of affinity with
this, is apt to ftrike us, in the contemplation of the fcriptural prophecies. There is
reafon to believe that more than one fenfe
was purpofely inclofed in fome of them;
and we find, in fact, that the writers of
the New Teftament give to many of the
old prophecies an interpretation very different and remote from that which may be
reafonably thought the primary and immediate view of the prophets themfelves.
This is what Divines call the DOUBLE
SENSE of prophecy: by which they mean
an accomplifhment of it in more events
than one; in the fame fyftem indeed; but
at diftant intervals, and under different
parts of that fyftem.

Now, as fufpicious as this circumftance
may appear, at firft fight, it will be found,
on inquiry, to be exactly fuited to that

idea

idea of prophecy which the text gives us
of it, as being, from the firft, and all along,
intended to *bear teftimony to Jefus.* For
from that idea I conclude again,

II. " That prophecies of a *double fenfe*
may well be expected in fuch a fcheme".

And where is the wonder that, if prophecy was given to atteft the coming of
Jefus and the difpenfation to be erected by
him, it fhould occafionally, in every ftage
of it, refpect its main purpofe ; and, though
the immediate object be fome other, it
fhould never lofe fight of that, in which
it was ultimately to find its repofe and
end ?

It hath been before obferved, That, between the earlier notices concerning Jefus,
and the advent of that great perfon, it
feemed good to infinite wifdom (I fpeak
in terms, fuited to the reprefentation of
fcripture) to inftitute the intermediate œconomy of the Jewifh Law. Among other
provifions for the adminiftration of this
Law, *prophecy* was one ; and, upon its

own

own pretenfions, a neceflary one; for the
government claims to be ftrictly *theocrati-*
cal; and the people, to be governed by it,
were to be made fenfible, at every ftep,
that it was fo. Therefore the interefting
events in their civil hiftory were to be regarded by them, as coming within the
cognifance, and lying under the controul,
of their divine governour : to which end,
a race of men were fucceffively raifed up
among them to give them warning of thofe
events, and, by this divine forefight of
what was feen to be accomplifhed in their
hiftory, to afford a clear conviction, that
they were, in fact, under that peculiar
government.

Add to this, that the *Law* itfelf, fo
wonderfully conftructed, was but a part,
indeed the rudiments, of one great fcheme;
was given, not for its own fake, but to
make way for a ftill nobler and more generous inftitution; was, in truth, a preparatory ftate of difcipline, or *pædagogy*, as

St.

St. Paul terms it, to bring the subjects of it, in due time, to *Christ* [b].

Jesus then, the object of the earliest prophecies, was not overlooked in this following dispensation ; which was, indeed, instinct with presages of that divine person. *It gave the shadow of good things to come, but the body was of Christ* [c]. The *legal* prophets, in like manner, while they were

[b] Gal. iii. 24.—ὁ νόμος παιδαγωγὸς ἡμῶν γέγονεν εἰς Χριστόν.—

[c] Coloff. ii. 17. Hence, St. Austin affirms roundly, " That, to such as consider the genius of the revealed " system, the Old Testament must appear a continued " prophecy of the New."— *Vetus Testamentum*, rectè *sentientibus*, PROPHETIA *est Novi Testamenti* [*contr. Faustum, l.* xv.].: and St. Jerom speaks of it as a generally received maxim, " That it is the manner of " sacred scripture, to deliver, beforehand, the truth of " futurity, in types"—*hunc esse morem scripturæ sanctæ ut futurorum veritatem præmittat, in* TYPIS [Hieron. T. III. 1127.]—I know, that the antient Fathers, and from them many moderns, have exposed themselves to much and deserved censure, by pursuing this principle too minutely and superstitiously, in their mystical and allegorical comments on the Jewish scriptures. But men of sense will consider, that a principle is not therefore to be rejected, because it has been abused. For in-

imme-

immediately employed, and perhaps believed themfelves to be folely employed,
in predicting the occurrences of the Jewifh
ftate, were at the fame time, preluding, as
it were, to the perfon and difpenfation of

ftance, that the Paffover was inftituted with a reference
to the facrifice of Chrift, that the pafchal Lamb was,
in the language of St. Auftin, a *prophecy*, or, in that of
St. Jerom, a *type*, of the lamb of God, will feem highly
credible to one who confiders the aptnefs of the correfpondence in two related parts of the fame fyftem : But,
that the famous Law in Deuteronomy, concerning the
marriage of a brother's widow, was *prophetic*, or *typical*
of the duty, incumbent on the minifters of the Gofpel,
to efpoufe the widowed church of Chrift, is certainly
much lefs clear, and will fcarcely be admitted even on
the authority of St. Auftin.—Hoc ipfum—quod uxo-
rem fratris ad hoc frater juffus eft ducere, ut non fibi,
fed illi fobolem fufcitaret, ejufque vocaret nomine,
quod inde nafceretur: quid aliud *in figurâ præmonftrat*,
nifi quia unufquifque Evangelii prædicator ita debet in
Ecclefiâ laborare, ut defuncto fratri, hoc eft Chrifto,
fufcitet femen, qui pro nobis mortuus eft, et quod fuf-
citatum fuerit, ejus nomen accipiat? *Contr. Fauftum*
l. 32.—St Auftin might, perhaps, fay for himfelf, that
he had an example of this practice in the myftical comments of St. Paul : it may be fo : but an *example*, followed without warrant, in this inftance, by the learned Father, and, not improbably, ill underftood by him.

F   Jefus ;

SERM.
III.
——— Jefus; the holy fpirit, which infpired
them, bearing out their expreffion, and
enlarging their conceptions, beyond the
worth and fize of thofe objects, which
came directly in their view.

There is nothing in this account of *prophecy*, but what falls in with our beft ideas
of the divine wifdom; intently profecut-
ing one entire fcheme; and directing the
conftituent parts of it to the general purpofe of his providence, at the fame time
that *each* ferves to accomplifh its own.

This *double*, or *fecondary fenfe* of prophecy was fo far from giving offence to
Lord Bacon, that he fpeaks of it with admiration, as one ftriking argument of its
Divinity. *In forting the prophecies of fcripture with their events* (a work much defired
by this wife author, and intended by this
Lecture) *we muft allow*, fays he, *for that
latitude which is agreeable and familiar unto
divine prophecies, being of the nature of the
author, with whom a thoufand years are but*

                                        as

as one day; and therefore they are not fulfilled punctually at once, but have springing and germinant accomplishment throughout many ages, though the height, or fullness of them may refer to some one age[d].

But, that we may not mistake, or pervert, this fine observation of our great philosopher, it may be proper to take notice, that the reason of it holds in such prophecies only as respect the several successive parts of one system; which, being intimately connected together, may be supposed to come within the view and contemplation of the same prophecy : whereas, it would be endless, and one sees not on what grounds of reason we are authorized, to look out for the accomplishment of prophecy in any casual unrelated events of general history. The Scripture speaks of prophecy, as respecting Jesus, that is, as being one connected scheme of providence, of which the Jewish dispensation makes a

[d] Adv. of Learning, B. II.

F 2   part :

part: fo that here we are led to expect that *fpringing and germinant accomplifhment,* which is mentioned. But had the Jewifh Law been complete in itfelf, and totally unrelated to the Chriftian, the general principle—*that a thoufand years are with God but as one day*—would no more juftify us in extending a Jewifh prophecy to Chriftian events, becaufe perhaps it was eminently fulfilled in them, than it would juftify us in extending it to any other fignally correfponding events whatfoever. It is only when the prophet hath one uniform connected defign before him, that we are authorifed to ufe this latitude of interpretation. For then the prophetic fpirit naturally runs along the feveral parts of *fuch* defign, and unites the remoteft events with the neareft: the ftyle of the prophet, in the mean time, fo adapting itfelf to this double profpect, as to paint the near and fubordinate event in terms that *emphatically* reprefent the diftant and more confiderable.

So

So that, with this explanation, nothing can be more juſt or philoſophical, than the idea which Lord Bacon ſuggeſts of divine prophecy.

The great ſcheme of Redemption, we are now conſidering, being the only ſcheme ·in the plan of providence, which, as far as we know, hath been prepared and digni‑ fied by a continued ſyſtem of prophecy, at leaſt this being the only ſcheme to which we have ſeen a prophetic ſyſtem applied, men do not ſo readily apprehend the doc‑ trine of *double ſenſes* in prophecy, as·they would do, if they ſaw it exemplified in other caſes. But what the hiſtory of man‑ kind does not ſupply, we may repreſent to ourſelves by many obvious ſuppoſitions; which cannot juſtify, indeed, ſuch a ſcheme of things, but may facilitate the conception of it.

Suppoſe, for inſtance, that it had been the purpoſe of the Deity (as it unqueſtiona‑ bly was) to erect the FREE GOVERNMENT of antient Rome; and that, from the time

F 3 of

of Æneas' landing in Italy, he had given prophetic intimations of this purpose. Suppose, further, that he had seen fit, for the better discipline of his favoured people, to place them, for a season, under the *yoke* of the Regal government; and that, during that state of things, he had instructed his prophets to foretell the wars and other occurrences which should distinguish that period of their history.—Here would be a case somewhat similar to that of the Jews under their theocratic regimen : not exactly indeed, because prophecy, as we have seen, was essential to the Jewish polity, but had nothing to do with the regal, or any other polity of the Romans.   But allow for this difference, and suppose that, for some reason or other, the spirit of prophecy was indulged to this people, under their *kings,* as it was to the Jews, under their *theocracy* ; and that it was *primarily* employed in the same way, that is, in predicting their various fortunes under that regimen : Suppose, I say, all this, and would it surprize us to find that their prophets, in dilating

on

on this part of their fcheme, fhould, in a
fecondary fenfe, predict the future and more
fplendid part of it? That, having the whole
equally prefented to their view, they fhould
anticipate the coming glories of their *free*
ftate, even in a prophecy which directly
concerned their *regal*, and much humbler
fucceffes? That, in commenting on their
petty victories over the Sabins and Latins,
they fhould drop fome hints that pointed at
their African and Afiatic triumphs; or,
in tracing the fhadow of freedom they en-
joyed under the beft of their kings, they
fhould let fall fome ftrokes, that more exprefly defigned the fubftantial liberty of
their equal republic: the *end*, as we fuppofe, and completion of that fcheme, for
the fake of which the prophetic power
itfelf had been communicated to them?
Still more: fuppofing we had fuch prophecies now in our hands, and that we found
them applicable indeed in a general way to
the former parts of their hiftory, but frequently more expreffive of events in the

latter,

latter, fhould we doubt of their being prophecies in a *double fenfe*, or fhould we think
it ftrange that two fucceffive and dependent
difpenfations in the fame connected fcheme
fhould be, at once, the object of the fame
predictions? And laftly, to put an end to
thefe queftions, could there feem to be equal
reafon for applying thefe predictions to
fuch events as might poffibly correfpond to
them in fome *other* hiftory, the Græcian,
for inftance, as for applying them to fimilar events in the *Roman* hiftory?

Let me juft obferve further, that, from
what hath been faid under thefe two articles, we may clearly difcern the difference
between *Pagan oracles*, and *Scriptural prophecies*. Both have been termed obfcure
and ambiguous; and an invidious parallel
hath been made, or infinuated, between
them[*]. The Pagan oracles were indeed
obfcure, fometimes to a degree that no reafonable fenfe could be made of them:

[*] DR. MIDDLETON, *Works*, vol. III. p. 177.
London, 1752, 4to.

they

they were also *ambiguous*, in the worst
fenfe; I mean, fo as to admit contrary interpretations. The fcriptural prophecies
we own to be *obfcure*, to a certain degree:
And we may call them, too, *anbiguous*;
becaufe they contained two, confiftent,
indeed, but different meanings. But here
is the diftinction, I would point out to
you. The obfcurity and ambiguity of the
Pagan oracles had no neceffary, or reafonable caufe in the fubject, on which they
turned: the obfcurity and ambiguity of
the fcriptural prophefies have an evident
reafon in the fyftem, to which they belong. As the Pagan predictions had near
and fingle events for their object, the fate
perhaps of fome depending war, or the
fuccefs of fome council, then in agitation,
they might have been clearly and precifely
delivered; and in fact we find that fuch of
the Jewifh predictions as foretold events of
that fort and character, were fo delivered:
But, the fcriptural prophecies under confideration refpecting one immenfe fcheme

of

of providence, it might be expedient that
the remoter parts fhould be obfcurely revealed; as it was furely natural that the
connected parts of fuch a fcheme fhould be
fhewn together.

We fee then what force there is in that
queftion, which is afked with fo much
confidence—" *Is it poffible, that the fame*
" *character can be due to the Jewifh prophe-*
" *cies, which the wife and virtuous in the*
" *heathen world confidered as an argument*
" *of fraud and falfhood, in the Pythian*
" *prophecies* [f] *?*"

Firft, we fay, the character is *not* entirely
the fame in both : and, *fecondly*, that, fo
far as it *is* the fame, that character is very
becoming in the Jewifh, but utterly abfurd
in the Pythian prophecies. What was
owing to fraud or ignorance in the Pagan
Diviner, is reafonably afcribed to the depth
and height of that wifdom, which informed the Jewifh Prophet [g].

[f] DR. MIDDLETON, vol. III. p. 177.
[g] See further on this fubject, D. L. vol. V. p. 290.

To

To proceed with our fubject. It further S E R M.
appears,   III.

III. On the grounds of the text, we now
ftand upon, " to be very conceivable and
credible that the line of prophecy fhould
run chiefly in one family and people, as
we are informed it did, and that the other
nations of the earth fhould be no further
the *immediate* objects of it, than as they
chanced to be connected with that people."

Prophecy, in the ideas of fcripture, was
not ultimately given for the private ufe of
this or that nation, nor yet for the nobler
and more general purpofe of proclaiming
the fuperintending providence of the deity
(an awful truth, which men might collect
for themfelves from the eftablifhed confti-
tution of nature) but *fimply* to evidence the
truth of the Chriftian revelation. It was
therefore confined to one nation, purpofely
fet apart to preferve and atteft the oracles
of God; and to exhibit, in their public
records and whole hiftory, the proofs and
cre-

credentials of an amazing difpenfation, which God had decreed to accomplifh in Chrift Jefus [h].

This conclufion, I fay, feems naturally and fairly drawn from the great principle, that *the fpirit of prophecy was the teftimony of Jefus*, becaufe the means appear to be well fuited and proportioned to the *end*. The *Teftimony* thought fit to be given, was not one or two prophecies only, but a *fcheme* of prophecy, gradually prepared and continued through a large tract of time. But how could fuch a fcheme be executed, or rather how could it clearly be feen, that

[h] Quand UN SEUL HOMME auroit fait un livre des prédictions de Jefus Chrift pour le tems et pour la maniere, et que Jefus Chrift feroit venu conformément à ces propheties, ce feroit une force infinie. Mais il y a bien plus ici. C'eft une SUITE D'HOMMES durant quatre mille ans, qui conftamment & fans variation viennent l'un enfuite de l'autre prédire ce même avénement. C'eft UN PEUPLE TOUT ENTIER qui l'annonce, et qui fubfifte pendant quatre mille années, pour rendre EN CORPS témoignage des affurances qu'ils en ont, & dont ils ne peuvent être detournés par quelques menaces et quelque perfecution qu'on leur faffe: CECI EST TOUT AUTREMENT CONSIDERABLE. Pafcal.

there

there was fuch a fcheme in view, if fome
one people had not been made the repofitory, and, in part, the inftrument of the
divine counfels, in regard to Jefus ; fome
one people, I fay, among whom we might
trace the feveral parts of fuch a fcheme,
and obferve the dependance they had on
each other ; that fo the *idea*, of what we
call a fcheme, might be duly impreffed
upon us?

For, had the notices concerning the
Redeemer been difperfed indifferently among
all nations, where had been that uncorrupt
and unfufpected teftimony, that continuity
of evidence, that unbroken chain of prediction, all tending, by juft degrees, to the
fame point, which we now contemplate
with wonder in the Jewifh fcriptures?

It is not then that the reft of the world
was overlooked [i] in the plan of God's providence, but that he faw fit to employ the
miniftry of *one* people, This laft, I fay, and
not the other, is the reafon why the divine

[i] See the paffage before referred to in Serm. I. p. 7.

commu-

communications concerning Chrift were appropriated to the Jews.

Yes, but " fome one of the *greater* nations had better been intrufted with that charge." This circumftance, I allow, might have ftruck a fuperficial obferver more : but could the integrity of the prophetic fcheme have been more difcernible amidft the multiform and infinitely involved tranfactions of a mighty people, than in the fimpler ftory of this fmall Jewifh family ; or would the hand or work of God, who loves to manifeft himfelf by weak inftruments, have been more confpicuous in that defignation ?

On the whole, I forget not, with what awful diffidence it becomes us to reafon on fuch fubjects. But the *fact* being, that *one*, in preference to other nations, had the honour of conveying the prophetic admonitions concerning Jefus, it may be allowable to inquire, with modefty, into the reafons of that appointment ; and the *end* of prophecy being clearly affigned in facred fcripture,

fcripture, fuch reafons will not be haftily rejected, as obvioufly prefent themfelves to an inquirer from the *confideration* of that end.

The benefits of prophecy, though conveyed by one nation, would finally redound to all ; and the more *effectually*, we have feen, for being conveyed by one nation. May we not conclude then (having the *fact*, as I faid, to reafon upon) that, to obtain fuch purpofe, it was fit to felect *a peculiar people ?* And, if thus much be acknowledged, it will hardly be thought a queftion of much moment, though no anfwer could be given to it, why the *Jews* had that exclufive privilege conferred upon them.

It is true, a great fcheme of prophecy was once revealed to a Gentile King [k]; but a King, connected with the Jews, and who had a Jewifh prophet for his interpreter. It is, befides, obfervable of that prophetic fcheme, that it laid open the future fortunes of four great empires; but

[k] Daniel, c. ii.

all

all of them inftruments in the hand of God
to carry on his defigns, on the Jewifh
people firft, but ultimately, with regard to
Jefus. For, it hath been remarked with
equal truth and penetration, that Nebu-
chadnezzar's vifion of the four kingdoms
was defigned, as a fort of *prophetic chronology*, to point out, by a feries of fucceffive
empires, the beginning and end of Chrift's
fpiritual kingdom. So that the reafon,
why thofe four empires only were diftinguifhed by the fpirit of prophecy, was,
not becaufe they were greater than all
others, but simply becaufe the courfe
of their hiftory led, in a regular and
direct fucceffion, to the times and reign
of Chrift [1].

[1] Eft autem Quaternio ifte regnorum Danielis
(quod imprimis obfervari velim) CHRONOLOGIA QUÆ-
DAM PROPHETICA, non tam annorum quàm regnorum intervallis diftincta, ubi regnorum in præcipuâ
orbis terrarum parte, fimul ecclefiam et populum Dei
complexâ, fibi invicem fuccedentium ferie, monftratur
tempus quo Chrifti regnum à tot feculis promiffum et
primùm inchoandum fit, idemque demum certis temporibus confummandum.

We

We fee then, on the principle, *that pro-* phecy *was given for the fake of Jefus only,* that no prefumption lies againſt the truth of it, on account of its refpecting chiefly one people, how inconfiderable foever in itfelf, or from its filence in regard to fome of the largeſt and moſt flourifhing king-doms that have appeared in the world.

IV. Laſtly (for I now haſten to an end of this difcourfe) I infer from the fame principle, " That, if, even after a mature confideration of the prophecies, and of the events, in which they are taken to be

—Ex his, quæ dicta funt, ratio elucét, qua re, ex om-nibus mundi regnis, quatuor hæc fola felegit Spiritus fanctus, quorum fata tam infigni ornaret prophetiâ ; nempe quia ex his folis inter omnia mundi regna pe-ríodus temporum ejufmodi contexi potuit, qua rectâ ferie et ordinatâ fucceffione perduceret ad tempora et momenta regni Chriſti. Non verò quia nulla iſtis paria imperia, forfan et áliquîbus majora, per omniæ fecula orbis vifurus eſſet. Nam neque Saracenorum olim, neque hodie Turcarum, neque Tartarorum regna ditionis amplitudine Perfico aut Græco, puto néc Affyrio, quicquam concedunt; imò, ni fallor, excedunt.

MEDE's *Works,* B. III. *p.* 712. *Lond.* 1672.

G   fulfilled,

fulfilled, there fhould, after all, be fome
cloud remaining on this fubject, which
with all our wit or pains we cannot wholly
remove, this ftate of things would afford no
objection to prophecy, becaufe it is indeed
no other than we might reafonably expect.''

For, 1. If Jefus be the end of prophecy,
the fame reafons that made it fit to deliver
fome predictions darkly, will further account to us for fome degree of obfcurity in
the application of them to their correfponding events.

I fay—will *account* to us for fuch obfcurity — for, whatever thofe *reafons* were,
they could not have taken effect, but by
the intervention of fuch *means*, as muft
darken in fome degree, the application of
a prophecy, even after the accomplifhment
of it; unlefs we fay, that an object can be
feen as diftinctly through a *veil*, as without
one.   For inftance; *figurative language* is
the chief of thofe means, by which it
pleafed the infpirer to throw a fhade
on prophecies, unfulfilled: but figurative
language,

language, from the nature of it, is not
fo precife and clear, as *literal expreffion*,
even when the event prefigured has lent its
aid to illuftrate and explain that language.

If then it was *fit* that fome prophecies
concerning Jefus fhould be *delivered* obfcurely, it cannot be fuppofed that fuch
prophecies, when they come to be *applied*,
will acquire a full and abfolute perfpicuity[m].

2. If the difpenfation of Jefus be the
main fubject of the prophecies, then may
fome of them be ftill impenetrable to us,
becaufe the various fortunes of that difpenfation are not yet perfectly difclofed, and
fo fome of them may not hitherto have
been fulfilled. But the completion of a

[m] To this purpofe the late learned and ingenious
author of the *Difcourfes on Prophecy*—" A figurative
and dark defcription of a future event will be figurative and dark ftill, when the event happens." And
again—" No event can make a figurative or metaphorical expreffion to be a plain or literal one." Bifhop
Sherlock, *Difc.* II. *p.* 32 and 36, *London*, 1749.

prophecy

prophecy is that which gives the utmoſt degree of clearneſs, of which it is capable.

3. But laſtly and chiefly, if the end and uſe of prophecy be to atteſt the truth of Chriſtianity, then may we be ſure that ſuch atteſtation will not carry with it the utmoſt degree of evidence. For Chriſti-anity is plainly a ſtate of diſcipline and probation ; calculated to improve our moral nature, by giving ſcope and exerciſe to our moral faculties. So that, though the evi-dence for it be *real* evidence, and on the whole *ſufficient* evidence, yet neither can we expect it to be of that ſort which ſhould compell our aſſent. Something muſt be left to quicken our attention, to excite our induſtry, and to try the natural ingenuity of the human mind.

Had the purpoſe of prophecy been to ſhew, merely, that a predicted event was foreſeen, then the end had been beſt anſwered by throwing all poſſible evidence into the completion. But its concern being to ſhew this to ſuch only as ſhould be diſpoſed

poſed to admit a reaſonable degree of evidence, it was not neceſſary, or rather it
was plainly not fit, that the completion
ſhould be ſeen in that ſtrong and irreſiſtible
light.[n].

For all the reaſons, now given, (and
doubtleſs, for many more) it was to be expected, that prophecy would not be one
cloudleſs emanation of light and glory. If
it be clear enough to ſerve the ends, for
which it was deſigned, if through all its
obſcurities, we be able to trace the hand
and intention of its divine author, what
more would we have? How improvidently,
indeed, do we aſk more of that great Being,
who, for the ſake of the *natural* world,
clothes the heavens with blackneſs [Iſ. 1. 3.];
and in equal mercy to the *moral* world, veils
his nature and providence *in thick clouds, and
makes darkneſs his pavilion* [Pſ. xviii. 11]?

[n] Le deſſein de Dieu eſt plus de perfectionner la volonté, que l'eſprit. Or, la clarté perfaite ne ſerviroit
qu'à l'eſprit, & nuiroit à la volonté. Paſcal.

To

SERM.
III.

To THESE deductions from the text, more might be added. For I believe it will be found that if the *end* of prophecy, as here delivered, be steddily kept in view and diligently pursued, it will go a great way towards leading us to a prosperous issue in most of those inquiries, which are thought to perplex this subject. But I mean to reason from it no farther than just to shew, in the way of specimen, the method in which it becomes us to speculate on the prophetic system. We are not to imagine principles, at pleasure, and then apply them to that system. But we are, first, to find out what the principles are, on which prophecy is founded, and by which it claims to be tried; and then to see whether they will *hold*, that is, whether they will aptly and properly apply to the particulars, of which it is compounded. If they will, the system itself is thus far clearly justified. All that remains is to compare the prophecies with their corresponding events, in order to assure ourselves

that

that there is real evidence of their completion.

The *ufe* of this method has been fhewn
in FOUR capital inftances. It is objected
to the fcriptural prophecies, *that they are
obfcure—that they abound in double fenfes—
that they were delivered to one people—that,
after all, there is fometimes difficulty in making out the completion*—all of them, it is
faid, very fufpicious circumftances; and
which rather indicate a fcheme of human
contrivance, than of divine infpiration.

To thefe objections it is replied, that,
from the very idea which the fcriptures
themfelves give of prophecy, thefe circumftances muft needs be found in it; and
further ftill, that thefe circumftances,
when fairly confidered, do honour to that
idea: for that the obfcurity, complained
of, refults, *from the immenfity of the fcheme*
—the double fenfes, *from the intimate connection of its parts*—the partial and confined
delivery, *from the wifdom and neceffity of
felecting a peculiar people to be the vehicle and*

G 4 *repofi-*

S E R M. *repositotry of the sacred* oracles—And laftly,
III. the incomplete evidence, *from the nature of*
the subject, and from the moral genius of that
difpenfation, to which the fcheme of prophecy
itfelf belongs.

In conclufion, it is now feen to what purpofe thefe preliminary difcourfes ferve, and in what method they have been con‑ ducted.

The FIRST, fhewed the vanity and folly of reafoning on the fubject of fcriptural prophecy from our preconceived fancies and arbitrary affumptions. The SECOND, fhewed the only true way of reafoning upon it to be from fcriptural principles, and then opened and explained *one* fuch principle. In this LAST, I have fhewn that, by pro‑ fecuting this way of reafoning from the principle affigned, fome of the more fpe‑ cious objections to the fcriptural prophe‑ cies are eafily obviated.

Taken together, thefe three difcourfes ferve to illuftrate the *general* idea of pro‑ phecy,

phecy, confidered as one great fcheme of *teftimony* to the religion of Jefus; and con- fequently open a way for the fair and equitable confideration of *particular* prophecies, the more immediate fubject of this Lecture.

SER-

SERMON IV.

The general Argument from PROPHECY.

JOHN xiii. 19.

Now I tell you before it come, that when it is come to pafs, ye may believe, that I am He.

SERM.
IV.

IT hath been concluded (not on the flight grounds of an hypothefis, but on the exprefs authority of fcripture,) that prophecy was given TO ATTEST THE MISSION OF JESUS: to afford a reafonable evidence, that the fcheme of redemption, of which he was the great inftrument and minifter, was, in truth, of divine appointment;

ment; and was carried on under the
immediate cognizance and direction of
the Supreme Being, whofe prerogative it
is to fee through all time, and to *call*
thofe things, which be not, as though they
were ᵃ.

Our next inquiry will be, how the prophetic fcriptures *ferve* to that end, and
what that *evidence* is (I mean, taking for
granted, not the truth of the prophetic
fcheme itfelf, but the truth of the *repre-*
fentation, given of it in fcripture) which is
thus adminiftered to us by the light of
prophecy.

I. The text refers to a particular prophecy of our Lord, concerning the trea-
chery of Judas; of which, fays he to his
difciples, *I now tell you before it come, that,*
when it is come to pafs, ye may believe that I
am He: that is, " I add this, to the other
predictions concerning myfelf; that, when

ᵃ Rom. iv. 17.

ye

ye fee it fulfilled, as it foon will be, ye
may be the more convinced of my being
the perfon, I affume to be, the *Meffias
foretold.*"

The information, here given, was perhaps intended by our Lord to ferve a particular purpofe, To prevent, we will fay,
the offence, which the difciples might
have taken at the circumftance of his being
betrayed by one of them, if they had
not, previoufly, been admonifhed of it.
But the reafon of the thing fhews, that
the *ufe*, which the difciples are directed to
make of this prophecy, was the *general*
ufe of the prophecies concerning Jefus.
The completion was to verify the prediction, in all cafes; and to convince the
world, That HE was the Meffiah, in whom
fuch things fhould be feen to be accomplifhed, as had been expreffly foretold [b].

---

[b] Ταῦτα ὁ Θεὸς προεμήνυσε διὰ τῶ προφηλικῶ πνεύματ⁣@·
μέλλειν γίνεσθαι, ἵν᾽, ὅταν γένηlαι, μὴ ἀπιςηθῇ, ἀλλ᾽ ἐκ
τῶ προειρῆσθαι πιςευθῇ.

J. MARTYR, *Apol.* I. *c.* 74.

Indeed

Indeed prophecies, unaccomplifhed, may have their ufe; that is, they may ferve to raife a general expectation of a predicted *event* in the minds of thofe, who, for other reafons, regard the *perfon* predicting it, in the light of a true prophet. And fuch might be one, a *fubordinate*, ufe of the prophecies concerning Jefus: but they could not be applied to the *proof* of his pretenfions, till they were feen to be fulfilled. Nor can they be fo applied even then, unlefs the things predicted be, confefledly, beyond the reach of human forefight.

Under thefe conditions, the argument is clear and eafy, and will lie thus.—" A great variety of diftant, or, at leaft, future events, infcrutable to human fagacity, and refpecting one perfon (whom we will call, Meffiah) have been by different men, and at different times, predicted. Thefe events have accordingly come to pafs, in the hiftory and fortunes of one perfon; in fuch fort, that each is feen to be, in a proper fenfe,

                                    fulfilled

fulfilled in him, and all together in no other perſon whatſoever : Therefore the prediction of theſe events was divinely inſpired : or (which comes to the ſame thing) therefore the perſon, claiming under theſe predictions to be the Meſſiah, or perſon foretold, hath his claims confirmed and juſtified by the higheſt authority, that of God himſelf."

Such is the argument from prophecy : and on this foundation, Jeſus aſſumes to be the MESSIAH ; and his Religion, to be DIVINE.

II. Let us now ſee, what the amount of that *evidence* is, which reſults from this kind of proof.

Careleſs talkers may ſay, and ſometimes think, " that prophecy is but an art of conjecturing ſhrewdly ; that the ſagacity of one man is ſeen to be vaſtly ſuperior to that of another ; that, in ſome men, the natural faculty may be ſo improved by experience, as to look like *divination* ; and

that

that no precife bounds can be fet to its powers." Light or fceptical minds may, I fay, amufe themfelves with fuch fancies: but ferious men will readily acknowledge, That many future events, efpecially, if *remote,* or *extraordinary*[c], or defcribed with fome degree of *particularity*, are not within the ability of the human mind to predict. And, to cut off all occafion of cavil, let it be owned, that the argument under confideration is, or ought to be, drawn from the completion of prophecies, fo qualified.

[c] Socrates foretold that he fhould *dye within three days:* and the event followed.—*Eft apud Platonem Socrates, cùm effet in cuftodiâ publicâ, dicens Critoni fuo familiari, fibi poft tertium diem effe moriendum—quod, ut eft dictum, fic fcribitur contigiffe* [Cic. de Div. *l.* i. *c.* 25.] Jefus foretold that he fhould fuffer death by *crucifixion.* [John iii. 14. viii. 28. xii. 32.]: He, likewife, foretold that he fhould *rife from the dead,* within *three days* after his crucifixion [John ii. 19. Matth. xii. 39, 40.] —The *firft* of thefe predictions, might be a fagacious conjecture. Can it be faid of fuch as the *two laft*—

Augurium, ratio eft, et conjectura futuri?

Ovid. Trift. *l.* I. vIII. 51.

To

To evade the force, which this argu-ment apparently carries with it, it muſt then be ſaid, That the completion of any particular prophecy, alledged, was fortu-itous, or, what we call, a *lucky hit*.

" Coincidencies of this ſort, we may be told, are very frequent. In the ceaſeleſs revolution of human affairs, ſome event or other will be turning up, which may give a countenance to the wildeſt and moſt ha-zardous conjecture. Hence it is, that every groundleſs fear, every dream, almoſt, has the appearance of being realized by ſome correſponding accident ; which will not be long in occurring to thoſe, who are upon the watch to make ſuch diſcoveries. Upon theſe grounds, the ſuperſtition of *omens* hath, at all times, been able to ſuſ-tain itſelf ; and to acquire a degree of credit, even with wiſe men. We ſee, then, that *chance*, in a good degree, ſup-plies the place of inſpiration ; and that He, who ſets up for a Prophet, is likely to drive a ſafe, as well as gainful trade ;

eſpeci-

efpecially, if he have but the difcretion
not to deal too freely in precife defcriptions
of *times*, and *perfons*[d] : a confideration, of
great moment to the men of this craft[e];
and which hath not been overlooked by
thofe, whom we account *true* prophets."

Such libertine reflections, as thefe, thrown.
out with an air of negligent ridicule, have
too often the effect intended by them.   At
the fame time, they difguft fober men,
and are thought too light and trivial to
deferve a confutation.   But, becaufe I take
thefe fuggeftions, with whatever levity, or
difingenuity, they may be made, to contain the whole, or at leaft, the chief

---

[d] Hoc fi eft in libris, in *quem hominem*, et in *quod
tempus* eft ? Callidè enim, qui illa compofuit, perfecit,
ut, quodcunque accidiffet, prædictum videretur, *homi-
num et temporum definitione fublatâ*—faid, in difcredit of
the Sibylline oracles [*De Div. l.* ii. *p.* 295. *fol. Lutet.*
1565]: how far applicable to the fcriptural prophecies,
will be feen in its place.

[e] Διὰ τὸ ὅλως εἶναι ἁμάρτημα ἔλαττον, διὰ τῶν γενῶν
τᾶ πράγμαῖος λέγᾶσιν οἱ μάνῖεις.   And again—οἱ χρησ-
μολόγοι, ᾶ προσορίζονῖαι πότε.   Ariftot. Rhet. l. iii. c. v.

H   ftrength

ſtrength of the infidel cauſe, on this ſubject, I ſhall not decline to give them a very
ſerious anſwer.

IT IS TRUE, no doubt, what is here
alledged, That the conjectures of fanciful
or deſigning men, whether grounded on
caſual ſigns, or delivered in the direct way
of prophecy, have been frequently verified
in the events; that is, ſuch events have
actually come to paſs, in the ſenſe put
upon the *ſign*, when it was obſerved, and
in the literal ſenſe of the *prophecy*, as delivered.　Hiſtory and common life, it is
agreed, abound in ſuch inſtances[f]: and
I ſhall even make no ſcruple to produce
one of each ſort; as much, at leaſt, to the
purpoſe of theſe objectors, as any of thoſe,
which they have produced for themſelves.

Nothing is more famous in the annals
of antient Rome, than the ſtory of Romu-

[f] Permultorum exemplorum et noſtra plena eſt ref-
publica, et omnia regna, omneſque populi, cunctæque
gentes, augurum prædictis multa incredibiliter vera
cecidiſſe.

Cic. de Leg. l. iı. *p.* 337.

lus,

lus, and his TWELVE VULTURS; an *omen* SERM.
this, on which the aufpicious name of the IV.
rifing city, and the fortune of its founder,
were, at once, eftablifhed[g]. What further
conftruction was then put on this prodigy,
doth not appear: but, as the fcience of
augury advanced in fucceeding times, a
very momentous and ftriking prophecy
was grounded upon it. For we have it
affirmed[h], on the high authority of M. T.

[g] Certabant, urbem Romam, Remoramne vocarent.
Omnibu' cura viris, uter effet induperator.

- - - - - -

Cedunt de cœlo ter quatuor corpora fancta
Avium, præpetibus fefe, pulchrifque locis dant.
Confpicit inde fibi data Romulus effe priora,
Aufpicio regni ftabilita fcamna folumque.
            Cic. de Div. l. i. c. 48.

[h] Quot fæcula urbi Romæ debeantur, dicere meum
non eft: fed, quid apud Varronem legerim, non tace-
bo. Qui libro Antiquitatum duodevicefimo ait, fuiffe
Vettium Romæ in augurio non ignobilem, ingenio
magno, cuivis docto in difceptando parem; eum fe
audiffe dicentem: Si ita effet, ut traderent hiftorici, de
Romuli urbis condendæ auguriis, ac *duodecim vulturi-
bus*; quoniam cxx annos incolumis præteriiffet populus
Romanus, ad *mille et ducentos* perventurum.
    CENSORINUS *de die natali,* c. xvii. *p.* 97. *Cantab.* 1695.

            H 2   VARRO,

VARRO, that Vettius Valens, an augur of diftinguifhed name in thofe days, took occafion from this circumftance (and in the hearing of Varro himfelf) to fix the duration of the Roman empire. The TWELVE VULTURS, he faid, which appeared to Romulus, *portended,* that the fovereignty of that ftate and city, whofe foundations he was then laying, fhould continue for the fpace of TWELVE HUNDRED YEARS. It is of no moment to inquire, on what principles of his art the learned augur proceeded, in this calculation. The TRUTH is, that the event correfponded, in a furprizing manner, to the conjecture; and that the *majefty* of the weftern empire (of which Rome was the capital) *did,* indeed, expire under the mercilefs hands of the Goths, about the time limited by this augural prophet.

It fhould, further, be obferved that this prediction was of fuch credit and notoriety, as to take the attention of the later Romans them-

themfelves[i], who looked with anxiety for
the accomplifhment of it: and that it was
delivered by Valens, at leaft *five hundred
years* .before the event; when there was
not the leaft appearance, that this cataftrophe would befall, what was called, the
ETERNAL CITY, within that period.

THIS is an inftance of divination from
augury. The OTHER, I am about to
give, is a *prophecy*, in full form; refpecting a ftill more important fubject, and
equally accomplifhed in the event. A
poet, in the ideas of paganifm, was a prophet, too. And Seneca [k] hath left us, in

[i] Hence Sidonius, in perfonating the city of Rome,
makes her afk—

Quid, rogo, *bis feno* mihi *vulture* Thufcus arufpex
Portendit ?

Sidon. Carm. vii. 55.

And again, addreffing himfelf to the fame city,

Jam propè fata *tui biffenas vulturis alas*
Complebant (fcis namque tuos, fcis, *Roma*, labores.)

Ib. ver. 358.

And, before him, Claudian, to the fame purpofe—

Tunc reputant annos, *interceptoque volatu*
Vulturis, incidunt properatis fæcula metis.

B. G. ver. 262.

[k] Medea, ver. 374.

H 3   proof

proof of the infpiration to which, in his double capacity, he might pretend, the following oracle:

> ―― venient annis
> Secula feris, quibus Oceanus
> Vincula rerum laxet, et ingens
> Pateat tellus, Tiphyfque novos
> Detegat orbes; nec fit terris
> Ultima Thule.

This prediction was made in the reign of Nero; and, for more than *fourteen hundred* years, might only pafs for one of thofe fallies of imagination, in which poetry fo much delights. But, when, at length, in the clofe of the *fifteenth* century, the difcoveries of Columbus had realized this vifion: when that enterprizing navigator had forced the barriers of the vaft Atlantic ocean; had *loofened*, what the poet calls, *the chains of things*; and in thefe *later ages* [1], as was expreffly fignified, had fet at liberty an immenfe continent, fhut up before in furrounding feas from the commerce and acquaintance of our world;

[1] *Annis feris.*

wh

when this event, I fay, fo important and
fo unexpected, came to pafs, it might
almoft furprize one into the belief, that
the prediction was fomething more than
a poetical fancy; and that Heaven had,
indeed, revealed to *one* favoured Spaniard,
what it had decreed, in due time, to accomplifh by *another*.

THESE two inftances of cafual conjecture, converted by time and accident
into prophecies, I fhall take for granted,
are as remarkable, as any other that can
be alledged. Cicero, in his firft book of
Divination, where he laboured to affert the
reality of fuch a power in the pagan world,
was able to produce nothing equal, or com-
parable to them. We have the fulleft
evidence, that thefe two predictions were
delivered by the perfons, to whom they are
afcribed; and in the time, in which they
are faid to have been delivered, that is,
many hundred years before the event.
They, both of them, refpect events of the
greateft dignity and importance; one of

H 4   them,

them, the downfal of the *mightieſt empire*, that hath hitherto ſubſiſted on the face of the earth ; and the other, the diſcovery of a *new world.* Both, expreſs the *time*, when theſe extraordinary events were to happen : the *latter*, by a general deſcription, indeed, yet not more general, than is frequent in the ſcriptural prophets; but the *former*, in the moſt preciſe and limited terms. In a word, both theſe predictions are authentic, important, circumſtantial; they foretell events, which no human ſagacity could have foreſeen; and they have been ſtrictly and properly fulfilled.

Now, if ſuch coincidencies, as theſe, do not infer divine inſpiration; if, notwithſtanding all appearances to the contrary, it muſt ſtill be allowed (as it will, on all ſides) that they were ſimply *fortuitous*, or what we call the effects of hazard and pure chance, by what characters ſhall we diſtinguiſh genuine from pretended, prophecies ; or in what way ſhall it be diſcovered, that the ſcriptural prophets ſpake

by

by the fpirit of *God*, when thefe pagan diviners could thus prophecy, by their *own*
fpirit?

To this objection, put with all the force
which I am able to give to it, I reply directly, That the diftinction, fo importunately demanded, may very eafily and
clearly be affigned.

If *one or two* fuch prophecies, *only*, had
occurred in our fcriptures; if even *feveral*
fuch had occurred in the whole extent of
thofe writings, and in the large compafs
of time, they take up, without defcending
to a greater detail than is expreffed in thefe
pagan oracles; nay, if *a greater number ftill*
of fuppofed predictions, thus generally delivered in the facred writings, had been applicable only to fingle independent events,
difperfed indifferently through the feveral
ages of the world: In all thefe cafes, I
fhould freely admit, that the argument
from prophecy was very precarious and
unfatisfactory : I could even fuppofe, with
the deriders of this argument, that fo

many,

many, and fuch prophecies, fo directed,
might not improbably be accounted for,
from fome odd conjuncture of circumftances; and that the accomplifhment of
them did by no means infer a certainty of
infpiration.

But, if now, on the other hand, it be
indifputable, That a vaft variety of predictions are to be found in the fcriptures of
the Old and New Teftament; That a great
part of thefe predictions are delivered with
the utmoft degree of minutenefs and particularity; and, laftly, That *all* of them,
whether general or particular, refpect one
common fubject, and profefs to have, or
to expect, their completion in one connected fcheme of things, and, upon the
matter, in one fingle perfon : On this latter
fuppofition, I muft ftill think, that there
is great reafon to admit the divine infpiration of fuch prophecies, when feen to be
fulfilled.

To convert this fuppofition into a *proof,*
is not within the fcope and purpofe of
this

this Lecture. The work hath been under-
taken and difcharged by many others : or,
it may be fufficient, in fo clear a point, to
refer you directly to the Scriptures themfelves; which no man can read without
feeing, that the prophecies, contained in
them, are extremely numerous—that many
of thefe prophecies are minutely circum-
ftantial—and that one perfon, whoever he
be, is the principal object of them all. My
concern, at prefent, is only to fhew, that,
if the fuppofition itfelf be well founded,
the *inference*, juft now mentioned, is rightly made.

  1. Firft, then, if the prophecies in the
Old and New Teftament be very numerous,
and if thofe prophecies, fo many of them,
I mean, as are alledged in this controverfy
with unbelievers, have had a reafonable
completion (and I have a right to make
this laft fuppofition, when the queftion is
concerning the *account* to be given of fuch
a fact) : If, I fay, we argue from thefe two
affumptions, it muft appear highly credible
and

SERM.
IV.

and probable, that fo numerous prophecies, fo fulfilled, had not their origin from human conjecture, nor their accomplifhment from what we call, *Chance.* For mere conjecture is not ufually fo happy; nor chance, fo conftant [m]. Further ftill; if the fcriptural prophecies have been completed in numerous inftances, and if in *no* inftance whatfoever can it be clearly fhewn that they have failed in the event, the prefumption is ftill ftronger, that fuch coincidence could not be fortuitous; and a material difference between fcriptural prophecy, and pagan divination is, at the fame time, pointed out. For, that, in the multitude

[m] *Cafu,* inquis. Itáne verò quicquam poteft effe *cafu* factum, quod omnes habet in fe numeros veritatis? Quatuor tali jacti, *cafu* Venereum efficiunt. Num etiam centum Venereos, fi cccc talos jeceris, *cafu* futuros putas? *De Div. l.* i. *p.* 259, *Lutet.* 1565.— Had the fuppofed cafe been fairly applied to the fubject, there had been an end of the difpute; as may appear from the pitiful anfwer, made in the next book to this reafoning—dixifti multa de *cafu:* ut, Venereum jaci poffe cafu, quatuor talis jactis: quadringentis, centum Venereos non poffe cafu confiftere. Primùm, NESCIO, CUR NON POSSINT.—Was this, like a philofopher?

of

of pretended oracles in the days of paganifm, fome few only fhould come to pafs,
while the generality of them fell to the
ground, may well be the fport of *fortune* ⁿ.
But, that very many prophecies, recorded
in our fcriptures, have had an evident completion, when not *one* of all thofe, there
recorded, can be convicted of impofture,
muft furely be the work of *defign*.

The argument cannot be denied to have
real weight, though the expreffion of *all*
the prophecies were allowed to be *general*.
But this is, by no means, the cafe. It is further affumed, and is evident to all that have
read the Scriptures, that a great number
of them are delivered with the utmoft degree of minutenefs and particularity. And,
from this affumption, I infer,

ⁿ Multa, vera, inquit, evadere. Quid, quòd multo
plura, falfa? Nónne ipfa varietas, quæ eft propria for-
tunæ, fortunam effe caufam, non naturam, docet?
De Div. l. ii. *p.* 295. This, methinks, looks like
fenfe.

2. Secondly,

———

2. Secondly, that the accomplifhment of prophecies, fo circumftantially defined, can ftill lefs be imputed to mere chance.

Without doubt, if all the prophecies concerning the Mefiiah had been penned in the ftyle of the firft—*that the feed of the woman fhould bruife the ferpent's head*— though even then there might be reafon for applying them, exclufively, to the perfon of Chrift, yet, the evidence, that they were intended to be fo applied, would have been much obfcured by the mode of expreffion; the wide cover of which might feem to afford room for other applications. But when, to this general prophecy, the theme of all fucceeding ones, it is further added, That this feed of the woman, fhould be the feed of Abraham; of the tribe of Juda; of the family of David; that he fhould be born at Bethlehem; that he fhould appear in the world at a time, limited by certain events, and even precifely determined to a certain period:—when, after a particular defcription

of

of his life and office, it is said of him, that he should be betrayed by an intimate friend; and sold for a price, exactly specified; that he should suffer a particular kind of death; should have his hands and feet pierced; should have vinegar given him to drink; and should be buried in the sepulchre of a rich man—with innumerable other particularities of the like nature [o] —When all this, I say, is considered, the improbability, that these *specific* characters should meet in the same person by *chance*, is so great, that a reasonable man will scarce venture on so hazardous a position.

3. Still this is not all. Were we at liberty to apply even *numerous, and circumstantial* prophecies, to *any* person, indifferently, whom they might suit, and to *any*

[o] See the antient apologists, who are frequent and large on this subject; and, of the moderns, see especially Huetii *Dem. Evang. Prop.* IX.—Bishop Kidder's *Dem. of the Messias*, c ii. *p.* 17, 18. *London*, 1726, *fol.* —Dr. Clarke's *Evidences of Nat. and Rev. Religion.*— *Pensées de M. Pascal, p.* 108.

events

events indifcriminately, to which they might correfpond, fought out at large in the hiftory of mankind, the force of the argument for *defign* in fuch prophecies, might in good meafure be eluded. But, when we reflect on what, in part, hath appeared under the laft article, that all the fcriptural predictions profefs to refpect one certain fcheme of things; run in the line of one people; and point ultimately at one perfon, whofe country, and family, and age, and birth-place are exactly defined; the application of them is fo limited and reftrained, that, if they fuit at all, there is fcarce a poffibility of excluding actual fore-fight, and intention.

LET ME, further, obferve, that, as, upon this idea of a confined, connected, and dependent fcheme, in the prophecies, the detection of impofture, if there be any, is much facilitated; fo, on the other hand, if the prophecies can be fairly applied in this way, not only the prefumption, that they were given to be fo applied, is much
increafed,

increafed, but a clearer infight into the fcope and meaning of them, is obtained. For, in a fyftem of prophecy, directed to one and the fame general end, preceding prophecies prepare the way for interpreting thofe that follow, and every fucceeding prophecy reflects fome light on thofe that went before. Thus, the general evidence, arifing from this fpecies of argument, is, in all ways, augmented; while we fee, that lefs room is left to chance in verifying the more clear and direct prophecies, and that frefh light is let in upon fuch as are more ambiguous or obfcure.

It is faid, that many paffages in the prophets are applied to Jefus, on very flight grounds. This would be true, if the prophetic fcriptures, like the pagan oracles, had no determinate fcheme in view, and had, for their object, only detached and unconnected events. But, on this fcriptural principle, that one common purpofe is in the contemplation of that divine fpirit, which dictated all thofe

I   writings,

writings, That is *expreſſed*, which is barely intimated; and every applicable prophecy is *rightly* applied : whence it is, that even ſecondary prophecies have, in the ſyſtem of revelation, all the light and force of the primary ; as, in a former diſcourſe, hath been obſerved.

This aſſertion, I know, may ſtartle ſuch perſons, as have not attended to the genius of the prophetic writings, or to that gene-ral harmony of deſign and deſtination, which makes their diſtinctive character : but it may be rendered familiar to us by reflecting on the *manner*, in which we interpret other writings, ſomewhat ſimilar to theſe.

It is generally ſuppoſed, and on good grounds, that Virgil wrote his Æneid with the view of doing honour to the perſon and government of Auguſtus. But, the ſubject of his work being taken from a former age, this was either to be done, by introducing his encomiums under the form of *prophecies*, or by conveying them indirectly

indirectly in allufive defcriptions and what
we call, *fecondary* applications. The poet
hath employed both thefe methods, with
fuccefs. The purpofe of his *predictions* is
clear; for in them the emperour is exprefly
named: and the ableft critics make no
fcruple of applying to Auguftus all thofe
paffages in this poem, which, however
they may refpect, immediately, other perfons, are yet clearly feen to be *applicable* to
Him.

We have another instance of the fame
fort, at home. Our Spenfer wrote his
famous poem, to illuftrate the virtues and
reign of Queen Elizabeth. This we know
from himfelf. Though his fcene, therefore, be laid in *Faery Land*, yet, whenever we find his fictions agreeing to the
hiftory of that princefs, or the characters
of his knights expreffive of thofe virtues,
which diftinguifhed the great perfons of
her court, we make no doubt of applying
them in that way, or of the poet's intend-
ing that they fhould be fo applied. Thefe

appli-

applications would not be equally juſtifiable in *other* works of fancy, written in that time; but the knowledge, we have of the author's general purpoſe in writing, makes them reaſonable in *this.*

It may appear from theſe examples[p], that, whenever a general ſcheme is known to be purſued by a writer, whoſe real or aſſumed character gives him a right to deal in ſecondary ſenſes and prophetic anti-cipations, that ſcheme becomes the true key, in the hands of his reader, for unlock-ing the meaning of particular parts; of many parts, which would otherwiſe not be ſeen clearly and diſtinctly to refer to ſuch ſcheme. The obſervation applies to the inſpired writers, in all its force. We underſtand, that they had one common and predominant ſcheme in view, which was *to bear teſtimony to Jeſus.* Their writ-

---

[p] I take theſe examples to be more in point, than thoſe given by Biſhop Butler in his *Analogy*, P. II. c. vii. *p.* 386. *Lond.* 1740: not but thoſe, too, have their weight.

ings

ings are, then, to be interpreted in conformity to that ſcheme. Not only the more direct prophecies require this interpretation; but, if we will judge in this, as we do in other ſimilar inſtances, whatever paſſages occur in thoſe writings, which bear an apt and eaſy reſemblance to the hiſtory of Jeſus, may, or rather *muſt*, in all reaſonable conſtruction, be applied to him. SERM. IV.

Whence we ſee (to mention it, by the way) that, if no prophecy in the Old Teſtament had applied to Chriſt directly in its *primary* ſenſe, Chriſtianity might, yet, ſupport itſelf on the evidence of prophecy. For the evidence, ariſing from a *ſecondary* ſenſe of prophecies, is *real* evidence; and was certainly admitted, as ſuch, by that great man [q], whoſe miſtakes on this ſubject have afforded the occaſion of ſo much vain triumph to infidelity.

Fancy, no doubt, may grow wanton in this ſort of applications. It may find, in the prophet or poet, what was never de-

[q] Grotius.

signed by either : but, in the circumstances
supposed, the severest reader will not deny,
that *much* was probably designed by both.
It is impossible to lay down general rules,
that shall prevent all abuse in the interpretation of such writings. But good sense
will easily see, in particular cases, where
this liberty of interpreting is, in *fact*,
abused.

It is obvious to remark, that this use of
prophecy doth not commence, till the corresponding facts can be produced ; that is,
till the prophecies are seen to be fulfilled.
But this circumstance is no discredit to the
prophetic system ; which pretends not to
give immediate conviction, but to lay in,
beforehand, the *means* of conviction to such
as shall be in a condition to compare, in
due time, the prediction with the event.
Till then, prophecy serves only to raise a
general expectation of the event predicted ;
that is, it serves to make men attentive
and inquisitive, and to prepare them for
that full conviction, which it finally hath

in

in view. And this fervice, the prophecies of the Old Teftament actually did the Jews, who were led by them to expect the Meffiah, when he, in fact, appeared among them. And, had they purfued this reafonable method of interpreting the prophecies, not by their prejudices, but by correfponding events, they muft have been further led to acknowledge his miffion, as being evidently attefted by predictions, fo fulfilled. But their capital miftake lay in fuppofing, that their prophecies were fufficiently clear, without the help of any comment from fucceeding events; and thus, what they *could not* fee beforehand, they *would not* acknowledge, when thefe events came to pafs.

It follows from what hath been faid, that the obfcurity of the Jewifh prophecies concludes nothing againft the *ufe* of thofe writings, or againft the *application* of them, which Chriftians now make.

Their

Their *declared* ufe is pofterior to the facts, they adumbrate; whence the intervening obfcurity of thofe writings is no juft ground of complaint : and the *application* of them to Jefus, now that hiftory hath taught us to underftand them better, is made on principles, to which no fober man can object.

On the whole, the general evidence for the truth of Chriftianity, as refulting from the fcriptural prophecies, though poffibly not *that*, which fome may wifh or expect, is yet apparently very confiderable. *Some* coincidencies might fall out, by accident ; and *more*, might be imagined. But when *fo many*, and *fuch* prophecies are brought together, and compared with their correfponding events, it becomes ridiculous (becaufe the effect is, in no degree, proportioned to the caufe) to fay of fuch coincidencies, that they are the creatures of *fancy*, or could have been the work of chance.

The

The text fupplies the only juſt account of ſuch a phænomenon: and the ſpirit of God, methinks, calls aloud to us, in the language of his Son—*Theſe things have I told you before they come, that when they come to paſs, ye may believe, that I am* HE,

SERMON V.

Prophecies concerning Chrift's
FIRST COMING.

ISAIAH xlii. 9.

Behold, the former things are come to pafs, and new things do I declare: before they fpring forth, I tell you of them.

SERM.
V.

THE preceding difcourfes were de-figned, to open the *general idea* of prophecy; and to enforce the *general argument* from it, in proof of our holy Religion.

The way being thus far cleared, we now advance a ftep farther, and take a nearer view of THE PROPHECIES THEMSELVES.

Thefe

Thefe prophecies may be confidered
under *two* heads. They either refpect,
*the perfon and character and office of the
Meffiah*; or, *the fate and fortunes of that
kingdom*, which he came to eftablifh in the
world.

Divines call the *former* of thefe, Prophecies of his FIRST COMING : and the *other*,
Prophecies of his SECOND. Only, it may
be proper to obferve, That the *fecond* advent of the Meffiah is not, like the *firft*,
confined to one fingle and precife period,
but is gradual and fucceffive. This diftinction is founded in the reafon of the
thing. He could only come, *in perfon*,
at one limited time. He comes, *in his
power and his providence*, through all ages
of the church. His *firft* coming was then
over, when he expired on the crofs. His
fecond, commenced with his refurrection,
and will continue to the end of the world.
So that this *laft* coming of Jefus is to be
underftood of his *fpiritual kingdom*; which
is not one act of fovereignty, exerted at
once;

once; but a ſtate or conſtitution of government, ſubſiſting through a long tract of
time, unfolding itſelf by juſt degrees, and
coming, as oft, as the conductor of it
thinks fit to interpoſe by any ſignal acts
of his adminiſtration.   And in this ſenſe,
we are directed to pray, *that his kingdom*,
though long ſince ſet up, *may come*; that is,
may advance through all its ſtages, till it
arrive at that full ſtate of glory, in which
it ſhall ſhine out in *the great day*, as it is
called, the day of judgment.

It will be ſeen, as we advance in the
preſent inquiry, to what uſe this diſtinction
ſerves.

The *former* ſet of prophecies are preſumed to have had their completion, in
the hiſtory of *Jeſus*; The *latter* ſet, have
had, or are to find, their accompliſhment,
in the hiſtory of his *Religion*; And of
THESE only, it is the purpoſe of this
Lecture to ſpeak,

But

But, though the prophecies of Chrift's *firft* coming (fo largely and accurately con- fidered by many great writers) be not the immediate fubject of our inquiry, yet they muft not be wholly overlooked by us. It will contribute very much to rectify and enlarge our ideas of the divine conduct, in this whole difpenfation of prophecy, and to make way for that conviction, which the prophecies of Chrift's *fecond* coming were intended to give, if we ftop a while to contemplate the *method and œconomy* of that prophetic fyftem, by which the *firft* advent of the Meffiah was announced and prepared.

It is affumed, as a firft principle on this fubject, *That Jefus was the ultimate end and object of all the prophecies*[a]: which begin-ning from the foundation of the world[b], were, afterwards, occafionally delivered through many ages; till at length this great purpofe was profecuted more intently,

[a] Serm. II.

[b] A'π' αιῶνος. Luke i. 70.

by

by a continued and closely-compacted chain
of prophecy ; as we fee, firft, in the patri-
archal hiftory, but, chiefly, in the hiftory
of the Jewifh ftate.   For, when this people were felected from the other nations,
to anfwer many wife ends of providence, it
pleafed God to inftitute a form of government for them, which could not fubfift
without his frequent interpofition ; manifefted in fuch a way as might convince
them, that they were under the actual
and immediate conduct of their divine
fovereign.   Hence, it became a part of
this fingular œconomy, to be adminiftered
in the way of *Prophecy* ; by which it would
be feen that the hand of God was upon
them in all their more important concerns.

Upon this bafis of an *extraordinary providence*, the Jewifh government ftood : and
we are now to fee in what *manner* the prophetic fpirit, fo effential to that polity,
was employed.

1. Firft,

1. Firft, we may obferve, that, by means of this provifion for their civil regimen, an apt and commodious way was opened for carrying on the divine councils, in regard to *Jefus*; in whom, indeed, the Law itfelf was to be fulfilled. For, while the civil affairs of the Jewifh people furnifhed the occafion and fubftance of their prophecies, the divine wifdom, that infpired the prophets, fo contrived, as that their religious concerns fhould, alfo, be expreffed, or implied in them. The general theme of the *prophet*, was fome temporal fuccefs or calamity of the Jewifh ftate: the fecret purpofe of the *infpirer* was, occafionally at leaft, and when he faw fit, to predict the fpiritual kingdom of the Meffiah [c].

---

[c] This ufe and intent of prophecy was feen, and admirably expreffed, by the great *M. Pafcal*—"Les propheties font mêlées de propheties particulieres, et de celles du Meffie, afin que les propheties du Meffie ne fuffent pas fans *preuves*, et que les propheties particulieres ne fuffent pas fans *fruit.*" *Penfées,* p. 112.

We

We have innumerable inftances of this fort in the Jewifh prophets; but few, more remarkable than that of Ifaiah's prophecy, addreffed to Ahaz, king of Judah, concerning his deliverance from the two kings of Samaria and Damafcus. In the *primary*, but lower fenfe of this prophecy, the fign given was to affure Ahaz, that the land of Judæa fhould *fpeedily* be delivered from its two Royal invaders. But it had likewife *another*, and more important purpofe. The introduction of the prophecy, the fingular ftrefs laid upon it, and the exact fenfe of the terms, in which it is expreffed, make it probable, in a high degree, that it had fome fuch purpofe: and the event hath clearly proved, that the *fign given* had a refpect to the miraculous birth of Chrift, and to a deliverance much more momentous than that of Ahaz from his prefent diftrefsful fituation—*Hear ye now, O* HOUSE OF DAVID—*The Lord himfelf fhall give you a fign; Behold, a virgin fhall conceive,*

conceive, and bear a Son, and ſhall call his SERM.
name Immanuel. *Iſaiah,* vii. 13, 14. Admit that theſe words are capable of being
explained, in ſome ſort, of the *child* now
given to be a ſign, to the King of Judæa,
of his deliverance within two or three
years, as expreſſed in the following verſes;
ſtill, who ſees not that terms ſo emphati-
cal and energetic are more *properly* underſtood of *another* child, to whoſe birth and
character they are found, in the event, to
be exactly ſuited? And, if more properly,
who can doubt that theſe terms are *naturally,* that is, reaſonably underſtood of that
other child, when we conſider with what
ideas the mind of the prophet was ſtored,
and what the ultimate end and object was,
by ſuppoſition, of the prophet's inſpiration? The child promiſed was a *ſign* to
Ahaz of his deliverance; yet a ſign too,
that is, a *type,* to the houſe of David, of
another deliverance, which they expected,
which their prophets had frequently foretold, and which we have here announced

K   in

SERM.
V.

in the *name* of this miraculous child, IMMA-
NUEL, or eminently, *The Deliverer.*

There is nothing in this *sign* [d], thus interpreted, but what is eafy and unforced ;
I mean, if we bear in mind the genius and
character of the Jewifh prophecies. The

---

[d] *The Lord himfelf fhall give you a fign*, Ifai. vii. 14.—
This SIGN (and the extraordinary introduction of it, in
the words quoted, indicates no lefs) had plainly a re-
condite and even complicated meaning !

1. As addreffed to Ahaz, it was fimply an ASSURANCE,
that his deliverance from his two great enemies was
now at hand.

2. As addreffed to the *houfe of David—Hear ye now,
O houfe of David*—it was a TYPE of Chrift.

3. It was, further, a TOKEN, or pledge, that the
remote deliverance of the houfe of David by Immanuel,
fhould hereafter take place, juft as the approaching
deliverance of Ahaz, by the prophet's Son, would be
feen to do.

4. This fign, when fulfilled in the near event, would,
thenceforward, become a PROOF, or evidence, that it
would be fulfilled in the remote one.

5. Laftly, in the Antitype, the fign was a MIRACLE,
properly fo called.

So eminently was this Child, a SIGN ! A *fign*, in all
the *fenfes* of the word, as employed by the Jewifh prophets ; and to all the *purpofes*, for which figns were
given.

former

former event, fignified in the prophecy, was merely *civil:* the latter, concerned the *fpiritual* kingdom of Chrift. They were both predicted together: and the preceding event, when it came to pafs, was, further, to induce an *expectation,* that the other event would, in due time, follow. For

2. Secondly, it appears, that, to excite attention to thefe SPIRITUAL predictions, more obfcure than the other, and regarding events more remote, care was taken to fecure the authority of the prophet, by the completion of his *civil* predictions in events, diftinctly defcribed, and near at hand. Thus, Mofes might be believed by the Jews in what he faid, *of a prophet to be raifed up,* in a future age, *like to himfelf*; when they faw his prophetic bleffings and curfes upon them, according to their deferts in the land of Canaan, fo fpeedily and fo punctually executed. Thus, too, their prophet, Ifaiah, might reafonably expect to find credit with them, for the glorious things predicted by him of the

K 2   great

great deliverer, the Meffiah; when their deliverance from the Babylonifh captivity was feen fo certainly to verify his prediction of that event. The prophet himfelf exults in this argument, as decifive and unanfwerable. *Behold*, fays he, in the text, *the former things are come to pafs*, i. e. the prophecies, I have delivered to you concerning your redemption from the Affyrian bondage, will foon be fo exactly completed, that I regard them as things *paft*; *and therefore new things do I declare*; hence I claim your belief of other prophecies, concerning a much greater redemption, to take place hereafter, though there be no appearance, as yet, of any caufes tending to produce it; *for before they fpring forth, I tell you of them*. And this appears to be the general method of *all* God's prophets.

3. With thefe *new things*, thefe Spiritual prophecies concerning the *firft* coming of the Meffiah, were likewife intermixed other

other prophecies, which ran out beyond
that term and prefigured the great events
of his SECOND coming: and the warrant
for admitting *thefe*, would be the completion of thofe other prophecies, in the
perfon and fufferings of Chrift[f]. That
there are fuch prophecies in the Old
Teftament, will be fhewn hereafter. In
the mean time, it will not be thought in-
credible, that, if Jefus be indeed the end
of the prophetic fcheme, the revolutions
of his *government* fhould be foretold, as
well as the circumftances of his perfonal
appearance; in other words, that the confummation of that defign, which providence was carrying on, would not be overlooked, when the fteps and gradations of
it were fo diftinctly noted. For, in any
reafonable defign, whatfoever, the *end* is

[f] Επειδη τοινυν τα γενομενα ηδη παντα αποδεικνυμεν,
πριν η γενεσθ, προκεκηρυχθαι δια των προφητων, αναγκη
κ περι των ομοιως προφητευθεντων, μελλοντων δε γινεσθ,
πιστιν εχειν ως παντως γενησομενων.
JUSTIN MARTYR, *Apol.* i. c. 87.

K 3   firft

firſt and principally in view, though the *means* engage and may ſeem to engroſs, the attention of its author. It will then, I ſay, be no ſurprize to us to find, that prophecy ſet out with announcing the kingdom of the Meſſiah; that it never loſt ſight of that future œconomy; and only produced it into clearer view, as the ſeaſon approached for the introduction of it.

THUS MUCH concerning the *order and method* of the Jewiſh prophecies; in which one cannot but adore the profound wiſdom of their author. The *civil* prophecies are, at once, the vehicle, and the credentials, of the *ſpiritual*, concerning the *firſt* coming of Jeſus; and theſe laſt, in their turn, ſupport the credit of others, which point ſtill further at his *ſecond* coming: a ſubject, more than intimated by the *legal* prophets, but reſumed and amply diſplayed by the *evangelical*. Whence, we ſee, that the prophetic ſyſtem is ſo conſtructed, as, in the progreſs and various evolutions of it, to illuſtrate itſelf, and to afford an internal
evidence

evidence of its divinity. One great purpofe pervades the whole : and the parts, of
which it confifts, gradually prepare and
mutually fuftain each other.

But this fubject, fo curious and important, is not yet to be difmiffed. It remains to be confidered, whether *chance*, or
impofture, can in any degree account for fo
extenfive, fo connected, and fo intricate a
fyftem.

On the very face of the prophetic fcriptures it appears, that one ultimate purpofe
is in the contemplation of all the prophets.
This purpofe is unfolded by fucceffive predictions, delivered in diftant times, under
different circumftances, and by perfons,
who cannot be fufpected of acting in concert
with each other. It does not appear, that
the later prophets always underftood the
drift of the more antient; or, that either
of them clearly apprehended the whole
fcope and purpofe of their own predictions.
Yet, on comparing all their numerous prophecies with each other, and with the

K 4   events,

events, in which it is now prefumed they
have had their completion, we find a perfect harmony and confiftency between
them.   Nothing is advanced by one prophet, that is contradicted by another.   An
unity of defign is confpicuous in them all;
yet without the leaft appearance of *collufion*,
fince *each* prophet hath his own peculiar
views, and enlarges on facts and circumftances, unnoticed by any other.

Further ftill, thefe various and fucceffive
prophecies are fo intimately blended, and,
as we may fay, incorporated with each
other, that the credit of all depends on the
truth of each.   For, the accomplifhment
of them falling in different times, every
preceding prophecy becomes furety, as it
were, for thofe that follow;   and the
failure of any one muft bring difgrace and
ruin on all the reft.

Then, again, confider that the prophetic fpirit, which kept operating fo uniformly and perpetually in what is called the
former age, ceafed at that very time, when
                                            the

the great object, it had in view, was difclofed; when that future œconomy, which
it firft and laft predicted, was introduced:
a *time*, too, which was precifely determined by the old prophets themfelves. Could
they anfwer for what *defign* or *chance* might
be able to bring about ? Is it credible, that
this perennial fount of prophecy, which
ran fo copioufly from Adam to Chrift,
and watered all the ages of the Jewifh
church, fhould ftop, at once, in fo critical a feafon; and fhould never flow again
in any future age ; if fortune, or fraud,
or fanaticifm, had difpenfed its ftreams, if
any thing indeed, but the hand of God,
had opened its fource, and directed its
current ?

Nor let it be objected that a fucceffion
of prophets was *interrupted* for fome ages
before the coming of Chrift. It was fo:
but not, till preceding prophets had marked out the precife *time* of his comings ;
not, till Malachi, with whom the word

⁵ Ifaiah vii. 16, Daniel ix. 24.

of

of prophecy ceafed for a time, had foretold that this interrupted feries fhould be
refumed and finally clofed by Elijah, the
laft Jewifh prophet and *precurfor* of the
Meffiah [h]; and not, till it had been expreffly declared, that this eclipfed light of
prophecy fhould break forth again with
redoubled luftre, in the *days* of the Meffiah [i].
Who would not conclude, then, from this
very intermiffion, that prophecy was given,
or withheld, as the wifdom of God or-
dained, and not as the caprice or policy
of man directed?

It may not be pretended, that the age,
in which prophecy finally ceafed among
the Jews, will account for the fuppreffion
of this faculty, " for that it was an age of
the greateft turbulency and diforder, and
that their ruin and difperfion foon after
followed." This pretence, I fay, is altogether frivolous. For it was precifely in
thofe circumftances, that their antient pro-

[h] Mal. iv. 5. Luke xvi. 16.
[i] Joel ii. 28, 29.

phets

phets were moft numerous, and their
infpirations moft abundant. It was during
the calamitous feafon of their captivities,
that the prophetic power had been moft
fignally exercifed among the Jews. And
now, when they were carried captive into
all lands, not a fingle prophet arofe, or
hath arifen to this day, either for their reproof, or confolation[k].

If it be faid, "that the pagan oracles
ceafed, too, about the fame time; and
that the fame caufe, namely, the diffufed
light and knowledge of the Auguftan age,
was fatal to both;" befides, that this diffu-
fion of light, for obvious reafons, was not
likely to affect the Jewifh prophecies, and

---

[k] Is not their cafe exactly delineated by the prophet
Ezekiel—*Mifchief fhall come upon mifchief, and rumour
fhall be upon rumour*; *then fhall they* SEEK A VISION OF
THE PROPHET; i. e. they fhall feek what they fhall
not find, *for the* LAW *fhall perifh from the prieft, and*
COUNCIL *from the antients*; i. e. their ecclefiaftical and
civil polity, to which prophecy was annexed, fhall be
utterly abolifhed. See *Ezekiel* vii. 26. and compare
Ifaiah iii. 1, 2.

did

SERM.
V.

did not, as we certainly know, in any degree diminiſh the credit of them, with that people, the fact itſelf, aſſumed in the objection, is plainly falſe. For the pagan oracles continued for ſeveral ages after that of Auguſtus; they became leſs frequent, only, as Chriſtianity gained ground; and were not ſilenced, but among the laſt ſtruggles of expiring paganiſm[1]. So that if the Jewiſh prophecies, like thoſe of the Gentile world, had been the iſſue of *fraud*, or *fanaticiſm (principles*, that operate at all times, and, with redoubled force and activity, in the dark days of perſecution) one does not ſee, why they might not have continued to this day among the bigoted profeſſors of that religion.

· Now, put all theſe things together, that is, The long duration of the prophetic ſyſtem—the mutual dependance and cloſe connection of its ſeveral parts—the conſiſtency and uniformity of its views, all

[1] See A. VAN DALE, *de Oraculorum ethnicorum duratione atque interitu.*

termi-

terminating in one point—and the final SERM.
fuppreffion of it (as was likewife foretold) V.
at the very time, when thofe views were
accomplifhed; confider, I fay, all this, and
fee, if there be not fomething more than
a blind credulity in the advocates for the
divinity of fuch a fyftem. See, if there be
any inftance upon record—of fo numerous
prophecies—fo long continued—fo intimately related to each other and to one
common end—fo apparently verified—and
fo fignally concluded. If there be, I fhall
not wonder at the fufpenfe and hefitation
of *wife men*, on this fubject: but if, on
the other hand, no fuch thing was ever
feen, or heared of, out of the land of
Judæa, they muft excufe us if we incline
to think their diffidence mifplaced, and
their fcruples unneceffary, at leaft, if not
difingenuous.

I defcend no farther into a detail on the
fcriptural prophecies concerning Chrift's
firft coming. The immenfity of the fubject,
and the plan prefcribed to me in this

Lecture,

Lecture, equally reftrain me from this attempt. *Obfcurities* there may, and muft
be, in fo vaft a fcheme: *Objections* may,
and muft occur to the conftruction and application of particular prophecies. But
let any ferious man take the Bible into his
hands; let him confider, not *all* the prophecies in that book, but fuch as are more
obvious and intelligible; and let him compare fuch *prophecies*, as he muft acknowledge, and may, in part at leaft, underftand, with the *facts*, in which he fees
their completion, or fo far, as he may
think it *probable* that they have been completed; and I dare be confident that fuch
an inquirer will be much ftruck with the
amount of the evidence from prophecy, in
fupport of divine revelation. If, indeed,
on this general furvey, he find nothing to
affect him, I fhall not defire him to pufh
his refearches into the more fecret and myfterious prophecies: much lefs, fhall I ad-
vife him to wade through that cloud of
fmaller difficulties, in which the ignorant
temerity

temerity of ſome writers, and the *obſcure diligence* of others, hath involved *this*, as it eaſily may any other, ſubject.

To SPEAK PLAINLY, the only conſide-ration, which to me ſeems likely to per-plex fair ‚and candid minds, is this— "That the argument from prophecy is underſtood to be addreſſed ‚to thoſe, who admit the divinity of the Jewiſh ſcriptures —that the Jews themſelves were eminent-ly in this ſituation—that, beſides this ad-vantage, the Jews were better qualified, than any others, to interpret their own prophecies, and to judge of their comple-tion—and yet, that theſe very men nei-ther were, nor are convinced by this argu-ment.

Several things are here aſſerted, which deſerve to be explained. I take them in an inverted order.

·I. It is ſaid, " *that the Jews were not, and are not to this- day, convinced by the argument from prophecy.*" This allegation

is

SERM.
V.
is in part *false*: for multitudes [m], from among the Jews, were, in the apoftolic age, converted to chriftianity; and thefe are well known to have laid a peculiar ftrefs on this argument. The greater part of that people, indeed, difbelieved, and have continued to this day in their infidelity. But then let it be confidered, 1. that we have an adequate caufe of this effect, in the *prejudices* of the Jewifh nation; *prejudices*, of which their whole hiftory evidently convicts them. 2. That, notwithftanding their rejection of Jefus, they admit the exiftence and authority of thofe prophecies, which we apply to him; and that they themfelves have conftantly applied thefe very prophecies to their expected Meffiah: fo that the queftion between us is only this, Whether they, or we, *rightly* apply them. 3. That their perverfe obftinacy in refufing to fubmit to

---

[m] The facred text fays—*myriads*—Θεωρεῖς, ἀδελφὶ, πόσαι μυριάδες εἰσιν Ἰεδαίων τῶν πεπιςευκότων—Acts xxi. 20.

the

the evidence of their prophecies, is itfelf foretold by their own prophets.

II. But it is further faid, " *that their authority, in this controverfy, is greater than ours, for that they muft beft underftand their own prophecies, and judge beft of their completion.*"

1. I do not perceive on what ground of reafon, this is faid. The old prophecies belong to us, as well as to them; and have been confidered with as much diligence by Chriftian, as by Jewifh expofitors. Their cuftoms, their hiftory, their traditions, are equally known to both parties. Their very language hath been ftudied by Chriftians with a care, not inferior to that which the Jews themfelves employ upon it; with a *care*, that not unfrequently, in *both*, hath degenerated into fuperftition.

If it be faid, " that the *antient* Jews, that is, the Jews in the time of Chrift, muft have been better qualified, than we

L   now

now are, to interpret the prophecies, the language, they fpoke, being only a dialect of that in which the prophecies are written," the anfwer is already given, under the laft article: to which we may further add, that Chriftianity being much better underftood now, than it was then, the force of the prophetic language concerning it (if, indeed, the prophecies have any fuch thing in view) muft be more diftinctly apprehended, in many inftances, by Chriftians at this day, than it could be by the Jews, even when they fpoke a dialect of the Hebrew language. So that ftill I do not fee, upon the whole, what advantage the Jews, whether of antient or modern times, can be thought to have over us, in explaining the prophetic fcriptures. And then

2. As to the *completion* of the prophecies, the fame hiftories are in the hands of both: and if they do not apply them, as we do, the appeal is open to

common

common fenfe. Every man is left at liberty to judge for himfelf, which fide is beft fupported in the application of them. The prejudice might, indeed, be thought equal on *both* fides, if it were not decided by their own fcriptures, that no prejudice of any people upon earth was ever fo invincible, as that of the Jews.

3. Laftly, on both heads, there is a peculiar prefumption, that they, and not we, are mifled by prejudice: It is this: They were led by their prophecies, as interpreted by themfelves, to expect that they would be completed at the *time*, in which, we fay, they were completed; and it was not till after the coming of Chrift that they began to interpret them differently, and to look out for another completion of them. Judge then, if they, or we, are likely to have erred moft, through prejudice, in expounding and applying the prophecies. The natural and proper fenfe will be thought to be that, in which we take them; for that fenfe occurred firft to them-

L 2 felves,

selves, and was, in truth, *their* sense, before we adopted it.

When I say—*their sense*—I mean, especially, in respect to the *time*, which they
had fixed for the accomplishment of the
prophecies concerning the Messiah : for, as
to their giving a *temporal* sense to some.
prophecies, in which we find a *spiritual*,
that is another matter, concerning which,
as I said, the appeal lies to every competent and dispassionate inquirer. In the
mean time, it must be thought some presumption in favour of the Christian interpretation, that, whereas the Jews, in re-
jecting a spiritual or mystical sense of those
prophecies (which yet is admitted by them,
without scruple, on other occasions, and is
well suited to the genius of their whole
religion) are driven to the necessity of sup-
posing a *two-fold Messias* — a new conceit,
taken up, without warrant from their scriptures, and against their own former ideas
and expectations—WE, on the contrary,
by the help of that spiritual sense, are able

to

to explain all the prophecies of *one and the*
fame Meffias, conformably to the *event*, and
even to the *time* which the Jews themfelves
had prefixed for the completion of them.

Now, when, of two interpretations, *one*
has apparently all the marks of fhift, con-
ftraint, and diftrefs in it, and the *other*
comes out eafy, uniform, and confiftent;
we may guefs beforehand, as I faid, which
of them is likely to be well-founded.

III. Still it is pretended, " that the argument from prophecy is properly addreffed to thofe only who admit the divinity
of the Jewifh fcriptures, as the Jews have
invariably done; and that it hath no force,
but on that previous fuppofition. Why
then is the argument preffed on others,
who do not believe the divine authority of
thofe fcriptures? And how fhould it prevail with *any*, whether believers or not,
when the Jews themfelves, who of all
men moft firmly believe that authority,
are not convinced by it?"

L 3   The

S E R M.
V.

The *latter* part of the difficulty, which
refpects the incredulity of the Jews, hath
been already removed; fo far, I mean, as
it is founded on their prejudices. As for
the *affertion*, " That the argument from
prophecy prefuppofes the truth and divinity
of the Jewifh fcriptures, and muft therefore have moft weight with the Jews, or
rather hath no weight at all, but with
them, or with others, who admit that
common principle," though fomething,
like this, may have been faid, I take it to
be wholly unfupported as well by *fact*, as
by any *good reafon*.

1. I argue againft this affumption from
fact; that is, from the *method*, taken by
the early Chriftians to convert the Gentile
world, and from the *fuccefs* of that method.

If we look into the hiftory of the Gofpel,
we fhall find the Apoftle Peter, preffing
this argument from prophecy on the gentile Cornelius[a]; and the Apoftle Paul,

[a] Acts x.

urging

urging it with effect, on the Jews indeed
firſt, but alſo on the Aſiatic Gentiles[o].
If we turn to the Chriſtian apologiſts, we
ſhall find them addreſſing this ˏtopic to
Gentile unbelievers, nay, as venturing the
whole cauſe of Chriſtianity on this ſingle
argument [p].　Juſtin Martyr makes as free
uſe of it in his apology to the Antonines,
as in his dialogues with Trypho.　We
know, too, the ſucceſs of this argument,
thus employed, in many inſtances: and
therefore ſee, as well the *fitneſs* of the argument to produce this effect, as the *judgment* of the Apoſtles and primitive Chriſtians concerning its fitneſs.　But to come

　2. *to the reaſon of the thing.*

The Jews, who profeſſed to believe, and
did, in fact, believe, the divine inſpiration

---

　[o] Acts xiii. 42. 48.

　[p] Τίνι γὰρ ἂν λόγῳ ἀνθρώπῳ ϛαυρωθέντι ἐπειθόμεθα, ὅτι
πρωτότοκῶ τῷ ἀγεννήτῳ ἐϛι, κὶ αὐτὸς τὴν κρίσιν τῶ παντὸς
ἀνθρωπείκ γένϛς ποιήσεῖαι, εἰ μὴ μαρτύρεια, πρὶν ἐλθεῖν
αὐτὸν ἄνθρωπον γενόμενον, κεκηρυγμένα περὶ αὐτῶ εὕρο-
μεν, καὶ ὕτως γενόμενα ὁρῶμεν;　JUSTIN MARTYR,
　　　　　　　　　　　　　　　　Apol. i. *c.* 88.

　　　　　　　　　　　　　　of

SERM.
V.

of their facred oracles, were, doubtlefs, bound by their own principles, to expect with affurance the due completion of them. The Gentiles, who did not previoufly refpect thofe oracles, as of divine authority, but regarded them only in the light of human conjectures, yet faw that fuch paffages, whether we call them oracular or conjectural, did, in truth, occur in the Jewifh fcriptures; and were obliged to admit, on the faith of hiftorical teftimony, that thofe fcriptures were compofed by the perfons, whofe names they bear, and at the times fixed for the compofition of them. What then is the difference of the two cafes? Only this: the Jews believed that their oracles would be fulfilled, becaufe they held them to be divine; the Gentiles had to wait till thofe oracles were fulfilled, before they acknowledged their divinity. In either cafe, the argument is independent of the belief, or the expectation, and turns on the completion only. Then, indeed, the Jew fees that his belief was

well

well founded, and the Gentile admits that the prediction was divine.

The miftake would be equal, on the other hand, to conceive, that the argument from prophecy pre-fuppofes the divine infpiration of the New Teftament. It pre-fuppofes only the hiftorical truth of that book. Admit this, and compare the events recorded in that hiftory, with the prophecies, to which they correfpond, and the divinity of both Teftaments is proved. For then, the pretenfions of Jefus are made good, by the *completion* of the prophecies; and the infpiration of the prophets is concluded, from the *delivery* of them.

In both cafes (let me repeat it) it is not the authority of the books containing the prophecies, nor of the books recording the facts, in which they are fulfilled, but fimply the *completion* of the prophecies in thofe facts, feen and acknowledged, which infers the divinity of either Teftament. Even the Jew would retract his high opinion of the prophecies, if he did not

admit

SERM.
V.
admit or expect the accomplishment of them; and the Christian would renounce his faith in Jesus, if his history did not accord to the prophecies, alledged.

'Tis true, that, with either, the argument would gain more *attention*, than with such as professed no previous belief in the divinity of the Old or New Testament. But its force is really the same, on both suppositions. It lies merely in the conviction, which one hath from the evidence produced, that certain prophetic passages were delivered in the *Old* Testament, and have been fulfilled by certain corresponding events, related in the *New*.

On the whole, there is no reason to conclude, that we are not as good judges of the argument from prophecy, as the Jews were; or, that this argument ought to have the less weight with us, because the Jews were not convinced by it. For the argument doth, in no degree, depend on *faith*, but is calculated to produce it. It is equally strong, or equally weak, to a
Christian,

Chriftian, or Jew, or even to an unbeliever: the fole point in queftion being
this, Whether fuch things, as were pro-
phetically delivered, appear to have been
fulfilled : a point, on which common fenfe
and common honefty will equally decide,
on every fuppofition.

I know, indeed, that, unlefs we fuppofe the infpiration of the prophets, *fome*
paffages, delivered by them, will not fo
probably be thought to *intend* Chrift, as
they will be, if we acknowledge that principle: and, on the other hand, that there
are *fome* circumftances in the hiftory of
Jefus, which will not be fo readily feen
to *refer* to preceding prophecies, if the infpiration of Jefus and his Apoftles be not
previoufly admitted. But I do not argue,
at prefent, from either of thefe topics.
There are paffages enough, clearly *predictive* of the Meffiah, and clearly *accomplifhed* in him, to afford a folid foundation
for the argument from prophecy, as here
infti-

SERM.
V.

inftituted, without looking out for any other of more nice and ambiguous inter-pretation.

Hence we fee the dangerous miftake of thofe, who contend that the argument from prophecy hath not, of itfelf, the nature of a *direct pofitive pooof*, of our re-ligion. Prophecies fulfilled, I mean fuch prophecies as *thofe* in queftion, prove in-vincibly the divine infpiration of the pro-phets. But, if the prophets were infpired, the divine miffion of him, in whom the predicted marks of the Meffiah meet, muft needs be acknowledged. And what more is required to prove the truth of Chriftianity? Not even the evidence of *miracles*, per-formed by Chrift, if the prophecies had not made them one mark of his character. The truth is, *Prophecies* and *Miracles* are, in themfelves, two diftinct pofitive proofs. Either proof is *direct*, and would have been fufficient, if the other had not been given. But the divine goodnefs, for our more abundant fatisfaction, and to leave infidelity

without

without excuſe, hath made the one proof
dependent on the other: ſo that neither the argument from prophecy is complete, without the *miracles*; nor the argument from miracles, as applied to Chriſt, un- leſs he likewiſe appear to have fulfilled the *prophecies*. Can we deſire a ſtronger proof, that neither *they*, who predicted the *miracles*, were *falſe prophets*, nor *he*, who claimed to himſelf the application of ALL the *prophecies*, was a *falſe Meſſiah?*

Theſe reflexions, on the *method and order* of the prophecies, of thoſe eſpeci- ally concerning Chriſt's FIRST COMING; together with what has been ſaid on the *independency* of this argument on Jewiſh or Chriſtian conceſſions; may ſerve to convince us, That we ſhall do well to ſuſpend our concluſions concerning the evidence of prophecy, till we have ex- amined the *whole* ſubject. In the mean time, *this part* of the ſubject, thus far opened and explained, leads us, with ad-

vantage,

SERM.
V.
——— vantage, to the confideration of *that*, which
is yet behind and is the peculiar object of
this Lecture, I mean, *the prophecies concerning* CHRIST'S SECOND COMING.

SER-

SERMON VI.

Prophecies concerning Chrift's
SECOND COMING.

ISAIAH xlii. 9.

Behold, the former things are come to pafs,
and new things do I declare : before they
fpring forth, I tell you of them.

IT muft ftrike the moft carelefs reader
of the prophecies to obferve, that the
general fubject of them all was announced
from the earlieft time, and was only drawn
out more diftinctly by fucceeding prophets:
that, of the two *ages*, into which the
world of God, I mean his *religious* world,
is divided in holy fcripture, the *former*,
which

which abounds moſt in prophecy, was
plainly made ſubſervient to the *latter:*
that not only the events of that preceding
age are foretold by its own prophets, but
that the fortunes of the laſt, and very remote age, are occaſionally revealed by
them ; and that the ſame oracles, which
atteſt the *firſt coming* of Chriſt, as if impatient to be confined to ſo narrow bounds,
overflow, as it were, into the future age,
and expatiate on the principal facts and
circumſtances of his *ſecond coming.*

By this divine artifice, if I may ſo ſpeak,
the two diſpenſations, the Jewiſh and
Chriſtian, are cloſely tied together, or
rather compacted into one intire harmo-
nious ſyſtem ; ſuch, as we might expect,
if it were indeed formed, and conducted
by him, *to whom are known all his works
from the beginning* [a].

So that, in reſpect of the fortunes,
which were to befall the Chriſtian church,

[a] Acts xv. 18.

even

even in the *latter days*, we may ftill afk, in
the triumphant terms of the Jewifh prophet
—*Have ye not known? Have ye not heard?*
Hath it not been told you from the beginning?
Have ye not underftood from the foundation of
the earth [b]?

But, though this fubjeft was opened by
the old prophets, fo far as feemed expedient in that *age,* and clearly enough, to fhew
the integrity and continuity of the whole
fyftem, it was more illuftrioufly, becaufe
more diftinctly, difplayed by the evangelical prophets.

And here, again, the fame provifion of
wifdom and goodnefs meets us, as before.
The Chriftian prophets, like the Jewifh,
befpeak our attention to what they reveal
of the greater and more diftant events in
their difpenfation, by other lefs momentous prophecies, which were fpeedily to be
accomplifhed [c]; thus, impreffing upon us

[b] Ifaiah xl. 21.
[c] We fee this defign very plainly, in the prophecies
of Jefus concerning *his own death and refurrection;*

M   an

SERM.
VI.

———

an awful fenfe of their divine forefight, and procuring an eafy credit from us to their ' fubfequent predictions : *while the events, which both thefe prophetic fchemes point out, are fo diftributed through all time, as to furnifh, fucceffively, to the feveral ages of the world, the means of a frefh and ftill growing conviction* [d].

As THE ORDER of thefe Difcourfes, now, leads me to exemplify this *laft* obfervation, I fhall do it in THREE remarkable prophecies concerning the Chriftian church; I mean thofe, which refpect

1. THE DESTRUCTION OF JERUSALEM.
2. THE DISPERSION OF THE JEWS. And
3. THE CONVESRION OF THE GENTILES.

concerning *the defcent of the holy Ghoft on the day of Pentecoft* ; concerning *events, that were to befall his difciples* ; and in other inftances.

[d] La plus grande des preuves de Jefus Chrift, ce font les propheties. C'eft auffi à quoi Dieu a la plus pourvû ; car l'evenement, qui les a remplies, eft un MIRACLE SUBSISTANT depuis la naiffance de l'Eglife jufqu' à la fin. *M. Pafcal.*

I refer

I refer to thefe prophecies, ·as well known. They are in the number of thofe, which, in · part, were delivered by the Jewifh prophets ; and afterwards, more diftinctly revealed by the Chriftian.

I. THE DESTRUCTION OF THE JEWISH CITY AND TEMPLE, is an event of the utmoft moment in the view of revealed religion. It accomplifhed a great number of prophecies, and vindicated the honour of Jefus, by a fignal vengeance on his murderers. It anfwered, befides, *other* important purpofes of divine providence; by putting a vifible and neceffary end to the Jewifh œconomy, which was now to give way to the difpenfation of the Meffiah; and by difperfing the Jews into all lands, for many wife and admirable reafons. Hence, of all the prophecies, delivered by Chrift himfelf (who was a prophet, though indeed *much more than a prophet*) *This* alone is difplayed by him, at large, and in all its circumftances.

M 2

If

SERM.   If any man, unacquainted with thefe
VI.   matters, fhould doubt, whether this prophecy of Jefus, as recorded in three of the
four Gofpels, were not delivered, that is,
forged, after the event, I might refer him
to the numerous writers on that fubject.
But I hold it fufficient to fay, 1, On the
faith of all antiquity, that thefe Gofpels
were not only written, but publifhed to
the world, before the deftruction of Jerufalem—2, that the early date of their compofition is apparent from many internal
characters, difperfed through thefe writings—3. that no interpolation of this prophecy could afterwards take place, becaufe
the prophecy is interwoven with the general thread of the hiftory—and 4, laftly,
that no unbeliever of the primitive times,
whether Jew or Gentile, when preffed, as
both frequently were, by this prophecy,
appears to have had recourfe to the charge,
either of forgery, or interpolation [e].

[e] For thefe particulars, fee Dr. Jortin's *Rem. on
Ecclefiaftical Hiftory*, vol. I. *p.* 20—89.

The

The authenticity and early date of the prophecy is, then, on thefe grounds, af-. —————
fumed.

I will, further, fuppofe (becaufe the hiftory of Jofephus invincibly proves it) that all the particulars, mentioned in this prophecy, concurred in the *event.*

" But this, you will fay, might well be: for what more *uniform*, than the characters of diftrefs in a *great* city, forced and defolated by a fuperior enemy? And what more *probable*, than that, fome time or other, fuch fhould be the fate of *every* great city?"

It may further be infinuated, " That, if ever Jerufalem was to be deftroyed, the obftinate humour of its inhabitants, and the *nature of the place*, would probaby draw this deftruction upon it, in the way it actually happened, in the way of *fiege* [f]:

[f] An event, it muft be owned, the more likely to happen, as the Jews had always been difpofed to *truft to their high and fenced walls*; which yet could never defend them from their enemies, as their hiftory fhews, and, as Mofes had diftinctly foretold, *Deut.* xxviii. 52.

that,

that, then, all the miferies, endured by
the Jews, would naturally fall on a defpe-
rate people from an irritated and fuccefsful
conqueror; above all, in antient times,
when conqueft and clemency were little
acquainted with each other : that, as for
the preceding *wars, famines, peftilences, and
-earthquakes* (which are mentioned, in the
prophecy, as *figns* of the approaching defolation) *thefe,* are fuch ufual things in the
courfe of the world, as may be fafely made
the prognoftics of any predicted event
whatfoever : that Jefus, therefore, as any
other wife man, might form his prediction
on thefe principles; and truft to time, and
the paffions of mankind, for the completion
of it.''

Now, let all this be allowed (and fcepticifm itfelf will hardly make other or
greater demands upon us) ftill, the honour
of Jefus ftands fecure; and this fine fabric
of fufpicion is overturned at once, if we reflect on *two or three* circumftances, unluckily, and, if the prophet be not divine,

unne-

unneceffarily wrought into the texture of this famous prophecy.

Firft, I obferve, that this deftruction was to come from *the hands of the Romans*[s]; and, without doubt, if it were to happen in any reafonable time, it could not fo probably be expected to come from any other quarter. But, then, was it *likely* that Judæa, at that time a Roman province,

---

[s] Matth. xxiv. 28. and compare Luke xvii. 37. Οπε γαρ εαν η το πωμα, εκει συναχθησονlαι οι αετοι. —Meaning by *eagles*, the ftandards of the Roman army. —Some writers of name have, indeed, obferved, that this is only a *proverbial* expreffion. True: but proverbial prophecies are often fulfilled in the ftrict literal fenfe of the expreffion; as Grotius well, obferves on Matth. xxvi. 23.—hîc quoque accidit, quod in *multis aliis vaticiniis*, ut verba—non tantùm fecundùm proverbialem loquendi modum, fed etiam fecundùm *exactiffimam verborum fignificationem* implerentur.—If the reader calls to mind the prediction of our Lord, as it is elfewhere expreffed, without a figure—*when ye fhall fee Jerufalem compaffed with* ARMIES [Luke xxi. 20]— and compares it with the *event*, he will hardly make a doubt whether *eagles*, in thofe figurative predictions, which refpect the fame fubject, namely, the deftruction of Jerufalem, were not intended by our Lord to denote, the ROMAN armies.

M 4 fhould

should be thus defolated by its own mafters? Was it to be *prefumed*, that fo fmall a province fhould dare to engage in a formal conteft with Rome, the miftrefs of the world, as well as of Judæa? with Rome, then in the zenith of her power, and irrefiftible to all nations? Was it *conceivable*, if any future diftraction of that mighty empire fhould tempt the Jews to oppofe their feeble efforts to its high fortune, that a vengeance fo fignal, fo complete, fhould be taken upon them? that nothing lefs than a total *extermination* fhould be propofed, and effected? The ruin of the temple at Jerufalem was to be fo entire, that *one ftone fhould not be left upon another*. Allow for the exaggerated terms of a prophetic defcription; ftill, was it *imaginable*, that the Romans fhould, in any proper fenfe of the words, execute this denunciation? Was it *their* way, as it was afterwards that of the Goths, to wage war with *ftones?* Was it a principle with *them*, to beat down the *pride* of buildings, as well as

of

of *men*[h]? Would even their *policy*, or their *pride*, have ſuffered them to blot out an antient, a renowned, an illuſtrious temple, the chief ornament of their province, the glory of the eaſt, and the trophy of their own conqueſts?

Such an event was very improbable, in contemplation: and hiſtory ſhews, that it did not come to paſs in any ordinary way. For the inſtrument, in the hands of heaven, of this exterminating vengeance, was a man, the moſt unlikely of all others, to inflict it; a man, who by nature abhorred ſuch extremities; who, in fact, did his utmoſt to prevent this dreadful cataſtrophe, and *could not* prevent it[i].— Still, a more unmanageable circumſtance, than this, occurs in the prophecy. For,

[h] —debellare *ſuperbos.* Virg.

[i] Aſſuredly this prophecy was not in the number of thoſe, of which it hath been ſaid—*The prophecy is not occaſioned by the event, but the event by the prophecy*— *L'evenement n'eſt pas predit parce qu'il arrivera; mais il arrive parce qu'il a été predit.* ROUSSEAU, *Nouv. Hel.* t. iv. p. 314. n. *Neuf.* 2764.

Secondly,

SERM.
VI.

Secondly, it is implied that ONE of our Lord's difciples fhould furvive this defolation [k] : and it is exprefsly afserted, that the then *fubfifting generation fhould not pafs away, before all thefe things were accomplifhed* [l]. They WERE accomplifhed, within forty years from the date of the prophecy, and before the death of that difciple. The fact is certain and undeniable : I leave the reft to your own reflexions.

Thirdly, warning is given in this prophecy to the difciples of Jefus, to fly from this impending ruin; and a fignal is held out to them, for that purpofe [m]. It is further predicted, that they fhould avail themfelves of this fignal ; and fo entirely efcape the fnare, in which the reft of their countrymen fhould be taken, that *not a hair of their heads fhould perifh* [n]. And this

[k] Matth. xvi. 28.
[l] Matth. xxiv. 34.
[m] Luke xxi. 20.
[n] Luke xxi. 18. Acts ii. 21. Mark xiii. 20.

part

part of the prophecy was, it feems, completed °.

Laftly, this prophecy was incumbered
with another ftrange event, *needlefsly* incumbered with it, if the whole were an
impofture. It is faid, that *the Gofpel fhould
be preached in all the world, for· a witnefs
unto all nations*, before it fhould be fulfilled.
Was it not enough to fay, that the prophecy fhould be accomplifhed in the time
of that generation, and in the life-time of
St. John, without adding fo unlikely a·
circumftance, as that a general promulga-
tion of the Gofpel, by a few unlettered
and unfriended fifhermen, fhould precede
the accomplifhment of it?—I know, that
this part of the prophecy admits a fecondary
fenfe: but, in the primary fenfe, it was fo
far fulfilled, as to aftonifh us with the divine forefight of its author.

I omit other confiderations, that might
be alledged. But you fee that, fetting

° See the learned Bifhop Newton's *Differtations on the
Prophecies*, vol. ii, *p*. 268, *n*.

afide

afide fuch particulars in the prophecy, as fceptical men may think themfelves able to draw within the fphere of *human con- jecture*, there are feveral things exprefled in it, fo ftrange to all apprehenfion, fo unlikely to happen, fo impoffible for any natural fagacity to forefee, and yet fo cer- tainly and punctually fulfilled, that no- thing fhort of *divine infpiration* can poffibly account for them. The prophecy, in all its parts, is divine: but in *thefe*, its divi- nity is clear and inconteftable.

II. THE DISPERSION OF THE JEWS, is another event, which deferves your con- fideration.

Mofes himfelf had predicted this cir- cumftance of their fortune, in terms of the greateft energy. He had told them—*that they fhould be removed into all the kingdoms of the earth, and that they fhould be fcattered among all people from one end of the earth even unto the other*—that, among the na- tions, into which they fhould be driven,
they

they should find no ease, nor rest, and that they should be only oppressed and crushed alway—that they should *become an astonishment, a proverb, and a by-word among all nations*—and that *their plagues should be wonderful, and of long continuance* [p]. These prophecies had been, to a certain degree, fulfilled in other parts of their history: but there was to be a time, when *the wrath of God should come upon them to the uttermost* [q]. This time was now come, when their city was destroyed, and their land desolated, by the arms of Titus. Then, as Jesus prophesied of them, *were the days of vengeance, that all things, which were written, should be fulfilled*: then, were they *to be led away captive into all nations*: and thenceforth, *was Jerusalem to be trodden down of the Gentiles, until* THE TIMES OF THE GENTILES SHOULD BE FULFILLED [r].

[p] Deut. xxviii.
[q] 1 Thess. ii. 16.
[r] Luke xxi. 22. 24.

Nor

Nor fay, that this *laſt* prophecy is *indefinite*: for *the times of the Gentiles* is a
period, well known in the prophetic writings; a period, of long duration indeed,
as the event hath ſhewn; yet a period,
marked out by other prophecies (which
may come, in turn, to be conſidered in
this Lecture) no leſs diſtinctly, than their
other captivities had been.

For, to all theſe predictions there muſt
be added *one* more, which exprefly aſſerts
the return of this people, in ſome future
age, from their long and wretched diſperſion: for *blindneſs, in part*, only, *hath
happened to Iſrael*; and that again, *till the
fulneſs of the Gentiles be come in*[s]. This,
St. Paul terms *a myſtery*: and yet the
antient prophets had a glimpſe of it, when
they foretold, *that the Lord would not make
a full end of them*[t], and that a remnant of
them *ſhould remain, and ſhould return in the
latter days*[u]. Moſes himſelf, who had

[s] Rom. xi. 25.
[t] Jer. xlvi. 28.
[u] Iſa. x. 21. Ezek. vi. 8.

denounced

denounced ſuch heavy judgments upon SERM.
them, and of ſo *long continuance*, during VI.
their diſperſion, had mingled, with his
woes, this one note of mercy—*And yet
for all that, when they lie in the land of their
enemies, I will not caſt them away, neither
will I abhor them, to deſtroy them* UTTERLY
and to break my covenant with them ᵛ.

Conſider theſe predictions, and compare
them with the preſent and paſt ſtate of this
people for ſeventeen hundred years; and
ſee, if there be nothing to take your attention, or, rather, your aſtoniſhment, in
the completion of them.

Why is this dreadful vengeance; *ſingular*
in its circumſtances, and never yet ex-
perienced by any other people on the face
of the earth, why is this peculiar vengeance executed on the Jews?—Or, whatever the *cauſe* may be, is not the *fact*,
ſuch as was predicted?

ᵛ Lev. xxvi. 44.

" The

" The predictions, you will fay, have the appearance of being fulfilled. But where is the wonder, that a people, diftinguifhed by a *fingular* religion, and above meafure *addicted* to it, fhould continue to exift under that diftinction, and fhould be every where known by it ? That a people, on account of their profeffion, more than commonly obnoxious to the other religious fects, among whom the earth hath been chiefly parcelled out—to the *Heathen*, for their unconquerable averfion to idolatry — to the *Chriftians*, for the atrocious murder of their founder—to the *Mahome-tans*, for the conftant rejection of their prophet—fhould be the fcorn and outcaft of all three; and that, being excluded from the only country, to which they have any attachment, they fhould be vagabonds on the earth, and fhould difperfe themfelves indifferently through every quarter of it, as caprice, or intereft, or convenience invites them ? That, laftly, being thus diftinguifhed from all men,

men, and thus at enmity with all, they fhould never be fuffered to enter into any other civil community, or to eftablifh a diftinct community of their own?"

But the wonder doth not lie, altogether, where thefe queftions feem to place it. That the Jews, while they profefs them-felves fuch, fhould be thus treated, may be natural enough : but that they fhould *continue*, for fo many ages, under fuch treatment ; every where and always fpurn-ed, reviled, oppreffed ; yet neither worn out by this ufage ; nor induced by it to renounce their offenfive profeffion, and take refuge in the mafs of people, among whom they live ; that neither time, nor cuftom, nor fuffering, fhould get the better of their bigotry or patience ; but that they fhould ftill fubfift a numerous, a diftinct, a wretched people, as they do, to this day—all this hath fomething pro-digious in it, which the common princi-

N ples

SERM.
VI.
ples of human nature will not easily explain [x].

We, who admit the divine origin of their religion; and adore, with them, the extraordinary providence, by which their polity was so long administered and upheld; can better, than any others, explain this difficulty. For, what so likely to produce an invincible attachment to their Law, as the abundant evidence, they had of its authority? But neither will this account of the matter be found satisfactory. For, as if on purpose to discredit this solution, their history informs us, That *ten*, of the twelve tribes, which originally composed their nation, did, in fact, disappear under their last captivity, and were, in a good measure at least, absorbed in it. If

[x] Hear the profound and reflecting M. Pascal— L'etat où l'on voit les Juifs est une grande preuve de la Religion. Car c'est une chose étonnante de voir ce peuple *subsister* depuis tant d'années, & de le voir *toujours misérable*—et, quoique il soit contraire, D'ETRE MISERABLE, & DE SUBSISTER, il subsiste neanmoins toujours malgré sa misere. . PENSEES, p. 115.

such,

fuch, then, was the fate of *Ifrael* in its
difperfion, within the compafs of not many
generations, and yet the relics of *Judah*
are ftill preferved in all countries to this
day, what better or other reafon can we
affign for this difference of fortune in two
branches of the fame people, equally at-
tached to the fame divine Law, than that
the *former* were left to the natural confe-
quences of a difperfion, and that the *latter*
were purpofely kept from being affected
by them, as the prophecies had diftinctly
foretold ?

If it be ftill faid, " That there is nothing more extraordinary in this continu-
ance of the Jews, under their difperfion,
than of other religionifts in like circumftances ; of the *Chriftians* for inftance,
under the Turkifh dominion ;" the cafes
(to fay nothing of the difference in point
of *time*) are, in many refpects, entirely
unlike.

The Afiatic CHRISTIANS derive a confidence, and fome degree of protection,

**S E R M.
VI.**

from the many flourishing Christian empires, which subsist in other quarters of
the world.

THEY, can perform all the duties of
their religion, as perfectly in the countries,
where they reside, as in any other.

THEY, have the future hopes of the
Gospel, the proper sanction of their Law,
to support them in all the distresses, to
which their Christian profession may, at
present, expose them. What is it to them,
as St. Austin well observed in a like case,
that they suffer for a season in a strange
land; when even in their *own*, that is, a
Christian country, they are still obliged,
by the principles of their religion, to consider themselves, *as strangers and pilgrims
on the earth* ?

---

^y —Multò minus nomen criminandum, in captivi-
tate sacratorum suorum, qui supernam patriam veraci
fide expectantes, *etiam in suis sedibus peregrinos se esse
noverunt. Aug. De Civ. Dei, l. i. c. 15.*

The

The condition of the JEWS, on the other hand, is widely different. THEY, profeſs a religion, founded on temporal promiſes, only : and how miſerably theſe have failed them, the experience of many ages hath now ſhewn.

The JEWS, are ſhut out from the only country in the world, where the ſeveral rites and ordinances of their religion can be regularly and *lawfully* obſerved.

The JEWS, have, beſides, the ſenſible mortification of knowing, that all their brethren of the diſperſion are every where in equal diſtreſs with themſelves ; and that there is not one Jewiſh ſtate or ſovereignty ſubſiſting on the face of the whole earth.

It follows, that in the JEWS, we find nothing but their *deſtiny,* ſo plainly read to them by their own prophets, as well as ours, to account for their long continu-ance in their preſent diſperſion : whereas, the *Aſiatic Chriſtians* have many reſources of comfort within themſelves ; and may ſubſiſt, in Mahometan countries, on the

N 3   ſame

SERM. fame general motives and inducements,
VI.
——— which fuftain the courage of other unhappy
men.

Yet, notwithftanding the advantages,
here pointed out, on the fide of the Afiatic
Chriftians, the *fact* is, that they are reduced to a very fmall number, and are in-
fenfibly melting away under the oppreffions
of their Ottoman mafters; fo that in no
long time, if that enormous tyranny
fhould be permitted to continue, they may,
not improbably, quite vanifh out of thofe
countries, where they had formerly fo
many and flourifhing churches: whereas,
the Jews continue every where to abound
in great numbers; they thrive under their
oppreffions; and feem to multiply amidft
their diftreffes; as if the order of things
were reverfed in regard to them, and the
fame caufes operated to the confervation of
this people, which tend fo naturally to the
wafte and deftruction of every other.

Still, I have another reflexion, or two,
to make on this interefting fubject.

1. It

1. It deferves to be confidered, that the *natives* of any country, though fubdued and enflaved by a foreign nation, may, indeed, fubfift very long under that dif-tinction. Thus, the Gentoo Indians, have preferved their name and race, under their Mahometan invaders: and thus, the Moors, if they had not been violently expelled, might have continued a diftinct people for many ages, in their old Spanifh quarters. But that fmall colonies of men, tranfported into *ftrange* and populous nations, fhould preferve a diftinct exiftence, and not in-fenfibly moulder away, and mix themfelves with their numerous native mafters; This, I think, is without example in the hiftory of mankind. If the Jews might be ex-pected to abound any where, it fhould, methinks, be in Judæa; where the fight of the *holy land*, and the memory of their paft fortunes, might invigorate their pre-judices, and perpetuate their attachment to the Jewifh name and worfhip. But it fo happens, that the number of Jews

N 4 in

in that country hath now for many ages been inconfiderable, while they fwarm in every other.

2. It fhould, further, I think, be obferved, that a *fect*, whether you will call it of *religion*, or *philofophy*, may fubfift through a long tract of ages; I mean, that certain opinions may continue to be profefled by fome people, or other, without intermiffion; as may be true of the *doctrine* concerning *the two principles*, at all times fo prevalent in the eaft; of that fpecies of eaftern *idolatry*, which confifts in the worfhip of *fire*; and in other inftances. But that thefe opinions, in circumftances any thing like thofe of the Jews, fhould ftill be profefled not only by fome, but by the *fame* men, that is, by men known to be of the fame extraction, as well as of a certain perfuafion; this, again, is, I think, a circumftance of great fingularity, and altogether unprecedented in the cafe of any other people. Who knows, of what race

or

or family the prefent Manichees are de-
fcended, or the profeffors of the old Perfian
idolatry? The followers of the Mofaic
law, are every where known to be of the
ftock of Abraham.   They are diftinguifhed in all places, as being Jews by *defcent*,
as well as by *Religion*.

3. Suppofing, what I think cannot be
fhewn, that the hiftory of the world fur-
nifhes an inftance or two of a people cir-
cumftanced in all refpects, as the Jews are;
thefe extraordinary cafes would not much
abate the wonder, we are now contemplating. For how happened it, that a prophecy delivered above three thoufand years
ago concerning the fate of a *particular* people, fhould be fo exactly verified, as it has
hitherto been, when that fate is fo far
from being a common one, that it has
only taken place, in one or two inftances
befides, within the compafs of fo many
ages? And ftill more, how fhould it enter
into the head of Mofes to deliver this prophecy,

phecy, when, at the time of his delivering it, he had abfolutely no inftance before his eyes of fuch fate, in the cafe of *any* people?

Thefe things, then, deferve to be well and ferioufly confidered.

Laftly, We believe, on the faith of the facred oracles, that the Jews fhall *never be deftroyed utterly*, but fhall exift a diftinct people, as they have hitherto done, *till the times of the Gentiles are fulfilled*. But here, you will fay, the prophets indulged a natural prejudice in favour of their own nation; it being the way of all people to delight in fuch dreams of *exiftence and perpetuity*. It may be fo: But fee, whether this *dream* hath ever yet been fo far realized, in the cafe of any other people. The Romans, for inftance, were as partial to themfelves, and doted as much on the idea of their *perpetuity*, as the Jews. But what now is become of their *eternal empire?* Confider, therefore, the fingular fate of the Jews through fo many ages, and

fee

ſee whether it be not credible from what
is paſt, that the prophet was moved by
ſomething more than a ſpirit of *national
vanity*, when he ſaid, *Fear thou not, O
Jacob my ſervant, ſaith the Lord, for I am
with thee; for I will make a full end of
all the nations whither I have driven thee,*
BUT I WILL NOT MAKE A FULL END OF
THEE [z].

To theſe prophecies concerning *Jeruſa-
lem,* and the *Jews,* I add

III. *A third, concerning* THE CALL
AND CONVERSION OF THE GENTILES TO
CHRISTIANITY.

This prophecy is very remarkable,
whether we conſider—*the matter of it—
the perſons, by whom it was delivered*—or,
the manner, in which it hath been fulfilled.

1. As it had been declared from the beginning, that in the promiſed ſeed, *all the
nations of the earth ſhould be bleſſed,* ſo the
Goſpel, or, the good tidings of that bleſſ-

---

[z] Jer. xlvi. 28.

ing,

SERM. ing, was, in due time, to be communi-
VI.   cated to *all nations.* Further ſtill, this
Goſpel was not only to be publiſhed to all
nations, but to be acknowledged and received by them. There are numberleſs
prophecies to this purpoſe in the books of
the Old Teſtament : prophecies, which ſay
expreſſly—*that God would give unto the
Meſſiah the heathen for his inheritance, and
the uttermoſt parts of the earth for his poſ-
ſeſſion* [a]—*that from the riſing of the ſun even
unto the going down of the ſame, his name
ſhould be great among the Gentiles* [b]—*It is a
light thing,* ſays the prophet Iſaiah, addreſſing himſelf, in the perſon of the
Almighty, to the Meſſiah, *that thou ſhould-
eſt be my ſervant to raiſe up the tribes of Jacob, and to reſtore the preſerved of Iſrael; I
will alſo give thee for a light to the Gentiles,
that thou mayeſt be my ſalvation to the end of
the earth* [c]. And Jeſus himſelf, when

[a] Pſ. ii. 8.
[b] Mal. i. 2.
[c] Iſ. xlix. 6.

he

he commiſſioned his Apoſtles to publiſh
his doctrine, did it in theſe words—Go
YE INTO ALL THE WORLD, AND PREACH
THE GOSPEL TO EVERY CREATURE[d].

It is unqueſtionable, therefore, from
theſe and other paſſages[e], that not the
Jews only, but all nations were to be in-
ſtructed in the Chriſtian faith; that the
Goſpel was to be an univerſal religion;
and that, thus, the Meſſiah was to be, in
every ſenſe, the Saviour of mankind.
There is no doubt, I ſay, but that ſuch
is the language of the prophets; and that
they clearly ſuppoſe the diſpenſation of the
Goſpel to have theſe views, and to terminate in this event.

But now, let any man conſider with
himſelf, what it is to proſelyte the whole
race of mankind to one faith, and to one
religion. Let him revolve in his mind this

---

[d] Mark xvi. 15.
[e] The reader may ſee many of them collected, and
the general argument from them well inforced, by Mr.
Bullock, in his VINDICATION, *Part* II.

great,

‑‑‑‑‑‑ great, this magnificent idea. Let him, next, turn his thoughts on what hiftory and experience may fuggeft to him on the fubject. And then let him tell us, whe‑ ther there be not fomething extraordinary in this project; whether, indeed, there be any other example of this fort in the annals of mankind.

In the old world, the inftitutors of *pa‑ gan religion* looked no further, than to fingle communities : each deftined his ceremo‑ nies for his own people only ; and never prefumed fo far on the truth or importance of his religious fcheme, as to fet it up for a ftandard of belief or worfhip to the other nations of the earth. Even the *Jewifh ritual* was fo conftituted as to refpect the the Jews only, and was even practicable no where but in the land of Judæa.

But this idea of univerfality was equally ftrange to the *Doctors*, as to the Legifla‑ tors, of the antient world. Sects of philo‑ fophy, there were many ; efpoufed with zeal, and propagated with induftry ; and
some

fome of them, of no fmall extent. Yet the moft fanguine, or the moft fuccefsful of thefe fpeculatifts never conceived fo much as the idea of bringing all nations into their fyftem. They prefumed, indeed, that truth, or probability at leaft, was on the fide of their favourite opinions; but they beheld a negleɔt of them in others, with a fort of indifference; and, contenting themfelves with their own fuperior fkill or felicity, left it to the reft of the world to philofophize in their own way, and on their own principles. They feem not to have thought it either neceffary or poffible, that their own fentiments fhould become the ftanding, univerfal perfuafion of mankind.

Ambition, I know, hath been fometimes enterprizing enough to think of fubduing the whole world. But this was the ambition of *power*, not of religion, or philofophy: it was an ambition to fubdue the *bodies*, not the minds of men. This *laft* was a projeɔt, too big for a Cæfar or an

Alex-

Alexander, much more, for a Numa or an Ariſtotle, to entertain. And I think it certain, that, except in the ſcheme of Chriſtianity, or ſuch other ſchemes of revelation, as have been copied from it [f], we ſhall no where find the idea of *uni-verſality* to have taken place in any reli-gious or philoſophical ſect whatſoever [s].

If then this idea was *familiar* to the Jewiſh and Chriſtian prophets, you will, at leaſt, conclude that this circumſtance is remarkable enough to engage your atten-tion; and you will naturally aſk, how it

[f] As in the caſe of *Mahometaniſm*, for inſtance.

[s] What the philoſopher Celſus thought of ſuch a project, we learn from a curious paſſage in Origen. It being uſual with the Chriſtians of that time, as of every other, *to pray for the converſion of the whole world to the Chriſtian faith*, the philoſopher laughs at the extrava-gance of this petition. He obſerves upon it, ὅτι ὁ τᵘτο διόμενος οἶδεν ᵘδέν. The words are not eaſily tranſlated. But the *meaning* of them is, That he regarded an uni-verſal agreement in one mode of religious belief, as a perfect chimæra: and the *turn* of the words is ſo con-trived, as to expreſs the utmoſt contempt of thoſe, who, in their ſupreme ignorance of mankind, could entertain ſo ſenſeleſs an idea. *Contr. Celſum, l.* viii. *ſub fin.*

adopt

S E R M.
VI.

came to pafs that thofe prophets fhould adopt fo ftrange a fancy, which appears not to have entered into the views or conceptions of other men.

When you are in this train of inquiry, it will furprize you ftill more to find,

2. *By what perfons, thefe prophecies,* fo remarkable for the *matter* of them, *were announced.*

The publifhers of this extraordinary doctrine were, in one word, JEWS: that is, men of the moft narrow and contracted minds; men, brought up in the higheft conceit of themfelves, and in the utmoft fcorn and contempt of the Gentiles; men, accuftomed to think themfelves the only favourites of heaven, and to regard the reft of the world, as outcafts of its providence; men, in fhort, induced, partly, by the genius of their religion, ill underftood, and partly, by their carnal temper, long indulged, to believe with affurance the perpetuity, the eternity of their divine law; and to deem it impoffible that God fhould reign

O   any

anywhere but in the land of Ifrael, or
fhould impart his bleffings to any, that
lived out of the Jewifh pale.

Was it, now, to be expected of fuch
men, as thefe, that they fhould enlarge
their ideas fo far as to form the project of
a new and univerfal religion; a religion,
not imprinted outwardly on the flefh, but
written in the heart; a religion, that was
to fuperfede and evacuate the law of Mofes,
to which they were fo immoderately addicted, and to enlighten and blefs and
fave the heathen, whom they fo perfectly
defpifed and abhorred?

You will fufpect, perhaps, that the
meaning of thefe prophecies was no more,
than that the Jewifh Law fhould finally
prevail over all other Laws, and be the
fole predominant religion of the whole
earth: a prejudice, very likely, it may be
faid, to poffefs the minds of fuch a people
as the Jews; and fuitable enough to that
zeal, which prompted them *to compafs fea*

and

and land, as Jefus himfelf obferved of them, S E R M.
to make one profelyte[h].

But the contrary is apparent from the
ftructure of the Jewifh Law, which, as I
faid, was fo contrived, that it could not
be obferved out of Judæa—from the *tenour*
of that Law, addrefled only to the houfe
of Ifrael, and not obligatory to any other
people—from exprefs *declarations* of the
prophets themfelves; who call the difpenfation of the Meffiah, *a new Covenant*,
a covenant *written in the heart*, in oppofition to the law of circumcifion[i]; who fay,
that the Lord will *create new heavens and
a new earth*, that is, in the prophetic
language, will inftitute a *new* difpenfation
of religion, different from that, which he

[h] Matth. xxiii. 15.
[i] Behold, the days come, faith the Lord, that I will
make a *new covenant* with the houfe of Ifrael, and with
the houfe of Judah, not according to the covenant that
I made with their fathers—but this fhall be my covenant that I will make with the houfe of Ifrael, after
thofe days, faith the Lord, *I will put my Law in their
inward parts, and write it in their hearts*, &c. Jer. xxxi.
31—33. See alfo Jer. iii. 16.

O 2   had

had given to the Jews, and *fubverfive* of
it [k]; who, laftly, fpeak of this difpenfation, as of *one*, that fhould be eftablifhed
under *a new name*, and fhould be embraced
by the Gentiles, as *fuch*, that is, by men,
converted immediately to this new religion
from their ftate of Gentilifm, without
paffing through the ftrait gate of the
Jewifh Law [l].

Judge then, whether the prophets did
not mean more than a *profelytifm* to their
own religion, when they predicted, and
in fuch terms, the future converfion of
the Gentiles; and whether fuch ideas, as
thefe, could ever have entered into the
hearts of Jews, if fomething, befides and
above the natural fuggeftion of their own
minds, had not infpired their prophecies.

[k] For behold, *I create new heavens and a new earth:
and the former fhall not be remembered nor come into mind.*
If. lxv. 17.

[l] The *Gentiles* fhall fee thy righteoufnefs, and all
Kings, thy glory: And thou fhallt be *called by a new
name*, which the mouth of the Lord fhall name.
If. lxii. 2.

Add

Add to all this, if you pleafe, that Jefus
was himfelf a Jew, and (to regard him as a man only) in the loweft clafs of the Jews, that is, of the moft confined and bigoted education; and yet was not reftrained by his prejudices from giving that fublime command to his followers — Go AND TEACH ALL NATIONS.

But enough on the *doctrine* itfelf, and on the *character* of its teachers. It remains only

3. To add one word, *on the manner, in which this prophecy*, concerning the converfion of the Gentile world, *appears to have been completed.*

There are efpecially TWO prophecies on this fubject, which merit our attentive confideration. ONE of them afferts, that the converfion of the Gentile world fhall take its rife from fmall and very unpromifing beginnings, and yet fhall prevail fpeedily and to a vaft extent; the OTHER, that it fhall prevail by pacific means only, without the intervention of any force or violence whatfoever.

O 3   1. The

SERM.
VI.

1. The FORMER of thefe prophecies is exprefled thus—*A little one fhall become a thoufand, and a fmall one a ftrong nation: I the Lord will haften it in his time* [m]. In allufion to this prophecy, concerning the rife and progrefs of Chriftianity, is that parable of our Lord applied to the king-dom of heaven—*the kingdom of heaven,* fays, he, *is like to a grain of muftard-feed, which a man took and fowed in his field: which in-deed is the leaft of all feeds: but when it is grown, it is the greateft among herbs, and becometh a tree: fo that the birds of the air come and lodge in the branches thereof* [n]. And, with regard to the *celerity,* with which this tree fhould grow up, we have a prophecy from Chrift himfelf, and that wonderfully fulfilled—that *his Gofpel fhould be preached to all the world for a teftimony to all nations,* before the deftruction of Jerufalem, or within forty years from the date of the prophecy.

[m] If. lx. 22.
[n] Matth. xiii. 31, 32.

Now

Now, confider the ftate of the Gofpel, at our Lord's afcenfion. It was left in the hands of a few, mean, unlearned, difpirited perfons: without any countenance from authority; and with every difficulty, every terror, oppofed to them, and placed diftinctly within their view. *Math.* xxiv. 9. Yet thefe men were commiffioned to fpread this Gofpel through the world, and had an exprefs promife, that they fhould fucceed in their attempt. Againft all appearance, the fuccefs followed. In lefs than half a century, *the found of the Gofpel went out into all lands;* and, within three centuries from the death of Chrift, Chriftianity afcended the impe- rial throne; *and had the utmoft parts of the earth for its poffeffion.*

To encreafe the wonder, this amazing revolution was brought about, by *pacific methods only*; as was, likewife, foretold

2. In the LATTER of the *two* prophecies, to which I before alluded.

Jefus himfelf quotes this prophecy from Ifaiah in the following words—*Behold, my*

O 4 *fervant,*

SERM.
VI.
servant, whom I have chosen, my beloved, in whom my soul is well pleased: I will put my spirit upon him, and he shall shew judgment, i. e. declare a new Law, *to the Gentiles. He shall not strive, nor cry, neither shall any man hear his voice in the streets; a bruised reed shall he not break, and smoaking flax shall he not quench,* i. e. (as all interpreters explain these proverbial expressions) he shall not employ the least degree of force or violence in the propagation of this law, *till he send forth judgment unto victory,* till it finally prevail against all opposition; *And in his name shall the Gentiles trust.* Matth. xii, 18—21.

Let any man read the history of Christianity, from its first publication in Judæa, to the conversion of Constantine, and then see whether this prophecy hath not been exactly and illustriously completed. The followers of Jesus were numerous enough, long before the empire became Christian, to have attempted the way of force, had

it

it been permitted to them°: and the in-
fults, the oppreffions, the perfecutions,
which they fuffered from their Pagan enemies, were enough to provoke the moft
paffive tempers to fome acts of hoftility
and refiftance ᵖ. But every one knows, that
they had recourfe to no arms, but thofe of

° Si enim et hoftes *exertos,* non tantùm vindices oc-
cultos, agere vellemus, *deeffet nobis vis numerorum et co-
piarum?* *Tertull. Apologet. c.* 37.

ᵖ Could it be *forefeen,* that nothing of this fort would
happen? When the *Reformation* was fet on foot in Ger-
many, Luther and his adherents refolved to carry it on
in the fpirit of the Gofpel, that is, by *pacific meafures.*
But how foon did paffion and policy ftrike in, to drive
them from this purpofe? The Catholics were intolerant: the Reformed grew powerful: and then, what
was too naturally to be expected, followed.

If it be faid, that the Gofpel hath not been always
propagated, *without force;* I reply, 1. that it was in-
conteftably fo propagated, till the converfion of the
Roman empire; in which event, alone, the prophecies
appear to have had a reafonable completion. 2. that
the *force employed,* has generally been the force of one
Chriftian fect, directed againft fome other, (in which
fcandalous contentions the prophecies have no concern),
not in the propagation of Chriftianity itfelf in unbelieving countries. 3. That the *ufe of force,* when at
any time it hath been ufed againft unbelievers, appears
the

SERM.
VI.
——

the fpirit: they took no advantage of dif-
tracted times, to raife commotions in be-
half of the *new* religion, or to fupprefs the
old one: *a bruifed reed did they not break,
and fmoaking flax did they not quench:* yet
with meeknefs, and patience, and fuffering; by piety, by reafon, by the fecret
influence of a divine blefling attending on
thefe feeble efforts, the doctrine of the crofs
infenfibly gained ground, fpread itfelf far
and wide, and in the end became *victorious* over all the rage and power and fophif-
try of an unbelieving world⁹.

not to have profpered, or to have been followed by any
confiderable effects; of which the *crufades againft the
Mahometans* are a ftriking inftance; and 4. laftly, that
we expect the *final univerfal* prevalence of the Chriftian
faith from the fame fpiritual arms only, which were firft
employed with fuch fuccefs in the propagation of it.

⁹ An eminent writer, with the view, indeed, of dif-
gracing the Reformation, hath fet this matter in a very
juft light: "Que nos freres, fays he, ouvrent donc
les yeux; qu'ils les jettent fur l'ancienne Eglife, qui
durant tant de fiécles d'une perfecution fi cruelle ne
s'eft jamais échapée, ni un feul moment, ni dans un
feul homme, & qu'on a vûë auffi foûmife fous Diocle-

That

That this *victory* hath not been, hither- SERM.
to, fo complete, as to anfwer the promife   VI.

tien, et même fous Julien l'apoftat, lorfqu'elle rem-
pliffoit deja toute la terre, que fous Neron & fous
Domitien, lorfqu'elle ne faifoit que de naitre : c'est-
là qu' on voit véritablement le doigt de Dieu."
Hift. des Variations, l. x. c. 53.

The finger of God, as the learned writer fays, was indeed
confpicuous in this conduct of the primitive Chriftians,
becaufe it fulfilled the prophecies (fo unlikely to be
fulfilled) concerning the *manner* in which Chriftianity
was to obtain an eftablifhment in the world. If the
conduct of the *reformed* had not this merit, it was
becaufe the prophecies did not extend to the reformation of Chriftian religion, but to the introduction and
firft fettlement of it. The agents, in this laft work of
providence, were therefore left to the natural influence
of their paffions, and they acted too frequently as thofe
paffions impelled them.

For the reft, how far the *general* precepts of the
Gofpel require a paffive fubmiffion and non-refiftance
to outrageous intolerance, whether abfolutely, and in
all cafes, is a point of nice difcuffion; in which I take
no part, at prefent, becaufe I am not now making the
apology of the *reformed*, but fhewing the completion of
the prophecies concerning the *propagators* of Chriftianity : and the wonder to fee them fo punctually completed, is not leffened, but increafed by fuppofing, that
the precepts of the Gofpel leave mankind to the free ufe
of their natural rights, in the cafe of extreme violence
and injuftice.

of

of an *abſolute univerſality*, we readily acknowledge; but are in no pain for the
event[r]; as the ſame oracles, which have
thus far been verified, ſuppoſe the preſent
condition of things; and, what is more,
aſſure us of a time to come, when *the
fulneſs of the Gentiles ſhall come in.*

One word more, and I have done. If
it be now thought, that theſe THREE prophecies—*concerning the deſtruction of Jeru-
ſalem—the diſperſion of the Jews*—and *the
call of the Gentiles*—have been clearly accompliſhed; and yet were of that nature,
that no human foreſight could deliver
them, nor any probable conjuncture of
human affairs account for the accompliſhment of them, you will conclude that
they were truly divine, and that we do
not abuſe your credulity in alledging ſuch
prophecies, in proof of our holy religion.

[r] *The viſion is yet for an appointed time, but at the end
it ſhall ſpeak, and not lye: though it tarry, wait for it,
becauſe it ſhall ſurely come, it will not tarry.* Habak-
kuk, ii. 3.

You

You will fee and acknowledge that there SERM.
are prophecies, recorded in fcripture, *con-* ^{VI.}
cerning the Chriftian Church; and that *thefe*
prophecies, in particular, concerning it,
have been remarkably fulfilled. Ye will,
therefore, the lefs wonder to find, that
there are ftill *other* prophecies, relative to
the kingdom of Chrift, as adminiftered in
this world; and will, of courfe, be difpofed to confider, with lefs prevention,
what may further be faid in fupport of
them.

S E R-

SERMON VII.

[Prophecies concerning ANTICHRIST.

1 Ep. JOHN ii. 18.

*—Ye have heared that Antichrist shall
come—*

SERM.
VII.

AMONG the more remarkable prophecies concerning the Christian
Church, there are several, which describe
the rise, progress, and downfal of a certain
Power, represented under various symbols
or images, and distinguished by many ap-
pellations; but more especially known by
the name of ANTICHRIST.

These prophecies come now, in the
order of this Lecture, to be considered.

The

The subject is, in a high degree, curious and important; but of no easy discussion: not so much on the account of any peculiar difficulty in the prophecies themselves, as from the prejudice of party in *explaining* them, and still more, from the general prejudice that lies against every *attempt* to explain them.

To make my way through all these obstructions, I shall begin with laying before you a clear and distinct state of the question itself, which is chiefly agitated by inquirers into these prophecies.

It is admitted, that many predictions in the Old and New Testament, particularly in the book of Daniel, in St. Paul's Epistles, and in the Revelations of St. John, clearly point out a very extraordinary power, which was to manifest itself *in the latter times*, that is, in the times subsequent to the introduction of Christianity. The characters, by which this power (acknowledged by all under the name of Antichrist) is
chiefly

chiefly diftinguifhed, are thofe of *Tyranny* ᵃ,
Idolatry, and *Intolerance*. And, to abridge
our trouble in fearching after this *three-
headed* monfter, we are directed by the
prophets to look for him within the bound-
aries of what was properly called, the
Roman Empire, and even in the city of
Rome itfelf.

Thus far there is no difpute. The only
queftion is, To what Roman power, ex-
hibiting thofe characters, the prophecies
are to be applied. And even this queftion
is reduced within narrow · limits. For
TWO Powers only have fubfifted in Rome,
from the Chriftian æra to the prefent times
(within which period we are, again, allowed to expect the reign of Antichrift); the

---

ᵃ By the word *Tyranny*, here and elfewhere in thefe
difcourfes, as applied to the Pope, I would be underftood to mean, that *fuper-eminent dominion*, which he
exercifed, or claimed a *right* of exercifing, over the
princes and ftates of his communion,· in all affairs both
temporal and fpiritual.—I ufe the word (fomewhat
improperly, perhaps) for the fake of brevity, as I know
of no other fingle term, that fo well expreffes my meaning.

Roman

Roman Emperor, in the firſt place; and,
afterwards, the Roman Pontifs. So that,
on the whole, the ſingle point in debate is
merely this, Whether Imperial, or Papal
Rome, be that Antichriſtian Power, which
the prophets foretold. The church of
Rome holds, for obvious reaſons, that the
Imperial power is the objeſt of the prophecies: the Proteſtants have, on the contrary, their reaſons for maintaining, that *Papal*
Rome is that power, which the prophecies had in view, and in which alone they
are truly and properly verified.

This, then, is the meaning of that famous inquiry concerning Antichriſt: and
I muſt deſire you to keep your attention
ſteadily fixed on the queſtion, as here ſtat-
ed; while I endeavour to furniſh you with
the proper means of deciding upon it.

The obvious method of doing this, would
be, To lay before you, direſtly, the prophecies themſelves, and to examine them
by the light of ſober criticiſm, and authentic hiſtory. But, becauſe it is no new

P

or

or difficult thing to mifreprefent *facts*, and
to mifinterpret *fcripture*, to pervert, in fhort,
thefe two inftruments of truth to any ends,
which prejudice hath in view; and becaufe
I know how natural it is for you to fufpect
fuch management in the prefent cafe, where
the zeal of party is fuppofed, on either fide,
to exclude, or over-power, the love of
truth; for *thefe reafons*, it may be convenient to take a larger compafs, and, by a
previous hiftorical deduction of this controverfy, to let you fee in what light it has
been regarded, through the feveral ages of
the Chriftian Church.

I. THE FIRST ACCOUNT, we meet with
in fcripture, of the power in queftion, I
mean, under his proper name of *Antichrift*,
is in the firft epiftle of St. John, from
which the text is taken. The whole paffage runs thus—*Little children, it is the laft
time: And, as ye have heared that Antichrift
fhall come, even now there are many Anti-
christs;*

chrifts; *whereby we know that it is the laft time.*

To underftand thefe words, we muft call to mind what hath been already, more than once, obferved concerning the fcriptural divifion of time into two great portions, The FORMER, and LATTER times. By the *former*, is meant the times preceding the Chriftian æra; by the *latter*, the times fubfequent to it. Correfpondent to this partition of time, is the double advent of Chrift, of which I before gave a diftinct idea. His *firft* advent was, when he came in the flefh at Jerufalem: his *fecond* advent is to be underftood of his coming in his kingdom, through all the ages of the Chriftian Church.

But though the *latter times*, in the general fenfe of fcripture, be thus comprehenfive, they are further fubdivided into other conftituent portions, in which fome particular ftate of Chrift's kingdom is adminiftered, and within which it is completed. In reference to this fubordinate

P 2   divifion

divifion of time in the Chriftian difpenfation, the *coming* of Chrift is, alfo, proportionably multiplied. He *comes* in each
divifion; that is, as oft as he thinks fit to
interpofe by any fignal act of his power and
providence. The whole period, in which
any diftinct ftate of his kingdom is carrying on, is likewife called *the latter time*;
and the concluding part of that period is
diftinguifhed by the name of the *laft hour*:
as if the whole of each period were confidered as *one day*; and the clofe of each
period, as the end, or *laft hour*, of that day.

Thus, the time that elapfed from Chrift's
afcenfion to the deftruction of Jerufalem,
being one of the fubdivifions, before mentioned, is called the *latter times*; and the
eve of its deftruction, is called the *laft hour*.
He *was coming* through the whole time:
he *came* in the end of it. And the like ufe
of thefe terms is to be made, in other inftances. We are to apply them in the fame
manner to the *reign of Antichrift—to the
Millennium*—to the *day of judgment*. Each
of

SER M.
VII.

of thefe ftates, into which the *latter times*, or the times of Chriftianity, are divided, is likewife fpoken of under the idea of the *latter times*; and the feafon, in which each is drawing to an end, is the *laſt hour* of that ftate [b].

Thus much being premifed, it is eafy to give a juſt expofition of the text. *Little children, it is the laſt time,* or *hour*—that is, the deſtruction of Jerufalem is at hand; as indeed it followed very foon after the date of this Epiſtle. *And, as ye have heard that Antichriſt ſhall come*—that, in fome future period, called *the laſt times,* an hoſtile power, which we know by the name of Antichriſt, ſhall arife and prevail in the world, *even now,* we may fee the commencement of that power; for, *there are*

[b] What is here faid of the fcriptural divifion of *time*, with regard to the affairs of the *Church*, is enough for my purpofe. There is another divifion of time, in the prophetic fcriptures, with regard to the *kingdoms of the world*; concerning which the reader may confult BISHOP KIDDER's *Dem. of the Meſſiah, Part* iii. *ch.* ix.; and efpecially Mr. MEDE's *Apoſtaſy of the latter times, ch.* xi.

many

SERM.
VII.
many Antichrifts; many perfons, now, appear in the fpirit of that future Antichrift,
and deferve his name: *whereby, indeed,
we know that it is the laft hour*: for Chrift
himfelf had made the appearance of falfe
Chrifts and falfe prophets, that is, of Antichrifts, to be one of the figns by which
that *hour* fhould be diftinguifhed ᶠ.

The meaning of the whole paffage, then,
is clearly this: " That the appearance of
falfe Chrifts and *falfe Prophets* (of which
there were many, according to our Lord's
prediction, in St. John's time) indicated
the arrival of that *hour*, that was to be fatal to the Jewifh ftate: and that they
were, at the fame time, the types and
forerunners of a ftill more dreadful power,
which fhould be fully revealed in *the latter
times*, in a future period, when that calamity was paft." · For the truth of the
affertion, That fuch a power fhould arife in
the Chriftian church, he appeals to a tradition, then current among the difciples:

ᶠ Matth. xxiv. 24. Mark xiii. 21.

and

and his hated name of *Antichrift* is here S E R M. VII.
applied, by way of anticipation, to the
falfe prophets of that time; as poffeffing
much of his character, and acting with his
fpirit.

Hence we fee the meaning of the word,
Antichrift; which ftands for a perfon or
power, actuated with a fpirit oppofite to
that of Chrift. And fo indeed the Apoftle
explains himfelf, in another place of this
very Epiftle. For, fpeaking of certain
falfe teachers, who preached up a doctrine,
contrary to that of the Gofpel, he adds—
" This is that *fpirit* of Antichrift, whereof
" ye have heard that it fhould come, and
" even now already is it in the world[d]."
And I lay the greater ftrefs on this obfervation, becaufe the etymology of the word,
Antichrift, makes it capable of two different
meanings. For it may either fignify one,
who *affumes the place and office of Chrift*, or
one, who *maintains a direct enmity and oppo-*

[d] 1 Ep. John, iv. 3.

P 4 *fition*

SERM.
VII.

sition to him [e].　But the *latter*, is the sense
in which the Apostle useth this term;
although it be true that, in the *former*
sense, it very well suits the Bishop of Rome,
who calls himself the *Vicar* of Christ, as
well as the successor of St. Peter.　Nor can
there be any difficulty in fixing the charge
of Antichristianism, in the sense of *an enmity and opposition to Christ*, on the Roman
Pontif (though I know how absurd the attempt seems to the writers on that side;)
for, to merit this charge, it is not necessary that he should formally reject Christ,
which undoubtedly he does not, but that
he should act in defiance to the true genius
and character of Christ's religion : a charge,
which may be evidently made good against
him.

In short, as the word, *Christ*, is frequently used in the Apostolic writings for
the *doctrine* of Christ; in which sense we
are said to *put on Christ*, to *grow in Christ*,

[e] 'Αντίχριστος — αντι, in the sense either of *pro*, or
contra.

to

to *learn Chrift*, and in other inftances : So
Antichrift, in the abftract, may be taken
for a doctrine fubverfive of the Chriftian ;
and when applied to a particular man, or
body of men, it denotes *one*, who fets
himfelf againft the *fpirit* of that doctrine [f].

---

[f] Grotius fays, " Sicut *Anticæfarem* dicimus qui
contra Cæfarem fe Cæfarem vult dici atque Cæfar haberi,
fic *Antichriftus* eft qui fe vero Chrifto opponit *eo modo* ut
ipfe Chriftus haberi velit." OP. t. iv. *p*. 490.—The
learned commentator did not reflect, that words are not
always ufed according to the ftrict import of their ety-
mologies. *Falfe Chrifts*, we will fay, are, in the ftrict
fenfe of the word, *Antichrifts*. But the queftion is, in
what fenfe this word is ufed of the perfon called, by way
of eminence, THE ANTICHRIST. This muft be collected from the attributes given to him in the prophecies themfelves, not from the rigorous etymology of
the term. The cafe was plainly this. St. John is
fpeaking of the *falfe Chrifts*, who had appeared in his
time ; and, to difgrace them the more effectually in the
minds of thofe to whom he writes, he brands them
with the name of *Antichrifts*: not fo much refpecting
the exact fenfe of the word, as the ideas of averfion,
which, he knew, it would excite. For the tradition
of the church concerning *Antichrift*, had made this ap-
pellation, of all others, the moft opprobrious, and
hateful.—Befides, it is not fo clear, as Grotius fuppofes, that the ftrict fenfe of the word, *Antichriftus*,

In

In this laſt ſenſe, the word *Antichriſt* is clearly employed by St. John: and from his example, the word grew into general uſe in the Chriſtian church; and is ſo to be underſtood, whenever mention is made of Antichriſt by the primitive fathers, or any other ecclesiaſtical writers.

II. I am now to ſhew in what manner the prophecies concerning *Antichriſt*, or a perſon or power, ſo called, and, though variouſly deſcribed, always conſidered under the idea of an adverſary to the true doctrine of Chriſt, have been conſtrued and applied by many eminent members of the Chriſtian Church, in all ages.

muſt be—*is, qui ſe vero Chriſto opponit eo modo ut ipſe Chriſtus haberi velit.* Cæſar, who generally expreſſed himſelf with exact propriety, thought fit, on a certain occaſion, to aſſume the name and character of, ANTICATO. Was it Cæſar's purpoſe to ſay, or was it his ambition to pretend, " *that he oppoſed himſelf to the true Cato,* EO MODO *ut ipſe* CATO *haberi vellet ?*"

I, When

I. When the canon of fcripture was formed, and now in the hands of the faithful, the prophecies concerning Antichrift were too remarkable not to take their early attention. They accordingly cite thefe prophecies in their apologies and commentaries, or refer to them, very frequently. But one thing is fingular. Though Antichrift be every where fpoken of in the prophecies as a perfecuting power, and though the Chriftian church then was, and fo continued to be for near three centuries, in a ftate of perfecution under the Roman emperors, yet this opprobrious name was not ufually given to their perfecutors. I do not fay, that none of the early Chriftian writers ever applied that character to the Emperors. Some few of them, in a fit of zeal and refentment, did [s]. But the moft,

---

[s] Eufebius mentions, JUDAS, H. E. *l.* vi. *c.* 2; and DIONYSIUS, E, H. *l.* vii. *c.* 10.—*Others,* feemed to expect that Antichrift would appear as the Meffiah of the Jews; but in the perfon of a Roman Emperor; as will be explained prefently. See the next note.

and

and the ablest of the Fathers, were clearly of another opinion.

It may be thought, that they forbore this application of so odious a term, out of respect to the government under which they lived, and from prudential considerations. These motives had, without doubt, their weight with them, and made them more cautious, than they would otherwise have been, in interpreting the prophecies. But, if they had been at liberty to speak out, and declare their full sense, on the subject, it is certain they would not, and could not, consistently with their avowed principles, apply the prophecies concerning Antichrist to the Roman Emperors. For they had learned from tradition, and from the letter of the prophecies, that Antichrist was to be revealed in some distant age; and they even collected from a remarkable passage in one of St. Paul's Epistles (which will be considered hereafter) that the removal of the Roman empire was to make way for his appearance. Hence, they

they give it as a reafon for their ardent prayers to heaven for the prefervation of the empire, that the dreaded power of Antichrift could not commence, fo long as the Imperial fovereignty fubfifted. And it is obfervable that, of thofe few writers, who were in different fentiments, the greater part conceived the time of his coming to be *remote* ; and were even driven to the ftrange neceffity of fuppofing that Nero, the firft perfecuting Emperor, was miraculoufly kept alive, or would be raifed up from the dead, in order to be revealed in a future age, as the Antichrift of the prophets, or at leaft as the *Precurfor* of Antichrift [h].

In fhort, the idea, which the early Chriftians, in general, formed of Antichrift, was that of a power, to be revealed in diftant times, after the diffolution of the Roman empire ; of a power, to arife out of the ruins of that empire. Not to multiply quotations, on a point which admits no doubt, Jerom, the ableft of the antient Fathers,

[h] See many citations to this purpofe in Dr. Lardner's *Cred. p.* ii. *vol.* v. *p.* 210, 11, 12.

and

and the moſt eſteemed, ſhall ſpeak for the reſt.   He ſays expreſſly, that ſuch was the idea of *all the eccleſiaſtical writers,* down to his time, as is here repreſented[i].

Now this circumſtance ye will ſurely think not a little remarkable, that they, who lived under the emperors, and felt the whole weight of their tyrannous perſecution, ſhould not apply the prophetic notes and characters of Antichriſt, to *them,* if indeed the prophecies had been fairly capable of ſuch application.   This, I ſay, is exceedingly remarkable : for men are but too apt even to wreſt the ſcriptures to a ſenſe, which favours their own cauſe, or gratifies their paſſions ; and to find a completion of prophecy in events, which fall out in their own days and concern themſelves (as we ſee from ſo many abſurd applications of the Apocalypſe, juſtly objected to certain Proteſtant writers) ; though, when ſuch events are paſt, and impartially conſidered, no ſuch accom-

_____
[i] Jerom, in Dan. vii.   Mede, *p.* 657.

pliſhment

plifhment of prophecy can be difcerned in them.

When the church of Rome, therefore, now pretends, that Antichrift is to be fought in Imperial and Pagan Rome, ye will naturally afk how it came to pafs, that the antient fathers, who had the beft opportunity of feeing the conformity of the prophecies with the tranfactions of their times, and were fo much interefted in thofe tranfactions, fhould yet overlook fuch conformity, if it had been real, and fairly marked out by the prophecies, when interpreters of thefe days are fo quick-fighted! And to this queftion, no juft and fatisfactory anfwer can be given, but that, in the opinion of thofe fathers, the characters of Antichrift were not fufficiently applicable to the Roman emperors; or, if they were, that certain exprefs claufes in the prophecies themfelves forbade that application of them. Either way, their conduct forms a ftrong prefumption, that the Antichrift

of

of the prophets was not, and could not be, the Roman Emperor.

I know indeed, that, when the empire became Chriſtian, and factions ſprang up in the church, the name of Antichriſt, as a term of reproach, was not unfrequently beſtowed on ſuch of the emperors as had made themſelves obnoxious to the orthodox party.   But this flippancy of language proves nothing but the paſſion of the men who indulged themſelves in it, unleſs it be, that this term of reproach was thought better ſuited to an eccleſiaſtic, than a civil power: for the Emperor, being now the head of the Chriſtian church, his perſecutions of the faith were deemed the more *Antichriſtian,* as they eſpecially diſgraced his *religious character.*   And how natural this idea was, I mean the idea of *Antichriſt,* as intended by the prophets of a *religious,* not civil power, we may learn from the hiſtory of the ſchiſms, which afterwards diſtracted the church under the papacy;
when

when the Antipopes very liberally, and constantly branded each other with the name of *Antichrist :* as if they had found a peculiar aptnefs in the prophetic language to exprefs ecclefiaftical tyranny and ufurpation.

But, whatever ufe we may make of thefe facts, it is clear, on all hands, that the Roman Emperor, *as fuch,* was thought to have no concern in the predictions concerning Antichrift; at leaft, that the more intelligent Chriftian writers of the three firft centuries had no idea of his having any fuch concern in them : while, yet, they held very unanimoufly, that fome future power was to arife in the church, in which thofe predictions would be completed.

II. This, in general, was the ftate of the controverfy concerning Antichrift, till the down-fall of the Weftern empire; when the Bifhop of Rome reared his head, and by degrees found means, amidft the

Q   ruins

ruins of that mighty power, to advance himfelf into the fovereignty of Rome, and, at length, of the Chriſtian world; fixing his reſidence in the very ſeat and throne of the Cæſars. It remains to ſee, in what light the reign of Antichriſt was, thenceforth, conſidered by many eminent members of that church, which now called itſelf, and was, in a manner, *univerſal*. In other words, we are to inquire, now that the imperial power, which the fathers would not acknowledge to be Antichriſtian, had deſerted Rome, whether the papal power, which took its place on *the ſeven hills*, did not, in the opinion of ſober men, fill up all the meaſures of the prophetic characters, and perfectly correſpond to that idea.

1. So early, as about the cloſe of the ſixth century, Gregory the firſt, or, the *Great*, as he is uſually called, the moſt revered, and in ſome reſpects not undeſervedly ſo, of all the Roman pontifs, in a famous diſpute with the Biſhop of Conſtantinople, who

who had taken to himſelf the title of *Oecu-*
menical, or Univerſal Biſhop, objeċts to him,
the arrogance and preſumption of this
claim, and treats him, on that account,
as the fore-runner, at leaſt, of Antichriſt.
His words are remarkable enough to be
here quoted. *I affirm it confidently,* ſays He,
that whoever calls himſelf Univerſal Biſhop,
or is deſirous to be ſo called, demonſtrates him-
ſelf, by this pride and elation of heart, to be
the fore-runner of Antichriſt [k]. And, again,
From this preſumption of his [in taking the
name of Univerſal Biſhop] *what elſe can be*
collećted, but that the times of Antichriſt are
now at hand [l] *?*

It is to be obſerved of this Gregory, that
he diſclaimed, for himſelf, the title of
Univerſal Biſhop, as well as refuſed it to
his aſpiring brother of Conſtantinople.
How conſiſtently he did this, when at the

---

[k] Quiſquis ſe univerſalem vocat, vel vocari deſide-
rat, in elatione ſuâ Antichriſtum præcurrit. GREG.
M. Op. *Ep.* xxx. *l.* 6. *Par.* 1533.

[l] In hâc ejus ſuperbiâ, quid aliud niſi propinqua
jam Antichriſti eſſe tempora deſignatur? *Ep.* xxxiv. *l.* 4.

ſame

fame time, he exercifed an authority, which can only belong to that exalted character, it is not my bufinefs to inquire. Perhaps, he did not advert to the confequence of his own actions: perhaps, like an able man, he meant to fecure the thing, without troubling himfelf about the name: perhaps, he was jealous of a rival to this claim of catholic authority, and would not permit the Bifhop of Conftantinople to decorate himfelf with a title, which was likely to be favourable to the pretenfions of that fee, and injurious to his own. Whatever the reafons of his conduct were, the *fact* is, as I here reprefent it; and clearly fhews that, in the judgment of this renowned Roman Bifhop, Antichrift had not yet been revealed in the perfon of the Roman Emperor; and if ever he were to be revealed, that not a civil, but ecclefiaftical character, agreed beft with the prophetic defcriptions of him [m].

[m] With all his merits, Gregory the Great, it is to be feared, had fome Antichriftian marks upon him;

2. Pope

2. Pope Boniface III, had not, it feems, the fcruples, whatever they were, of his predeceffor, Gregory. He readily accepted, or rather importunately begged, this proud title of *Oecumenical Bifhop*, from the Emperor, Phocas; and tranfmitted it to all his fucceffors. And now, it might be expected, that the Bifhop of Rome would be Antichrift, in his turn. But, fuch was the fortune of that fee, or the devotion of the faithful to it, that this charge was not prefently brought againft him: as if the fpirit of dominion, which had fo long poffeffed that city, were a thing of courfe, and could not mifbecome the Bifhop of Rome, though it looked fo *Antichriftian* in him of Conftantinople.

Other reafons concurred to fave the honour of the papal chair. It's authority grew, every day, more abfolute: and the

and his adverfary of the Eaft might have gone fome way towards *fixing* them upon his *Grandeur*, if he had but obferved, that Antichrift, whoever he was, and whenfoever to appear in the world, is clearly marked out in the prophecies, as having his feat in *old Rome*.

Q 3   tradition

tradition of the church (which had hitherto been the chief fupport of the doctrine concerning Antichrift) gradually funk
under the apprehenfion of that power, to
which alone it could, with any apparent
propriety, be applied : while the ignorance
of the times became fuch, that, except
perhaps in the minds of fome few retainers
to the fee of Rome, there was fcarce light
enough left in the Chriftian world to point
out the meaning of the prophecies ; if it's
grofs fuperftition would have otherwife permitted the application of them to the facred
perfon of the Pope.

3. Under the cover of all thefe advantages, *the Man of Sin* had a convenient time
to difplay himfelf, and to grow up into
that full fize and ftature, in which he could
no longer be overlooked, or miftaken, by
thofe who had any knowledge of the prophecies, or fkill in applying them. Accordingly we find that at the fynod of
Rheims,

Rheims, held in the Xth century[n], Arnul- S E R M.
phus, Bifhop of Orleans, appealed to the VII.
whole council, whether the Bifhop of
Rome were not the Antichrift of the prophets; *fitting in the temple of God*; and
perfectly correfponding to the marks, which
St. Paul had given of him. In particular,
fpeaking of John the XVth, who then
governed the church of Rome, he apoftro-
phized the affembly in thefe words—
" What think ye, reverend Fathers, of this
man, feated on a lofty throne, and fhining
in purple and gold? Whom do ye account
him to be? Surely, if deftitute of charity,
and puffed up with the pride of fcience
only, He is ANTICHRIST, *fitting in the
temple of God, and fhewing himfelf that he is
God*[o].

[n] A. 991.
[o] Quid hunc, reverendi patres, in fublimi folio refi-
dentem, vefte purpureâ et aureâ radiantem; quid hunc,
inquam, effe cenfetis? Nimirum, fi charitate deftitu-
itur, folâque fcientiâ inflatur et extollitur, ANTI-
CHRISTUS eft, *in templo Dei fedens, et fe oftendens tanquam fit Deus.* USSER. *de Chriftian. Eccl. fucceffione &*

Q 4 4. In

SERM.
VII.

4. In the former part of the XIth century, Berengarius, a man of principal note in those days, and diftinguifhed by his free writings concerning the Euchariſt, went fo far as to call the church of Rome, *the feat of Satan* (which is but another apocalyptic name of Antichriſt;) and to know from what ſource he derived this language, we need only reflect, that, in the catalogue of his works, we find a treatiſe written by him expreſſly on the book of Revelations P.

As this century advanced, the papal power roſe to its height. And all the characters of Antichriſt glared ſo ſtrongly

ſtatu, c. ii. p. 36. Lond. 1613.—ILLYRICI *Cat. Teſt. Ver. p. 1558. Officin. Jacob. Stoër et Jacob. Chouëi.* —This Arnulph, Biſhop of Orleans, was eſteemed, in his day, the wiſeſt and moſt eloquent of all the Gallican prelates. Arnulphus—de quo ſic initio ejus ſynodi ſcriptum eſt—*Inter omnes Galliarum epiſcopos ſapientiâ et eloquentiâ clariſſimus habebatur.* ib.

P " Eccleſiam vanitatis, & SEDEM SATANÆ vocabat." USSER. *de Chriſtian. Eccl. ſucceſ. & ſtatu, c. 7. ſ. xxiv. p. 196.*—In Apocalypſin ſcripſiſſe teſtatur Boſtonus Burienſis. CAVE, H. L. *vol. ii. p. 131. Oxon. 1743.*

in

in the perfon of Hildebrand, who took the S E R M.
VII.
name of Gregory VIIth, that the Romifh
hiftorian, Joannes Aventinus, fpeaks of it
as a point, *in which the generality of fair,*
candid, and ingenuous writers, were agreed,
That THEN *began the empire of Antichrift* [q].

5. Pafcal II, who had been brought up
at the feet of Hildebrand, and fate upon
the papal throne in the beginning of the
XIIth century, was treated with as little
ceremony, as his mafter had been; particularly, by Fluentius, Bifhop of Florence,
and by the whole church of Liege [r].

St. Bernard, too, the moft eminent perfon of that age, was fo ftruck with the
marks of Antichriftianifm in the church of

[q] Plerique omnes boni, aperti, jufti, ingenui, fim-
plices, tum imperium Antichrifti coepiffe, quod ea quæ
Chriftus fervator nofter tot annos ante nobis cantavit,
eveniffe eo tempore cernebant, memoriæ literarum pro-
didêre. ANNAL. BOIORUM, *l.* v. *p.* 591. *Ingolftad.*
1554.

[r] CAVE, H. L. *vol.* ii. *p.* 258. Conc. Flor. 1105.
USSER. *De Chrift. Eccl. fucc. & ftat. c.* v. *f.* v. *p.* 109.

Rome

Rome (to which, however, in other re-
spects, he was enough devoted) that he
employed all the thunder of his rhetoric
(in which faculty he excelled) againſt its
corruptions; exclaiming, *that the miniſters
of Chriſt were become the ſervants of Antichriſt; and that the beaſt of the Apocalypſe had
ſeated himſelf in the chair of St. Peter*[s].

[s] MINISTRI CHRISTI SUNT, ET SERVIUNT ANTI-
CHRISTO [*Serm. ſup. Cantic.* xxxiii.]—It is true, by
Antichriſt, he ſeems not to mean the Pope, but, in general, an evil principle, which then domineered in the
church.   Yet he refers us to the famous paſſage in the
firſt Epiſtle to the Theſſalonians, *ch.* ii.   And he tells
us in his 56th epiſtle, that he had heard one Norbert,
a man of exemplary piety, ſay, That Antichriſt would
be revealed in that age.   Hence it ſeems probable, that
ſome one perſon or power was in his eye.   After all,
he ſays, that Norbert's reaſons did not ſatisfy him.
Yet, in another epiſtle, he aſſerts expreſsly—Beſtia
illa de Apocalypſi, cui datum eſt os loquens blaſphemias,
et bellum gerere cum ſanctis, PETRI CATHEDRAM OC-
CUPAT, tanquam leo paratus ad prædam. Ep. cxxv:
which was, in other words, to call the Pope, Antichriſt.
It is evident that St. Bernard applied the prophecies in
the Revelations to the ſucceſſor of St. Peter.—I mention
theſe things ſo particularly to ſhew, what his ſenti-

But

But this charge was, now, so general, and founded so high, that it reached the ears of *others*, besides prelates, and churchmen. Historians relate, that it made an impression on our military king, Richard I.; who, being at Messina in Sicily, in his way to the Holy Land, and hearing much of the learned Abbot Joachim of Calabria, (a man, famous in those times for his warm invectives against the Roman hierarchy;) had the curiosity to take a lecture from him on this subject. His text was, *Antichrist*, and the *Apocalypse*; which he explained in so pointed and forcible a manner, as was much to the satisfaction, we are told, of his royal auditor [t].

ments on this head really were; which have been misrepresented by hasty writers, who transcribe from each other, without examining, themselves, the authorities, they quote.

[t] CAVE, H. L. v. ii. *p.* 278. ROG. DE HOVEDEN. ANNAL. PARS POST. *p.* 681. Ed. Franc. 1601. — In this age [XIIth], was composed a very remarkable tract on the subject of Antichrist, which may be seen in Mede's Works, *p.* 721. — Mr. Mede supposes, and seems indeed to have proved, that the *true* doctrine of

6. The

SERM.
VII.
————

6. The firſt appearance of the people, called Waldenſes or Albigenſes, was in

Antichriſt was, and was intended to be, a myſtery, or ſecret, till the 12th century. Whence it follows that the teſtimonies, hitherto alledged, are only paſſionate or declamatory exaggerations, or to be eſteemed, as he ſays, *pro parabolicè et* κάτ᾽ ἄυξησιν *diɛ̄tis, declamatorum more. Works, p. 722.*

I admit the truth of the obſervation ; but hold, that the *uſe* of the deduɛ̄tion, here made, is not in the leaſt affeɛ̄ted by it. For my purpoſe in giving this cata-logue of witneſſes to the doɛ̄trine of Antichriſt, was not to *juſtify* that doɛ̄trine, in the *true*, that is, Pro-teſtant ſenſe of it (for then, not only the preceding teſtimonies, but even ſome of the following, would have been omitted) but merely to ſhew that the general, at leaſt, and confuſed idea of ſome ſuch doɛ̄trine did, in faɛ̄t, *ſubſiſt* in the antient Chriſtian church. That what idea they had of this doɛ̄trine was founded on the *pro-phecies*, is clear from the terms in which they expreſs themſelves. And, though the doɛ̄trine itſelf was very imperfeɛ̄tly conceived, and inconſequentially applied by them, ſtill their language ſhews that they had ſome notion of *a corrupt ſpiritual power, which was*, in their ſenſe of the prophets, *to domineer in the church of Rome :* whence I draw this concluſion (for the ſake of which, this whole deduɛ̄tion is made,) That the preſent application of the prophecies concerning Antichriſt to papal Rome, is not wholly new and unauthorized ; as the prejudice, I am here combating, ſuppoſeth it to be.

this

this age; but, in the next, the XIIIth century, they prevailed to that degree, that
Crufades and Inquifitions were thought
little enough to be employed againft them.
We may know what the guilt of this people was, when we underftand from their
books, and from the teftimony of the great
hiftorian, Thuanus, that a leading principle of their herefy was, To treat the Pope
as *Antichrift*; and the church of Rome, as
Babylon; on the authority of the prophecies contained in the Revelations ᵘ.

Other ᵛ teftimonies occur in the hiftory
of this age. But I muft not omit that of

ᵘ VITRINGA in Apoc. *p.* 747. Amft. 1719. USSER.
De Eccl. fucc. & ftat. *c.* 6 and 8. THUANUS, *l.* vi.
f. 16. *vol.* i. *p.* 221. Ed. Buckley.
ᵛ See, efpecially, the famous fpeech of Everhard,
bifhop of Saltzbourg, at the affembly of Ratifbonne, in
the time of Gregory the IXth; inferted at large in
Aventinus, *Ann. Boior. l.* vii. *p.* 684. The following
extracts from it will be thought curious. Hildebrandus
ante annos centum atque feptuaginta primus fpecie re-
ligionis *Antichrifti* imperii fundamenta jecit. *p.* 684.
Flamines illi *Babyloniæ* [meaning the Bifhops of
Rome] foli regnare cupiunt, ferre parem non poffunt,
non defiftent donec omnia pedibus fuis conculcaverint,

our

_____ our famous hiſtorian, Matthew Paris;
who hath taken care to inform us, that
his contemporary, Robert Groſtête, Biſhop
of Lincoln, the moſt conſiderable of all
the Engliſh biſhops, and equally renowned
for his affection to civil and religious
liberty, was ſo much in earneſt in fixing
this charge on the ſee of Rome, that, as
it had been the common theme of his me-
ditations during life, ſo it occupied his
dying moments; the *Pope*, and *Antichriſt*,
being, as he tells us, among the laſt words
of this zealous prelate[w].

atque *in templo Dei ſedeant, extollanturque ſupra omne id,
quod colitur.* Ib.

Nova conſilia ſub pectore volutat, ut proprium ſibi
conſtituat imperium, *leges commutat,* ſuas ſancit; con-
taminat, diripit, ſpoliat, fraudat, occidit, perditus
homo ille *(quem Antichriſtum vocare ſolent)* in cujus
fronte *contumeliæ nomen* ſcriptum eſt, " Deus ſum,
errare non poſſum," *in templo Dei ſedet,* longè latèque
dominatur. *Ib.*

— *Reges decem pariter exiſtunt* — *Decem Cornua* —
Cornuque parvulum — Quid hâc prophetiâ apertius?
p. 685.

[w] MATTH. PARIS, ad ann. 1253. *p.* 874. *ed.* Watts,
1640.

7. The

7. The XIVth century affords many

authorities in point; among which the
immortal names of Dante [x] and Petrarch [y]
are commonly cited. But the example of

[x] Purgat. 32.

[y] Epiſtolarum ſine titulo Liber. Ep. xvi. *p.* 130.
Baſil. 1581.—Many ſtrokes in this epiſtle are, to the
laſt degree, ſevere and cauſtic. Addreſſing himſelf to
Rome, " Illa equidem ipſa es, ſays he, quam in ſpiri-
tu ſacer vidit Evangeliſta.—Populi et gentes et linguæ,
aquæ ſunt ſuper quas meretrix ſedes; recognoſce habi-
tum. Mulier circumdata purpurâ, et coccino, et in-
aurata auro, et lapide pretioſo, et margaritis, habens
poculum aureum in manu ſuâ, plenum abominatione et
immunditiâ fornicationis ejus.—Audi reliqua. Et vidi
(inquit) mulierem ebriam de ſanguine ſanctorum, et de
ſanguine martyrum Jeſu. Quid ſiles ?—And ſo goes on
to apply the prophecies of the Revelations to the church
of Rome, in terms that furniſh out a good comment on
the famous verſe in one of his poems—

Gia Roma, hor Babylonia falſa è ria—

Numberleſs paſſages in the writings of Petrarch
ſpeak of Rome, under the name of *Babylon.* But an
equal ſtreſs is not to be laid on all of theſe. It
ſhould be remembered, that the Popes, in Petrarch's
time, reſided at Avignon; greatly to the diſparage-
ment of themſelves, as he thought, and eſpecially of
Rome; of which this ſingular man was little leſs
than idolatrous. The ſituation of the place, ſur-
rounded by waters, and his ſplenetic concern for
the *exiled* Church (for under this idea, he painted

our

our Wicklif, who adorned that age, is moſt
to our purpoſe, and may excuſe the mention
of any other.   This extraordinary man ſaw
far into all the abuſes of his time : but he
had nothing more at heart, than to expoſe
the *Antichriſtianiſm* of the Roman Pontif[z].

8. Still, as the times grew more enlightened, the controverſy concerning
Antichriſt became more general and important.   The writings of Wicklif had
great effects both at home, and abroad ;

to himſelf the Pope's migration to the banks of Avignon) brought to his mind the condition of the Jewiſh
church in the Babylonian captivity.   And this parallel
was all, perhaps, that he meant to inſinuate in moſt of
thoſe paſſages.   But, when he applies the prophecies to
Rome, as to the *Apocalyptic* Babylon (as he clearly does
in the epiſtle under conſideration) his meaning is not
equivocal ; and we do him but juſtice to give him an
honourable place among the TESTES VERITATIS.

[z] See the catalogue of his works in Cave's Hiſt. Lit.
vol. ii. App. p. 63 ; in which is the following book of
Dialogues.   Dialogorum libri quatuor; quorum —
quartus Romanæ Eccleſiæ ſacramenta, ejus peſtiferam
votationem, ANTICHRISTI REGNUM, fratrum fraudu-
lentam originem atque eorum hypocriſim, variaque
noſtro ævo ſcitu digniſſima, perſtringit.

and,

and, with other caufes, contributed very much to the cultivation of free enquiry, and to the improvement of all ufeful knowledge, in the XVth century. The church of Rome was pufhed vigoroufly on all fides; and, in her turn, omitted no means of felf-defence. That the *worft* were not fcrupled, may be feen by what paffed in England, at that time, as well as by the fanguinary and faithlefs proceedings at the council of Conftance. Lord Cobham, and the two Bohemian martyrs, were committed to the flames, for nothing fo much, as for afferting the impious doctrine, ' That the Pope was Antichrift.'

9. We now enter on the XVIth century; diftinguifhed in the annals of mankind by that great event, The Reformation of long oppreffed and much adulterated religion. The Chriftian world had flumbered in its chains, for full ten ages. But Liberty came at laft—

Libertas, quæ fera tamen refpexit INERTEM.

R   This

This important work was begun, and prosecuted, on the common principle, That the bishop of Rome was Antichrist: and the great separation from the church of Rome, was every where justified on the idea, That Rome was the Babylon of the Revelations; and that Christians were bound by an express command in those prophecies, to *come out of her* communion.

Leo Xth was thunder-struck with this cry, which resounded on all sides; and, in the last Lateran council, gave it in charge to all preachers, that none of them should presume to call the Pope, Antichrist, or to treat this obnoxious subject in their discourses to the people [a]. But his edict came too late. The notion had taken deep root in the minds of men; and the name of Antichrist, as applied to the Pope, was current in all quarters.

[a] Mandantes omnibus, &c.—*tempus quoque præfixum futurorum malorum, vel* ANTICHRISTI ADVENTUM—*prædicare, vel afferere, nequaquam præfumant.* BIN. CONC. *Lateran.* v. *fub Leone* X. *Seff.* xi. *p.* 632.

10. From

10. From this time to the prefent, *the* SERM.
charge of Antichriftianifm againft the church VII.
of Rome is to be regarded, not as the language of private men, or particular fynods;
but as the common voice of the whole
Proteftant world : fo that it will be need-
lefs to bring down the hiftory of it any
lower.

THIS DEDUCTION, though made with
all poffible brevity, hath held us fo long,
that I have but time for one or two fhort
reflexions upon it.

1. *Firft,* It may feem probable from the
general prevalence of this opinion, in al-
the periods of the Chriftian church, that it
muft needs have fome folid ground in the
fcriptural prophecies : it not being otherwife conceivable, that it fhould fpread fo
far, and continue fo long ; or that the
more enlightened, as well as barbarous
ages fhould concur in the profeffion of
it.

2. *Secondly,* from the catalogue of illuftrious names, here produced, and from

the fingular ftrefs, which all Proteftant churches to this day have ever laid on this principle, we may fee the importance of the general queftion. The papal divines have an evident reafon for treating it with contempt. The men of thought and inqui-ry, who fpeculate within the Roman com-munion, may be reftrained by confidera-tions of fear or decency, from joining [b] in this inviduous charge againft the head of

[b] M. d'Alembert, indeed, goes further. He ac-quaints us, that this *charge* is now out of date, and that nobody, either within or without the Romifh com-munion, makes it any longer. For, fpeaking of a public infcription at Geneva, in which *the Pope is called Antichrift*, he animadverts on this difgrace of that Pro-teftant people, and very kindly fuggefts to them what their improved fentiments and language fhould be on that fubject. *As for the Catholics* (fays he, very gravely,) *the Pope is regarded by them, as the Head of the true Church: By fage and moderate Proteftants, he is feen in the light of a fovereign prince, whom they refpect, though they do not obey him: But, in an age like this,* HE IS NO LONGER ANTICHRIST IN THE OPINION OF ANYBODY. "Pour les Catholiques, le Pape eft le chef de la veritable Eglife; pour les Proteftants fages & modérés, c'eft un Souverein qu'ils refpectent comme Prince fans lui obéir: mais dans un fiécle tel que nôtre, il n'eft plus l'Antichrift

their

their church. But for any, that profefs S E R M.
Chriftianity, and call themfelves Protef-   VII.
tants, to make light of inquiries into the
prophecies concerning Antichrift, and to
manifeft a fcorn of all attempts to apply
them in the way, in which they have fo
generally, and with fuch effect been applied, is a fort of conduct, which will not
fo readily find an excufe, much lefs a jufti-
fication.

3. *Laftly*, whatever becomes of the *truth*,
or *importance* of the doctrine, the *antiquity*
of it is not to be difputed. For we are
authorifed to affirm, on the moft certain
grounds of hiftory, that a Roman power,
commonly called Antichrift, was expected
to arife in *the latter times*, by the primitive
Chriftians; and that the Imperial, was not
deemed to be that power, fo long as it fubfifted. It is, further, unqueftionable that

pour perfonne." Encyclopedie, Art. GENEVE.—If the
prefent age be, here, truly characterized, it was high
time, or rather it was too late, to found this Proteftant Lecture.

not the Emperor, but the Bishop or Church of Rome, was afterwards thought entitled to the name of Antichrist by many persons of that communion, for several successive centuries, previous to the æra of the Reformation.

These facts should abate the wonder, at least, which some express at hearing the names of the *Pope* and *Antichrist* pronounced together. They must surely convince every man, that this language, whatever foundation it may, or may not have, in the prophecies, is not taken up without precedents and authorities; and that the notion, conveyed by it, is not a conceit of yesterday, which sprung out of recent prejudices, and novel interpretations. This, I say, is a conclusion which every man must draw from the premises, laid down in this discourse: and this, for the present, is the main use I would request you, to make of those premises.

S E R.

SERMON VIII.

Prejudices againſt the Doctrine of ANTICHRIST.

1 Ep. John ii. 18.

—YE HAVE HEARÉD, THAT ANTICHRIST SHALL COME.

ONE of the principal prejudices againſt the doctrine of Antichriſt, as under-ſtood and applied by Proteſtant divines, ariſes out of a circumſtance, which was juſt touched in the cloſe of my laſt diſ-courſe, and is of importance enough to be now reſumed and more particularly con-ſidered.

SERM.
VIII.

R 4

I. It

I. It is well known that, when the Reformation was set on foot in the sixteenth century, this great work was every where justified and conducted on the general principle, " That the Pope, or at least the church of Rome, was Antichrist."

" Now men of sense, who have looked no farther into the subject, and yet remember, as they easily may, the bitterness, the policy, the fraud, too commonly observable in the conduct of religious (as of other) parties, easily fall into the suspicion, That this cry of Antichrist was only an artifice of the time, or at least an extravagance of it; when the minds of men were intensely heated against each other, and when of course no arms would be refused, that might serve to annoy or distress the enemy.

In these circumstances, it was natural enough, it will be said, for angry men to *see* that in the prophecies which was not contained in them ; or for designing men to *feign* that which they did not see ; in order

the

the more effectually to carry on the caufe
in which they had embarked, and to feduce
the unwary multitude into their quarrel.
In fhort, the paffions of the Reformed, it
is readily prefumed, had fome way or
other, conjured up this fpectre of Antichrift, as a convenient engine, by which
they might either gratify their own fpleen,
or excite that of the people; the prophecies all the while being no further concerned in the queftion, than as they were
wrefted for thefe purpofes (as they frequently have been, in like cafes) from their
true and proper meaning."

To remove this capital prejudice (which,
more than any other, hath, perhaps, diverted ferious men from giving a due attention
to this argument) was the main purpofe of
the preceding difcourfe; in which it was
clearly fhewn from hiftorical teftimony,
that the queftion concerning Antichrift
had its rife in the earlieft times; that the
prophecies concerning Antichrift, though
imperfectly enough underftood, and, it
may

may be, paſſionately applied, had yet, been
conſidered, very generally, as referring to
ſome corrupt Chriſtian and even eccleſiaſtical perſon or power; and that many eminent members of the Chriſtian church had
even applied thoſe propheſies to the *ſame*
perſon or power, to which Proteſtants now
apply them, and for the *ſame* end, which
Proteſtants have in view, when they apply
them to ſuch perſon or power, for many
ſucceſſive centuries, before the Reformation
began.   From all which it is undeniable,
that the Reformers did not innovate in the
interpretation of the prophecies concerning
Antichriſt; and that their application of
them to the ſee of Rome, was not a contrivance, which ſprung out of the paſſionate reſentments, or intereſted policies
of that time.

It is true indeed (for the truth ſhould
not, and needs not be concealed) that the
Reformers were forward enough to lay
hold on this received ſenſe of the prophecies, and to make their utmoſt advantage

of

of it; the account of which matter is, briefly, this: The Chriſtian church had now for many ages been held together in a cloſe dependence on the chair of St. Peter; and to ſecure and perpetuate that dependence, was the principal object and concern of the papal court. Various means were employed for this purpoſe: but the moſt effectual was thought to be, to inculcate in the ſtrongeſt terms on the minds of Chriſtians the abſolute neceſſity of communicating with the Biſhop of Rome, as the centre of unity, and, by divine appointment, the ſupreme viſible head of the Chriſtian world. Hence, to renounce in any degree the authority and juriſdiction of Rome, was deemed the moſt inexpiable of all ſins. The name of SCHISM was faſtened upon it; a name, which was founded higher than that of Hereſy itſelf, as implying in it the accumulated guilt of Apoſtacy, and Infidelity. The way of heaven was ſhut againſt all offenders of this ſort; and, to make their condition as

miſe-

miferable, as it was hopelefs, all the en-
gines of perfecution, fuch as racks, fires,
gibbets, inquifitions, and even Crufades
had been employed againft them : as was
feen in the cafe of the Albigenfes and
others, who, at different times had attempted to withdraw themfelves from the
papal dominion.

Such was the ftate of things, when the
bold fpirit of Luther refolved, at all
adventures, to break through this inve-
terate fervitude *, fo dextroufly impofed
on the Chriftian world, under the pretence, and in the name, of ecclefiaftical
union. Yet the peril of the attempt was
eafily forefeen, or was prefently felt. And,
therefore, the Reformers (to prevent the
ill effects which the dreadful name of
Schifm might have on themfelves and their
caufe, and to fatisfy at once their own
confciences and thofe of their adherents)
not only revived and enforced the old

* Rompons leurs liens, dit il, et rejettons leur joug
de deffus nos têtes. *Boffuet, H. V. l. i. c.* 26.

charge

charge of *Antichriſtianiſm* againſt the church
of Rome; but futher inſiſted (on the authority of thoſe prophecies which juſtified the
charge) that Chriſtians were bound in con-
ſcience, by the moſt expreſs command, to
break all communion with, her. The expedient, one ſees, was well calculated to
ſerve the purpoſe in hand: but ſtill the
command was truly and pertinently alledged; for it exiſts in ſo many words (however the blindneſs or the bigotry of former
times had overlooked it) in the book of the
Revelations [b]. So that whoever admitted
the *charge* itſelf to be well founded, could
not reject this *conſequence* of it, That Chriſt
and Antichriſt had no fellowſhip with each
other. And on this popular ground, chiefly, the Proteſtant cauſe, in thoſe early
times, was upheld; with no ſmall advantage to the patrons of it; it being now clear,
that the invidious imputation of Schiſm
had loſt its malignity in the general obli-

[b] *Come out of her, my people, that ye be not partakers of
her ſins, and that ye receive not of her plagues.* Rev. xviii. 4.

gation,

gation, which lay upon Chriſtians, to renounce all communion with the church of
Rome.

This being the true account of that zeal,
with which the doctrine of Antichriſt was
aſſerted in the days of Reformation, let
us ſee how the caſe ſtands at preſent ;
and whether any reaſonable prejudice
lies againſt the doctrine itſelf, from the
uſes, that were then ſo happily made of
it.

In the firſt place, The injunction, *to
come out of her*, was, as I obſerved, not
forged by the Reformers ; nor (admitting
that church to be Antichriſtian) was it
miſrepreſented by them. Every reader of
the prophecies muſt confeſs, that the
command is clearly delivered, and that the
ſenſe of it is not miſtaken. How ſervice-
able ſoever, therefore, this topic was to
the cauſe of reformation, it is not, on that
account, to be the leſs eſteemed by the
juſt and candid inquirer.

In

In the next place, I will freely admit, that the dread, in which moft men, if not all men [c], of that time, were held, of in-curring the imputation of Schifm, was much greater, than the occafion required, and, upon the whole, a fort of panic terror, For, though a caufelefs feparation from the church would indeed have loaded the Reformers with much and real guilt, yet when the abufes of it had rifen to that height as to reduce an honeft man to the alternative, either of committing fin, or of leaving its communion, they might

[c] Il [Luther] condamnoit les Bohemiens qui s'etoient feparez de nôtre communion, et poteftoit qu'il ne lui arriveroit jamais de tomber dans *un femblable Schifme. Boffuet, Hift. des Variat. l.* i. *p.* 21. *Par.* 1740. And again, *p.* 28 ; Apres, dit il [Luther,] que j'eus furmonté tous les argumens qu'on propofoit, il en reftoit un dernier qu'à peine je pus furmonter par le fecours de Jefus Chrift avec une extrême difficulté & beaucoup d'angoiffe ; *ce'ft qu'il falloit écouter l'Eglife.*—One fees for what purpofe M. Boffuet quotes thefe paffages, and others of the fame kind, from the writings of Luther. However, they fhew very clearly how deep an impreffion the idea of Schifm had made on the mind even of this intrepid Reformer.

well

——— well have juſtified themſelves on the evident neceſſity of the thing, and had no need
of a poſitive command to authorize their
ſeparation. All this is, now, clearly ſeen;
and if the firſt Reformers did not ſee thus
much (as very probably they did not) all
that follows, is, That the doctrine of Antichriſt, from which that command derived
its effect, was leſs neceſſary to their cauſe,
than they ſuppoſed it to be; not, that the
doctrine itſelf is without authority, or the
command without obligation.

Laſtly, I obſerve, that, though the *vi-
olences* of the time might force the Reformers to take ſhelter in this doctrine of
Antichriſt, and though the *prejudices* of the
time might induce them to take the advantage, they did, of it; yet, neither of theſe
conſiderations affords any juſt preſumption
againſt the doctrine, as it lies in ſcripture,
and is enforced by us at this time out of it;
becauſe we argue not from their authority,
but from the prophecies themſelves; which
are

are much better underftood by us, than they were by them ; and are ftill maintained to fpeak the fenfe, which they put upon them, I mean with refpect to the general application of them to the church of Rome, though we have nothing to apprehend either from the power of that church, or from the prejudices of the people.

Let no man, therefore, rafhly conclude, from the free ufe made of this doctrine by our old Reformers (and there is fcarce one of them that has not left behind him a tract or difcourfe on Antichrift) that it hath no better or other foundation, than in their interefts or paffions. A reafonable man fees, that it has no dependance at all upon them. That Luther, indeed, heated in the controverfy with the church of Rome, and fmoaking, as I may fay, from the recent blaft of the papal thunders, fhould cry out, ANTICHRIST [d], fhall pafs, if you

---

[d] *Contra Bullam Antichrifti* — a tract of Luther, fo called, againft the Bull of Leo X.

S   will,

will, for a fally of rage and defperation[c]. But that we, at this day, who revolve the prophecies at our eafe, and are in little more dread of modern Rome, than of antient Babylon, fhould ftill find the refemblance fo ftriking as to fall upon the fame idea; and fhould even be driven againft the ftrong bias of prejudice (which with us, in England, for above a century paft, has drawn the other way) to adopt the language of our great Reformer; this, I fay, is a confideration of another fort, and will not be put off fo flightly.

STILL, there are other prejudices, which oppofe themfelves to this great Proteftant principle, *That the Pope is Antichrift*; and thefe, it will not be befide the purpofe of this Lecture to confider. It may, then, be faid,

II. " That, although there be not the fame evident neceffity for bringing this

[c] Luther reconnoit après la rupture ouverte, que dans les commencemens il étoit *comme au defefpoir—*
Boffuet, H. V. c. 26.

odious

odious charge againft the Papacy, as there
was formerly in the infancy of Reformation,
yet obvious reafons are not wanting which
may poffibly induce the Proteftant churches
of our times to repeat and inforce it. So
long as the feparation is kept up, the parti-
zans of the caufe will not fcruple to lay
hold on every popular topic, by which it
may be promoted. But an *ill name,* is the
readieft of all expedients, and generally the
moft effectual, for this fervice. And as
Heretic is the term in ufe, when the
church of Rome would difcredit the Reformation ; fo, *Antichrift* ferves juft as
well, in the mouth of a Proteftant, to difgrace the Catholic party. Hence, the
people are gratified in a low fpite againft
the perfon of the Pope ; the better fort are
confirmed in their religious or politic averfion to the church of Rome ; and Princes
themfelves are invited to come in aid of
the prophecies, by turning their arms and
councils againft a godlefs antichriftian

tyranny :

tyranny: and all this, to the ruin of public peace, and in defiance of Chriſtian charity."

When men declaim, inſtead of arguing, or, what is worſe, when they argue from their ſuſpicions only, it may not be eaſy to give them an anſwer to their ſatisfaction. Otherwiſe, one might reply,

Firſt, That the queſtion is not, what uſe has been, or may be, made of this doctrine concerning Antichriſt; but whether there be reaſon to believe that ſuch doctrine is really contained in ſacred ſcripture. If there be, it will become us to treat it with reſpect, how much ſoever it may have been miſapplied, or perverted.

In the *next place*, one might obſerve that no man, who underſtood the ſtate of this controverſy, ever applied the prophecies concerning Antichriſt to the *perſon* of the Pope, but in general to the church of Rome, or rather to the Antichriſtian ſpirit, by which it is governed; or, if to the *Pope*, to
him

him only as reprefenting that fociety, of which he is the head ; and fo far only, as he acted in the fpirit of it. And there is nothing ftrange or unufual in this ufe of the term. When Hobbes wrote his famous book, called LEVIATHAN (a word, now at leaft, of almoft as ill found, as Antichrift itfelf) no man fuppofes, that he meant to apply this character, exclufively, to the perfon of any prince, then living ; but, in general, to *civil government*, according to the ideas he had formed of it. And this way of fpeaking, as I have before obferved, is efpecially familiar to the facred writers. Many of the Popes are faid to have been, and, for any thing I know, *may* have been, *Saints*, in their private morals : fo that when we apply the term, Antichrift, to them, we do not mean to ftigmatize their *perfons*, but merely to exprefs the fenfe which the prophecies lead us to entertain of the commnnion, over which they prefide ; though they may not exemplify in their own conduct, or not

in

in any remarkable degree, the avowed principles of that communion.

Conceive, therefore, with more reſpect
of Proteſtant divines, when they explain
and vindicate the prophecies concerning
Antichriſt, than to ſuppoſe, that they indulge in themſelves, or would encourage
in others, *a low ſpite againſt the perſon of the
Roman Pontif.*

Thirdly, It is to be obſerved, that,
although this prophetic language may tend
to confirm Proteſtants *in a religious, or,* if
you will, *politic averſion to the church of
Rome;* yet it is not therefore to be forborn,
if the ſcriptures do, indeed, authorize the
uſe of it: nor is there any hurt done, if
the principles of that church be not miſrepreſented; for then, ſuch averſion becomes the wiſdom and the duty of all
Chriſtians. Beſides, this averſion proceeds
no farther in well-informed Proteſtants,
than to keep them at diſtance from the
Romiſh communion, and to admoniſh
others of their obligation to forſake it.
And,

And, if the members, above all, if the rulers, of that communion would reftrain *their* zeal within the fame bounds (though they would not, we fay, be equally jufti-fied in this zeal) neither public peace, nor Chriftian charity, would fuffer by it.

Laftly, it fhould be remembered, That, when the prophecies foretell the downfall of Antichrift, and even go fo far as to point out to us the princes of that communion, as the deftined inftruments of fuch cataf-trophe; yet neither is hereby any duty im-pofed on thofe princes to make war upon the Pope, nor any encouragement given to Proteftants themfelves to concur in any fuch meafures. For the prophets fimply predict an *event*; and do not deliver in their prediction, or propofe to deliver, *rules* for our conduct. Our Saviour him-felf, fpeaking by the fpirit, and in the language of prophecy, faid—*I come not to fend peace on earth, but a fword.* But will any man fuppofe that this prediction jufti-

S 4   fies,

fies, or was meant in any degree to juſtify, that ſtate of things, which it deſcribes, and which the author of it foreſaw would too certainly come to paſs? Nor think, that the event predicted, I mean, *the fall of Antichriſt*, will not take place, unleſs our invectives, or hoſtile attempts, make way for it. If the prediction be divine, there is ONE, who will ſee that it be accompliſhed. Princes and States may have nothing leſs in view than to fulfill the prophecies of ſacred Scripture: yet, when the appointed time is come, they will certainly fulfill them, though they never thought *of coming in aid of the prophecies*—though we ſhould not encourage them in any ſuch preſumptuous deſign—nay, though we ſhould do our utmoſt, as it is our duty to do, to reſtrain vindictive and ill-adviſed men from turning their arms even againſt Antichriſt himſelf, for the ſake of religion.

This topic, I know, is much laboured by the advocates of the papal cauſe, in order to throw diſgrace on Proteſtant writers,

writers, whom they confider as fo many incendiaries, wickedly attempting to fpread the flames of war through Chriftian focieties. There might be a time when, in the cafe of fome few men, tranfported by paffion, becaufe outrageoufly oppreffed, there was, perhaps, fome colour for this charge. But to perfift in it, as they ftill do, only fhews that they neither conceive with due reverence of divine prophecy, nor do juftice to that fpirit of toleration by which the Proteftant churches, at leaft of our days, are fo eminently diftinguifhed.

III. " A *third* prejudice, which operates in the minds of many perfons againft the principle under confideration, arifes from the difagreeing opinions of learned men concerning the fenfe and application of the prophecies; while not only the papal Divines, but many writers of note even among ourfelves, have ftrenuoufly maintained that the church of Rome is no way con-

concerned in the predictions concerning
Antichrift."

To obviate this prejudice, I obferve

1. That arguments from authority, in all cafes where reafon and good fenfe muft finally decide, are very little to be regarded. Shew me the queftion in religion, or even in common morals, about which learned men have not difagreed; nay, fhew me a fingle text of fcripture, though ever fo plain and precife, which the perverfenefs or ingenuity of interpreters has not drawn into different, and often contrary meanings. What then fhall we conclude? That there is no truth in religion, no certainty in morals, no authority in facred fcripture? If fuch conclufions, as thefe, be carried to their utmoft length, in what elfe can they terminate, but abfolute univerfal fcepticifm?

2. I obferve that this authority, after all, whatever weight we may, in the general, fuppofe it to have, is, in the prefent cafe, no great matter; for it is, in effect, but the authority of ONE man, whofe
                                                    eminent.

eminent worth, however, and luftre of reputation, made it current with fome others.

The character of HUGO GROTIUS is well known. He is juftly efteemed among the ableft and moft learned men of an age, that abounded in ability and learning. Befides his other fhining talents, his acquaintance with hiftory was extenfive; and his knowledge of fcripture, profound. And yet, with two fuch requifites for unlocking the true fenfe of the prophetic writings, this excellent man undertook to prove in form, *That the Pope was not Antichrift.*

The account of this mifchance, is as extraordinary, as the mifchance itfelf. The moral qualities of Grotius were ftill more admirable, than his intellectual: and in thefe qualities, we fhall find the true fpring of his unhappy and mifapplied pains on the fubject before us.

He was in his own nature juft, candid, benevolent, to a fupreme degree; and the experience of an active turbulent life had

but

but fortified him the more in a love of theſe pacific virtues. He was, on principle, a ſincere and zealous Chriſtian; and conſequently impreſſed with a due ſenſe of that exalted charity, which is the characteriſtic of that religion: but he had ſeen and felt much of the miſchiefs, which proceed from theological quarrels: and thus every thing concurred to make him a friend to peace, and, above all, to peace among Chriſtians.

An union of the Catholic and Proteſtant churches ſeemed neceſſary to this end; and the apparent candour, whether real or affected, of ſome learned perſons, whom he had long known and valued in the church of Rome, drew him into the belief, that ſuch a project was not impracticable. Henceforth, it became the ruling object of his life; and, permitting himſelf too eaſily to conclude, that the Proteſtant doctrine of Antichriſt was the ſole, or principal obſtruction to the union deſired, he

he bent all the efforts of his wit and
learning to difcredit and overthrow that
doctrine.

Thus, was this virtuous man betrayed
by the wifdom and equity of his own character; and I know not if the obfervation
of the moral poet can be fo juftly applied
to any other—

> Infani fapiens nomen ferat, æquus
> iniqui,
> Ultrà quàm fatis eft, virtutem fi petat
> ipfam [f].

The iflue of his general fcheme was
what might eafily be forefeen: and of his
arguments, I fhall only fay thus much, That
the Romifh writers themfelves, for whofe
ufe they might feem to be invented, though
they continue to object his name to us,
are too wife to venture the ftrefs of their
caufe upon them.

To conclude this head of authority, let
me juft obferve,

[f] Hor. 1 Ep. vi. 15.

3. In

3. In the laſt place, that, if any regard be due to it, the advantage will clearly be on our ſide. For, though the name of Grotius made an impreſſion on ſome Proteſtant interpreters of ſcripture, not inconſiderable for their parts and learning, yet, when the grounds of his opinion came to be examined, the moſt and the ableſt of them have generally declared againſt him: and among theſe, let it be no offence to the manes of this great **s** man, if we particularly mention TWO, and prefer even to his authority that of Newton and Clarke; the one, the ableſt philoſopher, and the other, the cooleſt and moſt rational divine, that any age has produced.

IV. " Another, and *fourth* prejudice may have been entertained on this ſubject from

---

s Grotius was more than a great, he was a faſhionable man. No wonder therefore that, under the influence of two ſuch prejudices, his opinions ſhould find followers; which yet they would ſcarce have found with us, if the political ſtate of that time had not been a *third* prejudice in their favour. See the Biſhop of Gloucefter's Sermon, *On the riſe of Antichriſt.*

obſerv-

observing that many curious persons, who have employed themselves much and long in the study of the prophecies, especially of those concerning Antichrist, have been led (on their authority, as they pretend) to fix the time and other circumstances of great events, which yet have not fallen out agreeable to their expectations. Whence it is inferred, that no solid information can be derived from the prophecies, and that all our reasonings upon them are no better than fancy and conjecture."

Now, though the indiscretion of these curious persons, who would needs prophecy when their business was only to interpret [h], be injurious enough to their own character, I do not see how it affects that of the prophets; unless whatever may be abused (as every thing may) be answerable for the abuses made of it. But to reply more directly to this charge.

[h] " The folly of interpreters has been, to foretell " times and things by this prophecy, as if God de- " signed to make them prophets." *Sir I. Newton, p.* 251.

The

The ill fuccefs of men in explaining prophecies of events, not yet come to pafs, can in no degree difcredit thofe prophecies, unlefs it be effential to this fort of revelation to be fo clearly propofed, as that it may and muft be perfectly underftood, before thofe events happen; the contrary of which I have already fhewn, in a preceding difcourfe. The very idea of prophecy is that of *a light fhining in a dark place:* and a place is not *dark,* if we have light enough to difcern diftinctly and fully every remote corner of it. But the thing fpeaks itfelf. For to what end is the prediction delivered in obfcure and enigmatic terms, if the purpofe of the infpirer was that the fubject of the prediction fhould be immediately, and in all its circumftances, precifely apprehended? Why, then, is any diftinction made between Prophecy, and Hiftory? The mode of writing clearly demonftrates, that fomething, for a time at leaft, was meant to be concealed from us: and then, if men will attempt, out of feafon, to penetrate
trate

trate this myftery, what wonder if miftake be the fruit of their prefumption?

Again : the *declared* end of prophecy is, not that we may be enabled by it to fore-fee things before they come to pafs, but *when* they come to pafs, that we may acknowledge the divine author of the pro-phecy[1]. What difhonour, then, can it be to the prophet, that he is not perfectly underftood, till we be expected to make ufe of his information? Nay, in the cafe before us, it would difhonour him, if he was. For, of the prophecies concerning Antichrift we are exprefly told, that they are *fhut up and fealed, till the time of the end*; that is, till Time brings the key along with him. So that, if men could open them, by their own wit and fagacity

[1] " God gave this, and the prophecies of the Old " Teftament, not to gratify men's curiofities by enabling " them to foreknow things ; but that, after they were " fulfilled, they might be interpreted by the event; and " his own providence, not the interpreter's, be then " manifefted thereby to the world." *Sir I. Newton,* *p.* 251.

T   only,

only, they would give the lye to the prophet. And thus we ſee, that the very
miſtakes of interpreters attempting prc-
maturely to unfold the *ſealed* prophecies
concerning Antichriſt, far from ſubvert-
ing, ſupport the credit of thoſe prophecies [k].

But I have ſomething more to ſay on
this ſubject. Though we cannot ſee every
thing in the prophecies, which we are
impatient to ſee, it is not to be ſuppoſed
that we can ſee nothing in them. If this
were the caſe, we ſhould ſcarce regard them
as prophecies at all; at leaſt, we ſhould
hardly be prevailed upon to read and conſider them. For, it is on the ſuppoſition
that ſome *light* is communicated to us, that
we are diſpoſed, as well as required, to *take
heed to it*. In ſhort, if we ſaw nothing,
we ſhould expect nothing: ſuch prophe-

[k] " 'Tis a part of this prophecy, that it ſhould not
" be underſtood before the laſt age of the world; and
" therefore it makes for the credit of the prophecy,
" that it is not yet underſtood." *Sir I. Newton, p.* 251.

cies

cies would not engage our curiosity, or so much as take our attention. In one word, they would be utterly lost upon us.

This seems to have been, in some measure, the case with regard to this very book of the *Revelations*. The early Christians saw so little in this prophecy, that they were led by degrees to neglect the study of it. Otherwise, the little they did see, might have given them a glimpse, at least, of many things, that intimately concerned both their faith and conduct.

It being then necessary, as I said, that prophecy should, from the first, convey some light to us, and time having now very much increased that light, it follows, that men may excuseably employ themselves in studying and contemplating even unfulfilled prophecies. They may conjecture modestly of points which time has not yet revealed: but they should, in no case, pronounce confidently, or decide dogmatically upon them.

T 2   It

It feems therefore to be going too far, to pafs an indifcriminate cenfure on all thofe, who have propofed their thoughts on the fenfe of prophecies, not yet completed, though it be ever fo clear that a wrong conftruction has been made of them. Nay, it is worth confidering whether they may not even have conjectured right, when they have been thought to miftake the moft widely. I fay this, chiefly, with regard to the *time*, which fome writers have beforehand affigned for the accomplifhment of certain prophecies, and that, on principles apparently contained in thofe prophecies; but fo unhappily, as to draw much fcorn and ridicule upon themfelves.

I explain myfelf by a famous inftance. Nothing has been more cenfured in Proteftant divines, than their temerity in fixing *the fall of Antichrift*; though there are certain data in the prophecies, from which very probable conclufions on that fubject may be drawn. Experience, it is faid, contradicts their calculation. But it is

not

not confidered, that the fall of Antichrift, is not *a fingle event*, to happen all at once; but *a ftate of things*, to continue through a long tract of time, and to be gradually accomplifhed. Hence, the interpretation of the prophecy might be rightly formed, though the expectations of moft men are difappointed.

It is vifible, I fuppofe, that the papal power (if we agree to call that, *Antichrift*) is now on the decline; whenfoever that declenfion began, or how long foever it may be, before it will be finifhed. And therefore interpreters may have aimed right, though they feemed to others, and perhaps to themfelves, to be miftaken.

Suppofe, the ruin of the Weftern Empire had been the fubject of a prediction, and fome had collected, beforehand, from the terms of the prophecy, that it would happen at a *particular* time; when yet nothing more, in fact, came to pafs, than *the firft irruption of the barbarous nations.* Would it be certain that this collection

T 3   was

SERM.
VIII.

was groundlefs and ill made, becaufe the empire fubfifted in a good degree of vigour for fome centuries after? Might it not be faid, that the empire *was falling* [r] from that æra, or perhaps before; though, in the event, it *fell* not, till its fovereignty was fhaken by the rude hands of Attila, or rather, till it was laid flat by the well-directed force of Theodoric?

But we have an inftance in point, recorded in facred fcripture. It had been gathered from the old prophecies [m], that, *in the laft times,* (that is, when the Meffiah was come) *a new earth and new heavens fhould be created.* The ftyle is fymbolical; but the meaning is, and was fo underftood to be, that a new Law fhould be given to mankind and prevail over the whole world. This Law was accordingly promulged and began to prevail in the days of the Apoftles. Yet there were fome who faid, *Where is the*

[r] St. Jerom, who lived in this time, fpeaks in the very terms, here fuppofed, *Romanus orbis* RUIT. *Ep.* iii.
[m] Ifai. lxv. 17.—2 Pet. iii. 4. 13.

promife

promise of his coming? for, since the fathers fell asleep, all things continue, as they were from the creation of the world. It was taken for granted, we see, that this great and glorious work, equivalent to the production of a new world, would take place suddenly and at once; which not being the case, it seemed to follow, that the prophecies were false, or at least ill understood; when yet, surely, they were then fulfilling under the eyes of these *scoffers.*

It will be considered, how far these hints may go towards rescuing some respectable interpreters (for I speak only of such) from that contempt, which has fallen upon them, and, from them, on the prophecies themselves, for some hazardous conclusions, or, (if you will) predictions, formed and given out by them, concerning the reign and fall of Antichrist. My meaning, however, is not to make myself responsible for these conclusions. They may not be rightly drawn from the premises, laid down; or the premises may be

T 4   such,

———— fuch, that the precife date of those tranfactions can not be determined from them,
at leaft, not, till the fcene of prophecy be
clofed, or, in the prophetic language, *till
the myftery of God be finifhed* [n]. In the mean
time, it is not clear and undeniable that
there is no ground at all for fuch conjectures: or, if it were, it would only
follow that they, who made them, had
been rafh and indifcreet in commenting too
minutely and confidently on prophecies
unfulfilled; and it would be weak, as we
have feen, to contract a prejudice againft
the fubject itfelf from the miftakes of fuch
commentators.

V. After all, the main and mafter prejudice, I doubt, is, that levity of mind
which difpofes too many to take their
notions on this, and other fubjects of moment, from certain polite and popular, it
may be, but frivolous and libertin writers:
men, who have no religion, or not enough

[n] Rev. x. 7.

to

to venerate the prophetic fcriptures; who have no knowledge, or certainly not enough to underftand them.

But with fuch cavillers, as thefe, I have no concern ; this Lecture, and the fubject of it, being addreffed to men of another character, to fair, candid, fober, and enlightened inquirers, only : For fo the infpired perfon, who firft announced thefe wonders concerning Antichrift, to mankind, expreffly declares, or rather prophefies—*None of the wicked fhall underftand: but* THE WISE *fhall underftand*°.

° Daniel xii. 10.

S E R-

S E R M O N IX,

The Prophetic Style confidered.

EZEKIEL XX. 49.

*—They fay, of me, Doth he not fpeak
Parables ?*

IN recounting the various prejudices,
which have diverted many perfons from
giving a due attention to the prophecies
concerning Antichrift, I may be thought
to have overlooked ONE of the moft confiderable; which arifeth from *the peculiar
ftyle, in which they are delivered.* But this
being a fubject of larger compafs, and nicer
inquiry, than the reft, (in which, too, the
credit

credit of all the prophetic fcriptures, as well as thofe refpecting Antichrift, is con- cerned) I have purpofely referved it for a diftinct and feparate examination.

WITHOUT DOUBT, a plain man, brought up in our cuftoms and notions, and unac- quainted with theological ftudies, when he firft turns himfelf to the contemplation of the Jewifh and Chriftian prophecies, will be furprifed, perhaps difgufted, to find, that he underftands little, or nothing of them. His *modefty* may incline him to think, that fuch writings are too myfteri- ous for his comprehenfion : or, his *lazinefs and prefumption* may difpofe him to reject them, at once, as perfectly unintelligible; to confider the language of them, as a jargon, to which no ideas are annexed; or, at leaft, as a kind of cypher, of fo wild and fanatical a texture, that no clear and certain conftruction can be made of it.

Now, this prejudice, whichever way it points, will be obviated, if it can be fhewn,

1. That

1. That the prophetic ftyle was of common and approved ufe, in the times, when the prophecies were delivered, and among the people, to whom they were addreffed. And

2. That this ftyle, how dark or fanciful foever it may appear, is yet *reducible to rule* ; that is, is conftructed on fuch principles, as make it the fubject of juft criticifm and reafonable interpretation ; and, in particular, to us, at this day.

For a language is not *fanatical*, that is authorifed by general practice ; nor can it be deemed *unintelligible*, when it is capable of having its meaning afcertained.

I. The proof of thefe two points will moft conveniently be given together, in a deduction of the caufes, which produced the character of the prophetic ftyle.

That character, I believe, is truly given by thofe who affirm, That the ftyle of the prophets was only the poetical, and highly figurative ftyle of the Eaftern nations.

nations. But if you go farther and afk, How it came to pafs, that the oriental poetry was fo much more figurative than ours, it may not be enough to fay, as many others have done, that this difference of character was owing to the influence of the fun, and to the fuperior heat and fervour, which it gave to an eaftern imagination. For I know not whether there be reafon to think, that the fun hath any fuch effect on the powers of the mind ; or that the fancies of men are apter to catch, and blaze out in metaphor, within a warm climate, than a cold one : a figurative caft of ftyle being obfervable in the native poetry of all countries; and that, fo far as appears from hiftory and experience, in a pretty equal degree.

Befides, if the fact were allowed, the. anfwer would fcarce be fufficient. For, as we fhall prefently fee, the fymbolic language of Prophecy, is too confiftent and uniform, hath too much of art and method

in

in it, to be derived from the cafual flights
and fallies of the imagination *only*, how
powerfully foever you fuppofe it to have
operated in the prophets.

We then muft go much deeper for a true
account of the emblematic and highly
coloured expreffion, which glares fo ftrongly in the prophetic fcriptures : and we fhall
find it, partly, in the nature of the human
mind ; and, partly, in the genius, indeed,
of the oriental nations, and efpecially of
the Jews, but as fafhioned, not by the influence of their climate, but by the modes
of their learning and inftitution.

I muft be as brief, as poffible, on a fubject, which many learned writers [a] have
largely and fully difcuffed ; and, as the reflexions, I have to offer to you upon it, are
chiefly taken from them, I may the rather
befpeak your attention to what follows.

1. Firft, then, let it be obferved, that
the original language of all nations is ex-

[a] Mede, More, Daubuz, Vitringa, and, above all,
the learned Founder of this Lecture.

tremely

tremely imperfe&. Their ftock of words
being fmall, they explain themfelves very
much by *figns*, or reprefentative actions:
and their conceptions, in that early ftate
of fociety, being grofs and rude, the few
words, they have, are replete with material images, and fo are what we call highly
metaphorical ; and this, not from choice
or defign, or even from any extraordinary
warmth of fancy, but of neceffity, and
from the very nature of things.

Such is the primitive character of all
languages: and it continues long in all,
becaufe the figurative manner is thought
ornamental, when it is no longer neceffary;
and becaufe the neceffity of it is only, if
at all, removed by long ufe and habit in
abftract fpeculation: a degree of refine-
ment, to which the orientals, and the Jews
fpecially, never attained. And therefore
in their languages, very long
—*Manferunt, hodieque manent veftigia ruris.*

Thus far we may go in accounting for
the figured ftyle of the eaft, from general
princi-

principles. But this is by no means the whole of the cafe. For

2. We are to reflect, that, before an alphabet was invented, and what we call literary writing was formed into an art, men had no way to record their conceptions, or to convey them to others at a diftance, but by fetting down the figures and fhapes of fuch things, as were the objects of their contemplation. Hence, the way of writing in *picture*, was as univerfal, and almoft as early, as the way of fpeaking in *metaphor*; and from the fame reafon, the neceffity of the thing.

In procefs of time, and through many fucceffive improvements, this rude and fimple mode of *picture-writing* was fucceeded by that of *fymbols*, or was enlarged at leaft, and enriched by it. By fymbols, I mean certain reprefentative marks, rather than exprefs pictures; or if pictures, fuch as were at the fame time *characters*, and befides prefenting to the eye the refemblance of a particular object, fuggefted a general

idea

Idea to the mind. As, when a *horn* was made to denote *ſtrength,* an *eye and ſcepter,* *majeſty,* and in numberleſs ſuch inſtances; where the picture was not drawn to expreſs merely the thing itſelf, but ſomething elſe, which was, or was conceived to be, analogous to it. This more complex and ingenious form of picture-writing was much practiſed by the Egyptians, and is that which we know by the name of HIERO-GLYPHICS.

Indeed, theſe *ſymbolic characters* were likely, in a courſe of ſucceſſive refinements, to paſs into characters by *inſtitution:* and have, in fact, undergone that change among the Chineſe: and it might be expected that *both* would be laid aſide by any people that ſhould come to be acquainted with the far more convenient and expeditious method of alphabetic writing. But the event, in ſome inſtances, hath been different. The Chineſe adhere to their *characters,* though from their late intercourſe with the Euro-

U   pean

pean nations, one cannot but fuppofe, that the knowledge of *letters* has been conveyed to them: and the Egyptians, through all the extent of their long fubfifting and high-ly polifhed empire, retained their *hierogly-phics*, notwithftanding their invention and ufe of an *alphabet*.

Their inducement to this practice might be, the pleafure they took in a mode of writing, which gratified their inventive curiofity in looking into the natures and analogies of things; or, it might be a ftrain of policy in them to fecrete by this means, their more important difcoveries from the vulgar; or, vanity might put them on raifing the value of their know-ledge by wrapping it up in a vehicle, fo amufing at the fame time, and myfterious.

What account foever be given of it, the fact is, that the Egyptians cultivated the hieroglyphic fpecies of writing, with pe-culiar diligence; while the antiquity, the fplendor, the fame of that mighty king-

dom

dom excited a veneration for it, in the reft S E R M.
of the world. Hence it came to pafs, that
the learning of thofe times, which was
fpread from Egypt, as from its center,
took a ftrong tincture of the hieroglyphic
fpirit. The Eaft was wholly infected by
it; fo that it became the pride of its wife
men to try the reach of each other's capacity by queftions conceived and propofed
in this form. Even the Greeks, in much
later ages, caught the manner of fymbo-
lizing their conceptions from Egypt; and
either drew their mythology from that
quarter, or drefled it out in the old Egyptian garb. But the Ifraelites, efpecially,
who had their breeding in that country, at
the time when the hieroglyphic learning
was at its height, carried this treafure with
them, among their other *fpoils*, into the
land of Canaan. And, though it be credible that their great Law-giver interdicted
the ufe of hieroglyphic characters, yet the
ideas of them were deeply imprinted on
their minds, and came out, on every oc-

U 2   eafion,

casion, in those symbols and emblems, with which, under the names of *riddles*, *parables*, and *dark sayings*, their writings are so curiously variegated and imbossed.

This then is the true and proper account of that peculiar style, which looks so strangely, and to those, who do not advert to this original of it, perhaps so fantastically, in the writings of the prophets. And what more natural, than that a mode of expression, which was so well known, so commonly practised, and so much revered; which was affected by the wittiest, nay, by the wisest men of those times; which was employed in the theology of the eastern world, in its poetry, its philosophy, and all the sublimer forms of composition; What wonder, I say, that this customary, this authorized, this admired strain of language should be that in which the sacred writers conveyed their highest and most important revelations to mankind?

Nor

Nor let any man take offence at the condefcenfion of the divine Infpirer, as though
he degradèd himfelf, by this compliance
with the humours and fancies of thofe to
whom his infpirations were addreffed. For
let him reflect, that in what form of words
foever it fhall pleafe God to communicate
himfelf to man, it muft ftill be in a way,
that implies the utmoft, indeed the fame,
condefcenfion to our weakneffes and in-
firmities; nay, that immediate infpiration
itfelf, though coming through no medium
of language, is of neceffity to be accommo-
dated to our methods of perceiving and
underftanding, how imperfect foever they
are.

Befides, if external revelation be poffible,
it muft be given in fome one mode of
fpeech or writing, in preference to others.
And, if we confider how antient, how
general, how widely diffufed, this fymbolic ftyle has been, and ftill is, in the world;
how neceffary it is to rude nations, and
how taking with the moft refined; how

U 3   large

large a proportion of the globe this practice had over-run before, and at the time of writing the prophecies, and what vast regions of the South and East, not yet professing the faith, but hereafter, as we presume, to be enlightened by it, the same practice, at this day, overspreads; when we consider all this, we shall cease perhaps to admire, that the style in question was adopted, rather than any other ; or we shall only admire the divine goodness and wisdom of its author, who had contrived beforehand, in the very form of this revelation, what may possibly help to bring on and facilitate the reception of it. Certainly, it may become us, on such an occasion, to inlarge our ideas a little; and not to conclude hastily and peremptorily that, when a general blessing was intended by providence, the mode of conveying it should be instituted singly with an eye to our local notions and confined prejudices, and with no regard to the more prevailing sentiments and expectations of mankind.

In

In the mean time, it is paſt a doubt that the hieroglyphic ſtyle was predominant in the antient world; in Judæa, particularly, from the times of Moſes to the coming of Chriſt. There was indeed a degree of obſcurity in it, ſo far at leaſt as to furniſh the Jews, who had no mind to liſten to their Prophets, with a pretence of not underſtanding them (as we ſee from the complaint brought againſt the prophet Ezekiel in the text, *Doth he not ſpeak Parables?*) yet ſtill, it cannot be denied, *That this mode of writing was of common and approved uſe in the ages, when the prophecies were delivered, and among the people, to whom they were addreſſed.*

Our FIRST propoſition is then reaſonably made out; and ſo much of the SECOND, as affirms that the prophetic ſtyle *is conſtructed on ſuch principles as make it the ſubject of juſt criticiſm and rational interpretation.* For it was conſtructed, as we have ſeen, on the ſymbolic principles of the hieroglyphics;

U 4

which

which were not vague uncertain things;
but fixed and conſtant analogies, determinable in their own nature, or from the
ſteady uſe that was made of them.. And
a language, formed on ſuch principles,
may be reaſonably interpreted upon them.
So that what remains is only to ſhew, that
there *are* means, by which this abſtruſe
language may become intelligible to·us,
at this day.

II. That there are ſuch means, you will
eaſily collect, without requiring me to come
to a detail on ſo immenſe a ſubject, from
the following conſiderations.

1. Some light may be expected to ariſe
from the ſtudy of the prophecies themſelves. For the ſame ſymbols, or figures,
recur frequently in thoſe writings : and,
by comparing one paſſage with another;
the darker prophecies with the more per-
ſpicuous; the unfulfilled, with ſuch as
have been completed; and thoſe which
have their explanation annexed to them,

with

with thofe that have not ; by this courfe
of inquiry, I fay, there is no doubt but
fome confiderable progrefs may be made
in fixing the true and proper meaning of
this myfterious language.

2. Very much of the Egyptian hieroglyphics, on which, as we have feen, the
prophetic ftyle was fafhioned, may be
learned from many antient records and
monuments, ftill fubfifting; and from innumerable hints and paffages, fcattered
through the Greek antiquaries and hifto-
rians, which have been carefully collected
and compared by learned men.

3. The Pagan fuperftitions of every
form and fpecies, which were either derived from Egypt, or conducted on hieroglyphic notions, have been of fingular
ufe in commenting on the Jewifh prophets.
Their Omens, Augury, and Judicial Aftro-
logy feem to have proceeded on fymbolic
principles; the myftery being only this,
That fuch objects, as in the hieroglyphic
pictures

pictures, were made the symbols of certain ideas, were considered as omens of the
things themselves. Thus, the figure of a
horse, being the symbol of prosperity and
success in arms, when a *head* of this ani-
mal was found in laying the foundations
of Carthage, the Sooth-sayers concluded,
that the character of that state would be
warlike, and its fortune prosperous : or,
thus again, because the *sun* was the common emblem of a King, or supreme governour in any state, an *eclipse* of this lu-
minary was thought to indicate the ruin,
or diminution, at least, of his power and
fortune; and the superstition is not quite
extinct at this day [b].

But, of all the Pagan superstitions, that
which is known by the name of *Oneirocri-
tics*, or the art of interpreting dreams, is
most directly to our purpose. There is a

---

[b] Hence, the allusion of our great poet,
    — or from behind the moon
In dim eclipse disastrous twilight sheds
On half the nations, and *with fear of change*
Perplexes monarchs —. *P. L.* i. 596.

curious

curious treatife on this fubject, which bears the name of Achmet, an Arabian writer; and another by Artemidorus, an Ephefian, who lived about the end of the firft century[c]. In the former of thefe collections (for both works are compiled out of preceding and very antient writers) the manner of interpreting dreams, according to the ufe of the oriental nations, is delivered; as the rules, which the Græcian diviners followed, are deduced in the other. For, light and frivolous as this art was, it is not to be fuppofed that it was taken up at hazard, or could be conducted without rule; an arbitrary or capricious interpretation of dreams, confidered as a mode of divination, being too grofs an infult on the common fenfe of mankind[d]. But the rules, by which both the Greek and Oriental diviners

[c] See thefe two works, publifhed together, under the title of *Artemidori Daldiani et Achmetis Sereimi F. Oneirocritica,* by Nicolaus Rigaltius. *Lutet.* 1603.

[d] Non enim credo, *nullo percepto* aut cæteros artifices verfari in fuo munere, aut eos, qui divinatione utantur, futura prædicere. *Cic. de Fato, c. 6.*

juftified

juftified their interpretations, appear to have been formed on fymbolic principles, that is, on the very fame ideas of analogy, by which the Egyptian hieroglyphics (now grown venerable, and even facred) were explained. So that the prophetic ftyle, which is all over￼painted with hierogly-phic imagery, receives an evident illuftra-tion from thefe two works.

I have faid, that this fuperftition was *more immediately to our purpofe, than any other*. For fome of the more important prophecies are delivered in the way of dreams; and therefore, without doubt, the rules for interpreting the fymbols prefented to the mind of the prophet in thefe infpired dreams, were the very fame with thofe, that were laid down in the Gentile Oneiro-critics. The conclufion, I know, may ap-pear bold and hazardous. But you will reflect that there is really nothing more ftrange in applying this mode of interpre-tation to *dreams*, than to any other fpecies of prophecy, to vifions, for inftance, or parables,

parables, or even, in general, to any part of the prophetic ſtyle. The compliance, on the part of the inſpirer, is the ſame on every ſuppoſition; and only ſhews that, when the Deity thinks ſit to reveal himſelf to men, he does it in a way that is ſuitable to their ideas and apprehenſions. Nor is any ſanction, in the mean time, given, by this accommodation of himſelf, to the pagan practice of divining by dreams. For, though the ſame ſymbols be interpreted in the ſame manner, yet the *prophecy* doth not depend on the interpretation, but the inſpiration of the dream. A caſual dream, thus interpreted, is only a dream ſtill; the received ſenſe of the ſymbols, repreſented in it, no way inferring the completion of it. But when the Almighty ſends the dream, the ſymbols are of another conſideration, and not only ſignify, but *predict*, an event.

Now, if men will miſtake a *barely ſignificant emblem*, for *a prophetic inſpiration*, the fault is in themſelves, and not in the uſe

of

of the common emblems; which may be the vehicle of a true prophecy, though craft or fuperftition take occafion from them to *divine lies*[e]. It follows, that the rules, which the antient diviners obferved in explaining fymbolic dreams, may be fafely and juftly applied to the interpretation of fymbolic prophecies, and efpecially to fuch of them as were delivered in the form of dreams.

4. It is laftly to be obferved, that not only the Arabic and other oriental writers, but even the Greek and Latin poets may contribute very much to the expofition of the antient prophets. For thefe poets abound in ftrong metaphors and glowing images, which were either copied from the fymbolic language of the Eaft, or invented on the fame principles of analogy as prevailed in the Egyptian hieroglyphics. So that many expreffions, which feem dark and ftrange in the writings of the Jewifh prophets, may be clearly illuftrated and

[e] Ezekiel xiii. 9.

fami-

familiarized to us, even from claffic ufage and example.

And now from thefe feveral fources; that is, from *the fcriptures themfelves*—from the ftill *fubfifting monuments of Egyptian hieroglyphics*—from *the Gentile ceremonies and fuperftitions*—and from *the greater works of genius and fancy, tranfmitted to us both from the Eaftern and Weftern poets*—fuch a vocabulary of the prophetic terms and fymbols may be, nay hath been [f], drawn up, as ferves to determine the fenfe of them in the fame manner, as any common art or language is explained by its own proper key, or dictionary; and there is, in truth, no more difficulty in fixing the import of the prophetic ftyle, than of any other language or technical phrafeology whatfoever.

[f] See Dr. Lancafter's *Symbolical* and *Alphabetical Dictionary*, prefixed to his abridgment of the Commentary on the Revelations, by Mr. Daubuz.

III. But,

III. But, if the case be so clear, you may now be tempted to ask, " What then becomes of the obscurity, in which the prophecies are said to be involved ; and in particular, how comes it to pass, that they may not be as well explained, before the completion, as after it [g] ; which yet is con- stantly denied by writers on this subject, and, even, by your own principles, cannot be supposed ?"

To this objection, I shall not reply by saying, That the style of the prophets, though intelligible, yet requires much practice in the interpreter to unfold its meaning ; for that is the case of many other arts and sciences, which yet are ge- nerally understood : nor, that the symbo- lic terms are frequently capable of several senses, which must needs perplex the in- terpretation ; for there is no common language, in which the plainest words do not frequently admit the same difference

[g] See this objection urged by Mr. Collins in his *Grounds and Reasons,* &c. *p.* 220. *Lond.* 1737.

of

of conftruction, which yet creates no great difficulty to thofe who attend clofely to the fcope of a writer : I fhall not therefore, I fay, amufe you with thefe evafive anfwers, but reply, directly to the purpofe of your inquiry, by obferving,

" That there are feveral methods, or, if you will, artifices, by which the infpired writers, under the cover of a fymbolic expreffion, and fometimes even without it, might effectually conceal their meaning, before the completion of a prophecy, though the language, in which they write, be clearly explicable on fixed and ftated rules."

1. When the prophecy is of remote events, the *fubject* is frequently not announced, or announced only in general terms. Thus, an *earthquake* is defcribed —a *mountain* is faid to be thrown down— a *ftar*, to fall from heaven ; and fo in numberlefs other inftances. Now, an earthquake, in hieroglyphic language, de-

X   notes

notes a *revolution in government* ; a mountain, is the fymbol of a *kingdom,* or *capital
city*; a ftar, of *a prince,* or *great man:* but,
of *what* government, of *what* kingdom,
of *what* prince, the prophet fpeaks, we
are not told, and are frequently unable to
find out, till a full coincidence of all circumftances, in the event, difclofes the
fecret.

2. The prophetic terms are not only
figurative, but fometimes, and in no common degree, hyperbolical (of which the
reafon will be given hereafter), fo that nothing but the event can determine the true
fize and value of them. This feems to
have been the cafe of thofe prophecies in
the Old Teftament, which defcribe the
tranquillity and felicity of Chrift's kingdom; and may poffibly be the cafe of thofe
prophecies in the New, which refpect the
Millennium.   •

3. It being the genius of the prophetic
ftyle to be ænigmatical, this caft is fometimes

times purpofely given to it, even when the expreffion is moft plain and direct. Thus Jeremiah prophefies of Zedekiah, king of Judah, *that he fhould be delivered into the hands of the king of Babylon, that his eyes fhould behold the eyes of the king of Babylon, and that he fhould go to Babylon* [h]. Ezekiel, prophefying of the fame prince, fays, *that he fhould go to Babylon, but that he fhould not fee it, though he fhould die there* [i]. Now Jofephus tells us, that the apparent inconfiftency of thefe two prophecies determined Zedekiah to believe neither of them. Yet both were ftrictly and punctually fulfilled.

4. Laftly, the chief difficulty of all lies in a circumftance, not much obferved by interpreters; and, from the nature of it, not *obfervable*, till after the event; I mean, in *a mixed ufe of the plain and figured ftyle*: fo that the prophetic defcriptions are fometimes *literal*, even when they appear

[h] Jeremiah xxxiv. 3.
[i] Ezek. xii. 13.

X 4

moft

moft figurative; and fometimes, again, they are highly *figurative*, when they appear moft plain. An inftance of *literal* expreffion, under the mafk of figurative, occurs in the prophet Nahum, who predicts the overthrow of Nineveh in thefe words—*With an over-running flood he will make an utter end of the place thereof,* [*Nahum* xi. 8.] An *over-running flood*, is the hieroglyphic fymbol of *defolation by a victorious enemy*: and in this highly figurative fenfe, an interpreter of the prophecy would, in all likelihood, underftand the expreffion. But the event fhewed the fenfe to be literal; that city being taken, as we know from hiftory, by means of an *inundation*. Of *figurative* expreffion, under the form of literal, take the following inftance from a prophecy of Chrift himfelf; who fays to the Jews, *Deftroy this temple, and I will raife it up in three days,* [*John* i. 19.] It was natural enough for the Jews to underftand our Lord as fpeaking of the *temple* at Jerufalem; the rather, as this term had

not

not been, and, I think, could not be, applied, to any perfon, before Jefus: to *Him*, it might be fo applied; and we know that *he fpake of the temple of his body*, [*ver.* 21.]

The fame equivocal ufe was, fometimes, purpofely made of *proverbial expreffions*, as learned men have obferved [k].

I omit many other caufes of obfcurity in the prophecies; fuch as the feeming incredibility, fometimes, of the things predicted—the undefined chronology and geography—the intricacy of the method—and many other confiderations. But you will collect from thefe brief hints, refpecting the *expreffion* only, that, though the fymbolic language be reducible to rule, and therefore, in the main, fufficiently intelligible, yet that there is room enough for the introduction of fo much obfcurity into the prophetic writings, as may anfwer the ends of the infpirer, and conceal the full meaning of them from the moft faga-

[k] See Grotius on Matth. xxvi. 23.

X 3

cious

cious interpreter, till it be revealed, in due time, by the event.

Or, if it be thought that fuch difficulties as the event removes, are not, in their own nature, invincible, before it happens, it is ftill to be confidered, that the giver of the prophecy is, by fuppofition, divine; and as he, therefore, forefaw, in framing the texture of it, that fuch difficulties would, in fact, be invincible, they ferved the purpofe of a defigned concealment juft as well, as if, in nature, they were. Whence the conclufion is ftill the fame, That the prophetic ftyle might be the cover of impenetrable obfcurities in a prophecy, before its completion, and yet the terms of it be clearly explicable on eftablifhed rules; the event only enabling the expofitor more fkilfully and properly to apply thofe rules.

IV. To conclude this fubject; It will now be acknowledged, that the fufpicions which have been taken up againft the pro-

phetic

phetic way of writing, as if it were vague, illufory, or unintelligible, are utterly with-out foundation. The ftyle of the prophets was the known, authorized ftyle of their age and country, in all writings efpecially, of a facred or folemn character; and is even yet in ufe with a great part of man-kind. It further appears, that, as it was underftood by thofe to whom it was ad-dreffed, fo the principles, on which it was formed, are difcoverable by many obvious methods, and may be applied, with fuc-cefs, to the interpretation of it, at this day.

The prophetic ftyle is, then, a *fober and reafonable* mode of expreffion. But this is not all. We may, even, difcern the *ex-pediency,* I had almoft faid, th e *neceffity,* of this ftyle, confidered as the *medium,* or vehicle of prophetic infpiration.

For we have feen, that the fcheme of fcriptural prophecy extends through all time; and is fo contrived as to adumbrate future and more illuftrious events, in pre-

X 4   ceding

ceding and lefs important tranfactions: a
circumftance, which fhews the harmony
and connection of the whole fcheme, and
is not imitable by any human art, or forethought whatfoever.   But now a figurative
ftile is fo proper to that end, that we fcarcely conceive how it could be accomplifhed
by any other.   For thus the expreffion
conforms, at once, to the type, and anti-
type: it is, as it were, a robe of ftate, for
the one; and only, the ordinary, accuftomed drefs of the other: as we may fee
from the prophecies, which *immediately*
refpect the reftoration of the Jews from
their antient captivities, and, *ultimately*,
their final triumphant return from their
prefent difperfion—from the prophecies
concerning the deftruction of Jerufalem,
which prefigure, at the fame time, the
day of judgment—from thofe concerning
the firft coming of Chrift; which, alfo, fet
forth his reign with the faints on earth,
and even the glories of his heavenly kingdom—and in a multitude of other inftances.

Thefe

Thefe fucceffive, and fo different, fchemes of providence could only be fignified *together* in a mode of language, that contracted, or enlarged itfelf, as the occafion required. But fuch is the fingular property of a fymbolic ftyle. For none but this, hath fold and drapery enough, if I may fo fpeak, to inveft the *greater* fubjects; while yet (fo complying is the texture of this expreffion) it readily adapts itfelf to the *lefs confiderable*, which it ennobles only, and not disfigures. The difference is, that what is a metaphor in the former cafe, becomes an hyperbole, in the latter. And this double ufe of the fame fymbol, is the true account of fuch figures as are thought moft extravagant in the defcription of the prophets.

We fee, then, in every view, how reafonable, how expedient, how divine, the fymbolic ftyle is, in fuch writings, as the prophetic. So that if any be difpofed, in our days, to take up the complaint of the text, and to upbraid the prophets by afking,

Do

S E R M.   *Do they not fpeak Parables?* We may now
IX.
take courage to anfwer, Yes: but *parables,*
which, as dark as they are accounted to
be, may be well underftood; and, what is
more, *parables,* which are fo. exprefled, as
to carry an evidence in themfelves that
they *are* what they affume to be, of divine
infpiration.

SERMON X.

The Style and Method of the
APOCALYPSE.

EZEKIEL XX. 49.

—*They say of me, Doth he not speak*
Parables?

ALL the prophecies of the Old and
New Teſtament are written in *pa-*
rables; that is, in highly figurative terms;
which yet, on examination, have appeared to be explicable on certain fixed and rational grounds of criticiſm.

SERM.
X.

Sp

SERM.
X.

So far, therefore, as any prejudice may have been entertained againſt the prophecies concerning Antichriſt, as if the language of them were too abſtruſe or fanciful to be underſtood, enough hath been already ſaid to ſhew, that it is not well founded.

It muſt, however, be confeſſed, that the book of *Revelations* [a], which contains the moſt, and the chief prophecies on the

[a] As to the *authority* of this extraordinary book (although the diſcuſſion of this point be foreign to my preſent purpoſe) it may be proper to acquaint ſuch perſons, as have not made the enquiry for themſelves, and are perhaps incapable of making it, with the ſentiments, which our ableſt writers have entertained of it.

Mr. Mede, a capable inquirer, if there ever was any, ſays roundly—" The Apocalypſe hath more human " (not to ſpeak of *divine*) authority, than any other ".book of the New Teſtament beſides, even from the ".time it was firſt delivered." *Works, p.* 602.

—And to the ſame purpoſe, Sir Iſaac Newton—" I " do not find any other book of the New Teſtament " ſo ſtrongly atteſted, or commented upon ſo early, as " this of the Apocalypſe." *Obſervations on Daniel,* &c. *p.* 249.

Thus, theſe two incomparable men. What ſome minute critics have ſaid, or inſinuated to the contrary,

ſubject

subject of Antichrist, is of a deeper and more mysterious contrivance, than any other of the prophetic writings. Whence, our next step, in this inquiry, must be, To trace the CAUSES of that peculiar obscurity; and to suggest, as we go along, the MEANS, by which it hath been, or may be, removed.

The *causes*, are to be sought in the STYLE, and the METHOD, of that book. I say nothing of the *subject*: for, though the *things predicted* may darken a prophecy, unfulfilled, the *event* will shew what they are; and it is not necessary, that we should anxiously inquire into the meaning of a prophecy, till it be accomplished.

I. *First*, then, the STYLE of the Revelations (for I mean not to consider it, with

---

is not worth mentioning; farther, than just to observe, that, if the authority of this momentous book be indeed questionable, the church of Rome could hardly have failed long since to make the discovery, or to triumph in it.

Hoc Ithacus velit, et magno mercentur Atridæ.

regard

regard to the Greek tongue, in which it is
compofed, or, as it may be affected by the
Hebrew idiom) The *ftyle*, I fay, being fymbolical, like that of the other prophecies,
muft, in general, be explained on the fame
principles, that is, muft be equally intelligible, in both.   Yet, if we attend nicely
to the ftyle of this prophecy, fome difference will be found, in *the choice of the fymbols*, and in *the continuity of the fymbolic
form.*

    1. To explain my meaning, on the firft
article, I muft obferve, That, though the
prophetic ftyle abounds in *hieroglyphic* fymbols, properly fo called, yet the Ifraelites,
when they adopted that ftyle, did not con-
fine themfelves to the old Egyptian ftock
of fymbols; but, working on the fame
ground of analogy, fuperadded many others,
which their own circumftances and obfer-
vations fuggefted to them.   Their divine
ritual, their civil cuftoms, their marvel-
lous hiftory, and even the face and afpect of
                                      their

their country, afforded infinite materials for the conſtruction of freſh ſymbols: and theſe, when they came into common uſe, their prophets freely and largely employed. Thus, *incenſe,* from the religious uſe of it in the Moſaical ſervice, denotes *prayer,* or *mental adoration* [b] — *to tread a wine-preſs,* from their cuſtom of preſſing grapes, ſignifies *deſtruction, attended with great ſlaughter* [c] —*to give water in the wilderneſs,* in alluſion to the miraculous ſupply of that element, during the paſſage of the Iſraelites through the wilderneſs to the holy land, is the emblem of *unexpected relief in diſtreſs* [d];— and, to mention no more, a *foreſt,* ſuch as Lebanon, abounding in lofty cedars, repreſents a *great city, with its flouriſhing ranks of inhabitants* [e]; juſt as, a *mountain,* from the ſituation of the Jewiſh temple on mount Moria, is made to ſtand for the *Chriſtian church* [f].

[b] Mal. i. 11.　[c] Lament. i. 15.　[d] Iſaiah xl. 20.
[e] Ezek. xx. 47.　[f] Iſaiah ii. 2.

Now

Now, though the fymbols of this clafs be occafionally difperfed through the old prophets, yet they are more frequent, and much thicker fown, in the Revelations: fo that to a reader, not well verfed in the Jewifh ftory and cuftoms, this difference may add fomething to the obfcurity of the book.

If you afk the *reafon* of this difference, it is plainly this. The fcene of the apocalyptic vifions is laid, not only in Judæa, but in the temple at Jerufalem; whence the imagery is, of courfe, taken. It was natural for the writer to draw his allufions from Jewifh objects, and efpecially from the ceremonial of the temple-fervice. Befides, the declared fcope of the prophecy being to predict the fortunes of the Chriftian church, what fo proper as to do this under the cover of Jewifh ideas; the law itfelf, as we have before feen, and as St. Paul exprefsly tells us, having been fo contrived, as to prefent the *fhadow* of that future difpenfation?

This

This then (and for the reason assigned) is ONE distinguishing character of the Apocalyptic style. But the difficulty of interpretation, arising from it, cannot be considerable; or, if it be, may be overcome by an obvious method, by a careful study of the Jewish history and law.

2. The OTHER mark of distinction, which I observed in the style of this book, is the *continuity* of the symbolic manner. Parables are frequent, indeed, in the old prophets, but interspersed with many passages of history, and have very often their explanation annexed. This great parable of St. John is, throughout, carried on in its own proper form, without any such interruption, and, except in *one* instance [s], without any express interpretation of the parabolic terms.

Now, the prophecy, no doubt, must be considerably obscured by this circumstance. But then let it be considered, that we have proportionable *means* of understanding it.

[s] Chap. xvii.

Y   For,

SERM.
X.

For, if the fymbols be continued, they are ftill but the *fame* [h], as had been before in ufe with the elder prophets; whofe writings, therefore, are the proper and the certain key of the *Revelations*.

From thefe diftinctive characters, then, of the Apocalyptic ftyle [i], nothing more can be inferred, than the neceffity of ftudying *the Law, and the Prophets*, in order to underftand the language of this laft and moft myfterious revelation. And what is

---

[h] The learned Bifhop Andrews fays exprefly—"You fhall fcarce find a phrafe in the Revelations of St. John, that is not taken out of Daniel, or fome other prophet." *Vix reperias apud Johannem phrafin aliquam, nifi vel ex Daniele, vel ex alio aliquo prophetâ defumptam.* Refp. ad Bellarm. Apol. *p.* 234.

[i] An eminent writer gives an exact idea of it, in thefe words—"The ftyle [of the Revelations] is very prophetical, as to the things fpoken: And very hebraizing, as to the fpeaking of them. Exceeding much of the old prophets language and matter adduced to intimate new ftories: And exceeding much of the Jews language and allufion to their cuftoms and opinions, thereby to fpeak the things more familiarly to be underftood." Dr. LIGHTFOOT, *Harm. of the N. T. p.* 154, *London,* 1655.

more

more natural, nay what can be thought

more divine, than that, in a fyftem, compofed of two dependent difpenfations, the
ftudy of the former fhould be made neceffary to the comprehenfion of the latter; and
that the very uniformity of ftyle and colouring, in the two fets of prophecies,
fhould admonifh us of the intimate connection, which each has with the other,
to the end that we might the better conceive the meaning, and fathom the depth,
of the divine councils in *both ?*

But, without fpeculating further on the
final purpofes of this Judaical and Symbolical character, fo ftrongly impreffed on the
Apocalypfe, it muft evidently appear that
the difficulties of interpretation, occafioned
by it, are not invincible; nay, that, to an
attentive and rightly prepared interpreter,
they will fcarce be any difficulties at all [k].

---

[k] I have heard it affirmed, on good grounds, that
the late Dr. Samuel Clarke, on being afked in converfation by a friend, whether, as he had taken much
pains to interpret the other books of Scripture, he had
never attempted any thing on the Revelations, replied,

I pro-

I proceed, then,

II. To the SECOND, and more considerable cause of the obscurities, found in this prophecy, the METHOD, in which it is composed.

The other prophecies have, doubtless, their difficulties, arising from the abrupt manner, in which, agreeably to the oriental genius, they are delivered : But then, being short and unconnected with each other, the apparent disorder of those prophecies, has rarely any sensible effect in preventing the right application of them. The case is different with the prophecies,

That he had not ; *but that, notwithstanding, he thought he understood every word of it :* Not meaning, we may be sure, that he knew how to apply every part of that prophecy, but that he understood the *phraseology*, in which it was written ; which a man, so conversant as he was in the style of scripture, might very well do.——Calvin, indeed, has been commended for making the opposite declaration : And, it may be, with good reason : For (not to derogate in any respect from the character of this great man) the language of the Scriptures, and especially of the prophetical scriptures, was in no degree so well understood in his time, as it was in that of Dr. S. Clarke.

con-

contained in this book. For, having been all delivered at once, and refpecting a feries of events, which were to come to pafs fucceffively in the hiftory of the Chriftian Church, it is reafonable to expect that fome certain and determinable method fhould be obferved in the delivery of them; and the true fecret of that method, whatever it be, muft be inveftigated, before we can, with fuccefs, apply any fingle prophecy to its proper fubject.

The *firft*, and moft obvious expectation of a reader is, that the events predicted in this prophecy fhould follow each other in the order of the prophecy itfelf, or that the feries of the vifions fhould mark out and determine the fucceffion of the fubjects, to which they relate. But there is reafon to think, on the face of the prophecy, that this method is not obferved.

A *fecond* conclufion would, then, be haftily taken up, that there is no regular method at all in thefe vifions, but that each is to be applied fingly, and without

Y 3

any

any reference to the reſt, to ſuch events as
it might be found, in ſome tolerable degree, to ſuit: And then it is plain, that
fancy would have too much ſcope afforded
her in the interpretation of theſe viſions, to
produce any firm and ſettled conviction,
that they were rightly and properly applied. Yet, as this idea of the Apocalypſe
would favour the lazineſs, the precipitancy,
the preſumption, and, very often, the malignity of the human mind, it is no wonder
that it ſhould be readily and eagerly embraced. And, in fact, it was to this preconceived notion of a general diſorder in
the texture of theſe prophecies, that the
little progreſs, which, for many ages, had
been made in the expoſition of them, is
chiefly to be aſcribed.

But then, *laſtly*, if neither the order of
the prophecy be that of the events, nor a
total diſorder in the conſtruction of it can
be reaſonably allowed, the queſtion is, By
what *rules* was it compoſed, and on what
ideas of *method* is it to be explained?

This

This queſtion, as obvious as it ſeems, was not preſently aſked ; and, when it was aſked, not eaſily anſwered. The clear light, indeed, which the Reformation had let in on ſome parts of this prophecy, and a ſpirit of inquiry, which ſprung up with the revival of Letters, excited a general attention to this myſterious book. But, as each interpreter brought his own hypotheſis along with him, the perplexities of it were not leſſened, but increaſed by ſo many diſcordant ſchemes of interpretation: And the iſſue of much elaborate inquiry was, that the book itſelf was diſgraced by the fruitleſs efforts of its commentators, and on the point of being given up, as utterly impenetrable, when a ſublime Genius aroſe, in the beginning of the laſt century, and ſurprized the learned world with that great deſideratum, *A Key to the Revelations.*

This extraordinary perſon was, JOSEPH MEDE: of whoſe character it may not be improper to give a ſlight ſketch, before I

Y 4   lay

lay before you the fubftance of his difcoveries.

HE was a candid, fincere man; dif-
interefted, and unambitious; of no faction
in religion or government, (both which began in his time to be overrun with factions)
but folely devoted to the love of truth,
and to the inveftigation of it. His learning was vaft, but well chofen and well
digefted; and his underftanding, in no
common degree, ftrong and capacious.

With thefe qualities of the head and
heart, he came to the ftudy of the prophecies, and efpecially of the Revelations:
But, with fo little *bigotry* for the fcheme
of interpretation concerning Antichrift,
that, as he tells us himfelf, *he had even conceived fome prejudice againft it*[1]: And, what
is ftranger ftill in a man of his inventive

---

[1] " As for me, I am confcious of my weaknefs and
unworthinefs; being, when thefe kind of thoughts firft
poffeffed me, looking another way with a prejudice in-
compatible to this." *General Pref. to Mede's Works*,
p. 20, from a MS. Letter.

genius,

genius, with fo little *enthufiafm* in his S E R M.
X.
temper for *any* fcheme of interpretation ⎯⎯⎯⎯ .
whatfoever, that, when he had made his
great difcovery, he was in no haft to pub-
lifh it to the world ᵐ ; and, when at length
he did this, he was ftill lefs in haft to apply it, that is, to fhew its important ufe in
explaining the Apocalyptic vifions ⁿ. Cool,
deliberate, and fevere, in forming his judgments, he was fo far from being obfequious
to the fancies of other men, that he was
determined only, by the laft degree of
evidence, to acquiefce in any conclufions of
his own °.

ᵐ He printed only a few copies of his *Clavis Apoca-*
lyptica in 1627, at his own expence, and for the ufe of
his friends. *Pref. to his Commentary.*

ⁿ His Commentary, on the principles of his *Clavis,*
did not appear till 1632.

° " I am by nature *cunctabundus* in all things, but in
this [his Expofition] let no man blame me, if I take
more paufe than ordinary." MS. Letter in *Gen. Pref.*
p. 22. And again, in a Letter of reply *ad animadverfi-*
ones Ludovici de Dieu, " Eo ingenio fum (delicatulo,
an morofo) ut nifi ubi interpretatio commodè et abf-
que falebris eat, nunquam mihi fatisfacere foleam."
WORKS, *p.* 569. Yet of this *fage* man, could the

In

In short, with no *vanity* to indulge, (for
he was superior to this last infirmity of
ingenious men[p])—with no *interest* in view
(for the interest of Churchmen lay at that
time, as he well understood, in a different
quarter[q])—with no *spleen* to gratify (for

Bishop of Meaux allow himself to speak thus negligent-
ly—*Il s'est rendu de nos jours célébre en Angleterre* PAR SES
DOCTES REVERIES *sur l' Apocalypse. Hist. des Var. l.* xiii.
p. 257. But M. de Meaux knew what he did, when
he *affected* this contempt of Joseph Mede. He was then
at liberty to turn himself from the ablest advocate of the
Protestant cause, to the *weakest*; I mean, M. Jurieu,
whose indiscretions afforded, indeed, ample scope for
the raillery of this lively prelate. Mr. Mede was not a
man to be confuted in this way, and still less by a fanciful and ill-supported *Exposition of the Apocalypse.*

[p] As appears from his backwardness to publish his
discoveries and from his unconcern about the reception
of them. But see his Letter to Mr. Hartlib, Ep. 96,
p. 881; and compare with his answer to Dr. Twisse,
Ep. 51. *p.* 811. See also Ep. 98, to Mr. Hartlib, *Aug.*
6, 1638, not long before his death, in which are these
words :

" I have not been very obtrusive unto men, to acquaint them with my notions and conceits—for some of
them that are but lately known have lain by me above
these twenty years." *P.* 883.

[q] *The point of the Pope's being Antichrist, as a dead fly,
marred the favour of* THAT OINTMENT—meaning the

even

SERM.
X.

even neglect and folitude could not en-
gender this unmanly vice in him ʳ)—with
no oblique purpoſes, I ſay, which ſo often
miſlead the pens of other writers, but with
the ſingle, unmixed love of truth, he de-
dicated his great talents to the ſtudy of the
prophetic Scriptures; and was able to unfold, in the MANNER I am now to repreſent to you, this myſterious prophecy of
the Revelations.

---

merit he had of being knówn to entertain ſome opinions, then much cheriſhed by the ruling clergy. Ep.
56, *p.* 818. He ſays afterwards of himſelf, in the ſame
Letter,—*I thank God, I never made any thing hitherto the
caſter of my reſolution, but reaſon and evidence, on what
ſide ſoever the advantage or diſadvantage fell.*

ʳ His friends ſpeak much of his chearful diſpoſition.
—But I draw this concluſion from the tenour of his
life and *writings*; and, above all, from that famous declaration which he made in confidence to a friend, that,
*if he might but obtain a Donative ſine curâ, of ſo much
value aſ, together with his fellowſhip* [of Chriſt's College
in Cambridge,] *ſhould enable him to keep a horſe, for his re-
creation, he would ſet up his ſtaff for this world. App. to
his Life, p.* 40.—The ſimplicity of this declaration,
makes one confident of it's truth. And a man of ſo
moderate deſires, was in no danger of having his temper
ſoured by diſappointments.

He

He had obferved, that the mifcarriage of former interpreters had been owing, chiefly, to a vain defire of finding their own fenfe in this prophefy, rather than the fenfe of the prophet. Laying afide, then, all hypothefefes whatfoever, he fate down to the book itfelf, and refolved to know nothing more of it, than what the frame and texture of its compofition might clearly reveal to him. He confidered the whole, as a naked recital of facts, literally ex-preffed; and not as a prophetic fcheme, myftically reprefented. In this way of inquiry, he difcerned, that feveral parts of the hiftory, whatever their fecret and in-volved meaning might be, were *homoge-neous*, and *contemporary*; that is, they re-lated to the fame fubject, and were com-prifed within the fame period; and this, though they were not connected in the order of the narration, but lay difperfed in different quarters of it. Thefe feveral fets of hiftorical paffages (or, of *Vifions*, to fpeak in the language of the book itfelf) he

care-

carefully analyzed and compared; fhewed, from circumftances, not imagined, but found, in the hiftory, their mutual relation and correfpondency; and eftablifhed his conclufions, as he went along, not in a loofe way of popular conjecture, but in the ftricteft forms of Geometric reafoning. The coincident hiftories, thus claffed and fcrutinized, he diftinguifhed by the name of SYNCHRONISMS; and gave them to the learned world, in this fevere fcientific form, without further comment or illuftration, under the title of CLAVIS APOCALYPTICA, or A KEY TO THE REVELATIONS.

In confidering this difcovery, which did fo much honour to the profound genius and accurate inveftigation of its author, one clearly perceives how it ferves to the end propofed.

Firft, it appears that the order of the Vifions is not that of the events; in other words, that the prophecy is not to be fo explained, as if the events, predicted in it,

followed

followed each other in the fame train as the Vifions. For the *facts*, which conftitute the fcheme or fable of the prophecy, lite-rally and hiftorically confidered, do not fuc-ceed to each other in that train ; therefore the *events*, whatever they may be, which thofe facts adumbrate, moft certainly cannot.

Secondly, It appears what the true, or chronological order of the Vifions, is ; namely, that, which the nature and con-nexion of the things tranfacted in them, points out and declares. So that, if the real time of any one Vifion can be fhewn, the relative time of the reft may be eafily fettled. For (to quote Mr. Mede's own words) *fuch Vifions as contemporate with that, already afcertained, are of courfe to be applied to the fame times; while fuch as, in the order of the ftory, precede that Vifion, are to be referred to preceding events, and thofe, which follow it, are in like manner to be ex-plained of fubfequent tranfactions* [s].

---

[s] Siquidem, quæ ifti tuo Vaticinio jam, ut dixi, cog-nito, cætera contemporaverint Vaticinia, iifdem pro-

By

By this means, the whole plan or method of the Apocalypfe will be laid down. The feveral fynchronical prophecies will thus fall into their proper places; and there will be no doubt of the relative fituation, which each holds in the general fyftem.

Thirdly, as we now fee the true order of the prophecies (though for the wifeft reafons, no doubt, the order, in which they are delivered, be fometimes different) fo it is to be obferved, that the knowledge of this order is a great reftraint on the fancy of an expofitor; who is not now at liberty to apply the prophecies to events of any time, to which they appear to fuit, but to events only falling within that time, to which they belong in the courfe of this pre-determined method. And if to this reftriction, which of itfelf is confiderable, we add *another*, which arifes from the ne-

cul dubio temporibus funt applicanda; quæ autem præcedunt, non nifi de præcedaneis; quæ fuccedunt, pariter de fuccedaneis eventibus funt interpretanda.

Clavis Apocal. Works, p. 432.

ceffity

ceſſity of applying, not one, but many
prophecies (which are, thus, ſhewn to ſyn-
chronize with each other) to the *ſame* time,
we can hardly conceive how an interpretation ſhould keep clear of theſe impedi-
ments, and make its way through ſo many
interfering checks, unleſs it be the *true* one.
Juſt as when a Lock (to take the author's
alluſion) is compoſed of many, and intricate wards, the *Key*, that turns eaſily within them, and opens the Lock, can only be
that which properly belongs to it.

After all, it may be difficult, I know,
to convey a diſtinct idea of the uſes, to
which this ſynchronal method ſerves, to
thoſe who have not read, and even ſtudied,
Mr. Mede's work. But the ſum of the
matter is this, That the order of the events
and of the Viſions is *not* the ſame—that the
true order of the events, is to be ſought in
certain characters, not fancied at pleaſure,
but inſerted, in the Viſions themſelves—
and, laſtly, that the whole book of the
Revelations being thus reſolvable into a
                                        parti-

particular determinate order, in which the
feveral fets of fynchronal prophecies regularly fucceed to each other, no expofition of this book can be admitted, that
does not refer every fingle prophecy to its
true place in the fyftem, and provide at
the fame time that no violence be done to
any other prophecies, which fynchronize
with it.

And thus much concerning the TRUE
ORDER of the Apocalypfe; deduced, you
fee, from no precarious hypothetic reafonings, but from notes and characters, inclofed in that book; that is, from intrinfic
arguments, which have their evidence in
themfelves, and conclude alike on every
fuppofition.

If we would know more diftinctly what
the EXTERIOR FORM of it, is; and how it
comes to differ fo widely from the plan of
a chronological arrangement; here, too,
our fagacious expofitor will give us fatiffaction. For, in bringing together and
comparing his fynchronifms, he found

Z   (what

(what had efcaped the attention of all others) that the main body of the prophecy is made up of two [r] great parts; which are, alfo, fynchronical; fo that, fetting out from the fame goal, and meafuring the fame fpace, they both concur in the fame end: but with this difference, that the *former* divifion more immediately regards the affairs of the *Empire*; the *latter*, thofe of the *Church*.

Still, this is not all. Our attentive and penetrating commentator further difcovered, That the two great component parts of this prophecy, though diftinct, are very artificially connected, and fhewn to harmonize throughout with each other, by making the fame concluding event [t], once told, the cataftrophe of both. For the *former* part is purpofely, and with exprefs warning given [u], left unfinifhed, till a fummary de-

[r] From ch. iv. to the end of ch. ix: And from ch. x. to the end.

[t] The founding of the feventh trumpet.

[u] Ch. x. 7.

duction

duſtion of the *latter* part down to the ſame
point of time ᵛ, (by way of prelude to the
more extended viſions of this laſt part,
which follow to the end of the book, and
to ſignify, that both parts are contemporary) furniſhed the occaſion of ſhutting up
the two prophecies together in one common
term : which, however, had the appearance of being miſplaced, till the detection
of this ſingular contrivance, by means of
the ſynchroniſms, pointed out the uſe and.
end of the preſent diſpoſition ᵂ.

ᵛ Ch. xi. 15.

ᵂ The reader may form a diſtinct idea of the method,
in which the *whole* book of the Apocalypſe is diſpoſed,
by obſerving that it is reſolvible into THREE great parts.

The FIRST part, is that of the EPISTLES to the ſeven
churches, contained in the three firſt chapters, and is
not at all conſidered by Mr. Mede.

The SECOND part (with which Mr. Mede begins his
commentary) is that of the SEALED BOOK, from ch. iv.
to ch. x; and contains *the fates of the Empire*, or its
civil revolutions, yet, with a reference, ſtill, to the
ſtate and fortune of the Chriſtian Church.

The THIRD part, is that of the OPEN BOOK, with
what follows to the end; and exhibits, in a more minute
and extended view, *the fates of the Chriſtian Church*,

Z 2 *Another*

Another caufe of the feeming perplexity in which this Prophecy is involved, is, That, it being expedient to treat the fame

efpecially during its Apoftacy, and after its recovery from it.

This THIRD divifion may, further, be confidered as confifting of TWO parts. The FIRST contains, in ch. xi, a fummary view of what fhould befall the Chriftian Church, contemporary with the events deduced in the *fecond* part concerning the Empire; and is given in this place, in order to connect the *fecond* and *third* parts, and to fhew their correfpondence and con-temporaneity. See Mr. Mede's Clavis, *p.* 424; and Comment. Apocalypt. *p.* 476.

The SECOND part of the laft divifion, from ch. xii to the end, gives a detailed account of what fhould befall the Chriftian church in diftinct, and, feveral of them, fynchronical vifions.

It has been thought by fome an objection to Mr. Mede's fcheme, " That the prophecy of the *open book*, (which contains, according to him, all the remaining vifions to the end of the Revelations) is not only, for the *fubject*, more confiderable, but, for the *fize* of the volume, larger, than the Prophecy of the *fealed book*; whereas, the name given to it, βιβλαρίδιον, or *little book*, feems very clearly to exprefs the contrary."

If this objection be thought material (for I do not find that Mr. Mede condefcends to take any notice of it) it *might*, perhaps, be obviated by fuppofing, That the *little book* contains the xith chapter, only, being a compen-

                                              fubject

fubject in different refpects, and to give different views of it, according as two fets of men, the true worfhipers and the falfe,

dium of the *third* divifion, and inferted in this place to fhew the contemporaneity of the *two laft* and principal parts; and that all which follows to the end, is to be regarded as a fort of *comment* on the little book, or larger explication of its contents: As if the defign had been to confult our weaknefs, in prefenting us, *firft*, with an abridged view of a great fcheme, and, *then*, in drawing it out at large, for our more diftinct information.

But the *truer* anfwer to the difficulty I take to be, That the *fealed book* is reprefented under the idea of a *book*, properly fo called, which, upon being opened, prefents to the eye the feveral objects and fchemes of the prophecy, diftinctly delineated on the *roll*, or volume, when it comes to be unfolded, and which, therefore, muft needs be confidered as a *large* one. The *open book*, on the other hand, is to be regarded, not as a real, but *metaphorical* book; and is not produced to be read or contemplated, after a gradual evolution of it, but to be *eaten*, at once, by the prophet; like that book, to which it alludes, and from which the imagery is taken, in the vifions of Ezekiel [ii. 8. and iii. 1, 2, 3.]— to *eat a book*, being, in the hieroglyphics, to *meditate upon*, and to *digeft*, its contents. So that this book, to diftinguifh it from the other, is named a *little book*: not, that the revelations, conveyed by it, are lefs confiderable, or lefs numerous, than the other, but that the *ufe*, to which it is put, required only that

Z 3

were

were affected by the fortunes of the Chriſtian Church, this ſhifting and oppoſite face
of things could not be exhibited together;
but was to be ſet forth in ſeveral and
ſucceſſive, though contemporary, viſions.
Hence, the prophecy is thought to proceed, when, in fact, it ſtands ſtill, and
only preſents another proſpect of the ſame
tranſactions.

But I enter no farther into the myſterious
contexture of this book; through which,
however, the clue of the ſynchroniſms, if
well purſued, would ſafely conduct us.
It is enough to my purpoſe to have ſhewn,
That, as the *Language* of the Revelations
is intelligible, ſo the *Method* is not involved in ſuch intricacies, but that, in general, a regular, a conſiſtent, and, what

it ſhould be ſpoken of, as a *book* ſimply; the diminutive
form being here ſuggeſted in the term βιϐλαρίδιον, that
the metaphor of *eating* it might ſeem the eaſier; and
(becauſe the former *ſealed* book was of an immenſe ſize)
might, under this idea, preſent itſelf the more naturally, and give leſs offence, to the imagination.

is

is more, a *true* [x] conception may be formed of it. Whence no fober man needs be difcouraged from reading this book ; or will be in danger, I think, of lofing either his wits, or his reputation, in the ftudy of it. For what fhould hinder a book, though of prophecies, from being underftood, when its *method* may be clearly defined, and its *language decyphered?* Provided always, that we only interpret a prophecy by the event, and do not take upon us to determine the event by a premature conftruction of the prophecy.

With this Apocalyptic key then (of which fo much has been faid), this *key of knowledge*, in my hands, it may, now, be ex-

---

[x] I am not ignorant that many interpreters have thought otherwife. But poffibly they have not enough attended to the advice, which Mr. Mede ufed to give to fuch of his friends as did not enter into his ideas— EXPENDE. My meaning is, that, if they had poffeffed the patience, or the fagacity, to underftand this great Inventor, before they objected to him, they would perhaps have feen caufe to acquiefce in the *Method*, pointed out by him, inftead of attempting in various ways, and to little purpofe, to improve upon it.

Z 4   pected

pected that I fhould open this *dark parable* of the Revelation, by applying fo much of it, at leaft, as refpects Antichrift, to Apoftate Papal Rome. But, befides that there would not, in what remains of this courfe, be room enough for a detailed account of the prophecies, *other reafons* reftrain me from entering immediately on a tafk, not lefs eafy perhaps, than amufing. For Interpreters, I think, have generally been too much in haft to apply the prophecies, before they had fufficiently prepared the way for their application : So that, leaving many doubts unrefolved, which men of thought and inquiry are apt to entertain on this fubject, or not laying before them all the reafons and inducements, which fhould engage their attention to it, their cleareft expofitions are not received, and poffibly not confidered.

With regard, then, to the prophecies, concerning Antichrift, though the chief obftructions in our way feem fairly removed,

and it be now evident that there *are* certain
grounds, on which the moſt abſtruſe of them may be reaſonably interpreted, yet, becauſe the application of them is a work of time and induſtry, many perſons, before they undertake it, may deſire to know, What GENERAL ARGUMENTS there are, which may aſſure them, beforehand, that their labour will not be miſemployed, and that Papal Rome is, in fact, concerned in the tenour of theſe prophecies: And, when this demand has been made, they may further wiſh to be informed, To what ENDS OR USES this whole inquiry ſerves; of importance enough, I mean, to encourage and reward their vigorous proſecution of it?

Theſe deſires and expectations are apparently not unreaſonable: And to ſatisfy them, in the beſt manner I can, will be the ſcope and purpoſe of the two following Lectures.

SER-

SERMON XI.

Prophetic Characters of ANTICHRIST.

LUKE xii. 56.

—How is it, that ye do not discern this time?

SERM.
XI.

SO much having been said on the *manner*, in which the prophecies, respecting Antichrist, may be interpreted; I suppose that now, at length, ye may be disposed to ask, On what GENERAL GROUNDS we affirm, that the Church of Rome is actually concerned in them.

To

To fatisfy this queſtion, it will be ſufficient to ſet before you, in few words, ſome
of the more obvious *notes*, or *charaƈters*, by
which Antichriſt is marked out in the
prophecies: ſuch, and ſo many of them, as
may convince you, that they are fairly applicable to the Church of Rome; and that,
taken together, they cannot well admit any
other application.

Of theſe prophetic charaƈters

1. The FIRST, I ſhall mention, is, *That
we are to look for Antichriſt within the proper
limits of the Roman empire.*

On this head, there is no controverſy
among thoſe who acknowledge the authority of the prophet Daniel, and can be
none: For that prophet, in his famous
viſion of the four kingdoms, ſays expreſly,
that, *among* the ten kingdoms into which
the fourth, or Roman, ſhall be divided,
ANOTHER *ſhall ariſe* [a]; that is, as all in-

* Dan. vii. 7, 8.—I ſaw in the night viſions, and behold, a fourth beaſt—had *ten horns.* I conſidered the
horns, and behold, there came up among them *another*

terpreters

terpreters agree, the kingdom of Antichrist.
So that this power, whatever it be, muſt
have its birth and ſeat within the compaſs
of the ten kingdoms, that is, of the Roman
empire, when, in ſome future time from
the giving of Daniel's prophecy, it ſhould
be ſo divided.

But, to fix the ſtation of the antichriſtian
power more preciſely, it is to be obſerved,
that, as the four kingdoms of Daniel,
conſidered in ſucceſſion to each other, form
a *prophetic chronology*[b]; ſo in another view,
they form a *prophetic geography*[c], being
conſidered, in the eye of prophecy, as *co-
exiſtent*, as ſtill *alive*, and ſubſiſting together,
when the dominion of all, but the laſt, was
taken away[d].

little horn—Compare with *ver.* 24.—The ten horns out
of this kingdom are *ten kings* (or kingdoms) that ſhall
ariſe: and *another ſhall ariſe after them.*

[b] Mede, *p.* 712.

[c] Sir Iſaac Newton, *p.* 31.

[d] Dan. vii. 11, 12.—Concerning the reſt of the beaſts,
they had their *dominion taken away:* yet their *lives were
prolonged* for a ſeaſon and a time.

In.

In confequence of this idea, which Daniel gives us of his four kingdoms, fo much only is to be reckoned into the defcription of each kingdom, as is peculiar to each; the remainder being part of fome other kingdom, ftill fuppofed to be in being, to which it properly belongs. Thus, the SECOND, or Perfian kingdom, does not take in the nations of Chaldæa and Affyria, which make the body of the *firft* kingdom; nor the THIRD, or Græcian kingdom, the countries of Media and Perfia, being the body of the *fecond*. In like manner, the FOURTH, or Roman kingdom, does not, in the contemplation of the prophet, comprehend thofe provinces, which make the body of the *third*, or Græcian kingdom, but fuch only as conftitute its own body, that is, the provinces on this fide of Greece : where, therefore, we are to look for the *eleventh*, or Antichriftian kingdom, as being to ftart up *among* the ten, into which the Roman kingdom fhould be divided.

We

We fee, then, that, as Antichrift was to arife within the Roman kingdom, fo his ftation is farther limited to the European part of that kingdom, or to the *weftern empire*, properly fo called.

This obfervation (which is not mine, but Sir Ifaac Newton's) is the better worth making, becaufe, in fact, the papal fovereignty never extended farther than the weftern provinces; at leaft, could never gain a firm and permanent footing in the countries, which lie eaft of the Mediterranean fea. But, whether you admit this interpretation, or not, it is ftill clear that Antichrift was to arife fomewhere within the limits of the Roman empire. In what *part* of that empire he was to make his appearance, we certainly gather from

II, A SECOND prophetical note or character of this power, which is, *That his feat and throne was to be the city of Rome itfelf.*

The prophet Daniel acquaints us only that the power we call Antichriftian, would

fpring

spring up from *among* the ruins of the fourth, or Roman kingdom: But St. John, in the *Revelations,* fixes his refidence in the *capital city* of that kingdom. For, when, in one of his vifions, he had been fhewn a portentous *beaft with feven heads and ten horns, and a woman arrayed in purple,* riding upon him, an Angel is made to interpret this fymbolic vifion in the following words —*The feven heads are feven mountains on which the woman fitteth—and the ten horns, which thou fawest, are ten kings—and the woman, which thou fawest, is that great city, which reigneth over the kings of the earth* [e].

Words cannot be more determinate, than thefe. The *woman,* that rides this beaft, that is, the fourth empire, in its laft ftate of *ten horns,* or divided into ten kingdoms, is that Antichriftian power, of which we are now inquiring. She is feated on *feven hills,* nay, fhe is *that great city, which reign-*

[e] Rev. xvii. 3, 4, 9, 12, 18.

eth

——— *eth* [that is, in St. John's time which *reigned*] over the *kingdoms of the earth.* Rome, then, is the throne of Antichrist, or is that city, which shall one day be Antichristian. There is no possibility of evading the force of these terms.

It hath been said, that Constantinople, too, was situated on seven hills. It may be so : But Constantinople did not, in the time of this vision, *reign over the kings of the earth.* Besides, if its *dominion* had not been mentioned, *the city on seven hills* is so characteristic of Rome, that the name itself could not have pointed it out more plainly : As must be evident to all those, who recollect, what the Latin writers have said on this subject.

The — *septem domini montes* of one [f] poet is well known ; and seems the abridgement of a still more famous line in another [g] —

Septem urbs alta jugis, toto quæ præsidet orbi :
To which, St. John's idea of a *woman,*

_____
[f] Martial l. iv. ep. 64.   [g] Propert. l. iii. 10.

seated

seated on seven hills, and reigning over the
kings of the earth; so exactly corresponds,
that one sees no difference between the
poet and the prophet; except that the *latter*
personifies his idea, as the genius of the
prophetic style required.

But a passage in Virgil is so much to our
purpose, that it merits a peculiar attention.
This poet, in the most finished of his
works, had been celebrating the praises of
a country life, which he makes the source
and origin of the Roman greatness.

> *Hanc* olim veteres vitam coluere Sabini;
> *Hanc* Remus et frater : *sic* fortis Etruria crevit :
> Scilicet et rerum facta est pulcherrima Roma [b].

The encomium, we see, is made with
that gradual pomp, which is familiar to
Virgil. And the last line (from its ma-
jestic simplicity, the noblest, perhaps, in
all his writings) one would naturally expect should close the description. Yet he
adds, to the surprize; and, I believe, to the
disappointment of most readers,

> *Septemque una sibi muro circumdedit arces.*

[b] Georg. l. ii. ver. 532.

A a

Had

———— Had we found this paffage in any other of the Latin poets, we fhould have been apt to queftion the judgement of the writer; and to fufpect, that, in attempting to rife upon himfelf, he had fallen, unawares, into an evident anti-climax. But the correct elegance of Virgil's manner, and his fingular talent in working up an image, by juft degrees, to the precife point of perfection, may fatisfy us, that he had his reafon for going on, where we might expect him to ftop; which reafon can be no other, than that the *feven hills* were neceffary to complete his defcription of the imperial city. To an antient Roman, the circumftance of its *fituation* was, of all others, the moft auguft and characteriftic; and Rome itfelf was not Rome, till it was contemplated under this idea.

There was ground enough, then, for faying, "that the *name* of Rome could not have pointed out the city *more plainly.*" But I go farther, and take upon me to affert, That the *periphrafis* is even more

precife,

precife, and lefs equivocal, than the *proper name* would have been, if inferted in the prophecy. For *Rome*, fo called, might have ftood, like Sodom, or Babylon, fimply for an idolatrous City. But the city, *feated on feven hills*, and *reigning over the earth*, is the city of Rome itfelf, and excludes, by the peculiarity of thefe attributes, any other application.

Nor is it any objection to the remark, now made, that this city, whatever it be, is defcribed by *another* circumftance, not peculiar to Rome, indeed fcarce applicable to it, I mean that of its being *feated on many waters*[l]. For thefe *waters* are not given as a mark of Rome's *natural*, but *political* fituation: as the prophetic ftile might lead one to expect, if the facred writer had not taken care to prevent all miftake by affuring us, in fo many words, That *the waters, where the whore fitteth, are* PEOPLES, AND MULTITUDES, AND NATIONS, AND TONGUES [k].

[l] Rev. xvii. 1.   [k] Ibid. ver. 15.

A a 2   If

If it be, further, faid, " That the *feven hills* may, likewife, admit a fimilar conftruction from the frequent ufe of *hills,* as emblems of *power,* in hieroglyphic writing, and therefore in prophetic defcription," the remark is very juft : but then, unluckily, there is no fuch explanation of the *feven hills*, as we have of the *waters*, from the prophet himfelf; while yet it could not efcape him, that fuch explanation was more than commonly neceffary in this cafe, to prevent the reader from applying the *feven hills* to the beft-known city in the world, then fubfifting in all its glory, and univerfally acknowledged by this diftinctive character of its fituation.

Should it, laftly, be alledged, " That the explanation is fubjoined to the figure, for that the prophet adds immediately in the following verfe—*and there are feven kings*—meaning, that the *feven hills*, juft mentioned, were to be taken as emblems only of *feven kings*," I reply, that the *feven hills*,

in

in the figurative fenfe of the term, *hills,*
naturally fuggefted, and elegantly intro-
duce, the *feven kings;* but that the *former,*
neverthelefs, are clearly to be diftinguifhed
from the *latter.* ` For it is not faid—*and the*
feven hills are feven kings—as it was before
faid—*the feven heads are feven hills*—but—
AND *there are feven kings*—plainly advanc-
ing a ftep further in the prophecy, and
pointing out a new charaƈteriftic diftinƈtion
of the feven-hilled city, arifing from the
different forms of Government, through
which it had paffed.

The truth is (as Mr. Mede well obferves[1])
the feven heads of the beaft, are a DOUBLE
TYPE: *firft,* they fignify the *feven hills,*
on which the city is placed; and, *then,* the
feven kings, or governments, to which it
had been fubjeƈt; but ftill *on* thofe feven
hills, for which reafon the fame type is

---

[1] *Septem* BESTIÆ *capita,* duplex typus: primò, feptem montes feu colles funt, fuper quos urbs Beftiæ me-
tropolis fita eft; deinde, feptem quoque, idque in iifdem
(quod unitas typi denotat) Collibus, Regum feu Dy-
naftarum fucceffivorum ordines. Works, p. 524.

A a 3   made

made to fignify both : But, if the type had been defigned to carry a *fingle* fenfe, and *kings* had been that fenfe, as explicatory of *hills*, it had been very prepofterous to give the *interpretation* of the type, and then to *interpret* the interpretation, unlefs the ex-preffion had been fo guarded as to convey this purpofe in the moft diftinct manner, As it is now put, there are manifeftly TWO SENSES, and ONE TYPE[m].

On the whole, there can be no doubt concerning *the great city on feven hills.* It can be no other, than the city of Rome it-felf; In other words, the antichriftian, is a *Roman Power.*

Still, this Roman power, for any thing that hath hitherto appeared, may be a *Pagan* and *Civil* power. But

[m] The whole paffage in the original ftands thus—αἱ ἐπίὰ κεφαλαὶ, ὄρη εἰσὶν ἑπίὰ, ὅπε ἡ γυνὴ κάθηίαι ἐπ' αὐίῶν· καὶ βασιλᾶς ἑπίὰ εἰσιν—of which the following is the literal tranflation—The SEVEN HEADS are *feven hills,* where the woman fitteth upon them, AND are *feven kings*— Every one fees that the connective particle, AND, re-fers to *heads,* and not to *hills.*

III.

III. The prophecies feem very clearly to
point it out to us, *as an* ECCLESIASTICAL
and, in name and pretence, at leaft, *a*
CHRISTIAN *power.*

To begin again with the prophet, Daniel.
He tells us, that the Horn which fhall *arife*
after, and from *among*, the ten horns, that
is, the Antichriftian kingdom, as before explained, fhall be DIVERSE from the ten
kingdoms, out of which it fhall arife[n].
" But a kingdom may be *diverfe* from other
kingdoms, in various refpects." Without
doubt. And, therefore, we cannot certainly conclude from this fingle text, that
the *diverfity,* mentioned, will confift in its
being a fpiritual kingdom. Yet, if ye
reflect that this *diverfity* is given, as the
characteriftic mark of the antichriftian
kingdom; that, although there may be
other and fmaller differences between kingdoms, the greateft and moft fignal is that

[n] Dan. vii. 24.—The ten horns out of this kingdom
are ten kings that fhall arife: and another fhall arife
after them, and He fhall be *diverfe* from the firft—

which ſubſiſts between a temporal and ſpiritual power; nay, that Government, as ſuch, is, and can only be, of two ſorts, civil and ſpiritual, as correſponding to the two conſtituent parts of *man*, (the ſubject of all government in this world,) the Soul and the Body : Taking, I ſay, theſe conſiderations along with you, ye cannot eſteem it a very harſh and violent interpretation, if, without looking any farther, we incline to think that this *diverſity* of regimen, ſo emphatically pointed out, reſpects that great and eſſential difference in human government, *only*. At leaſt, it will be admitted, that, if, from other and more expreſs teſtimonies, the government of Antichriſt appear to be a ſpiritual government, we ſhall, then, be authorized to put ſuch a conſtruction on Daniel's prophecy, as will reach the full force and import of his expreſſion. Such a kingdom muſt be allowed to be eminently *diverſe* from ſecular kingdoms. So that the harmony between the

pro-

prophets on this fubject will be clear and ftriking.

Now, fuch a teftimony we feem to find in the Apoftle, St. Paul; who, prophefying of *the man of Sin*, or Antichrift, to be revealed in the latter days, makes it a diftinguifhing part of his character, *That he* SITTETH IN THE TEMPLE OF GOD°. Confider the force of thefe words. A power, *feated in the temple of God*, can be nothing but a power fuitable to that place, or a *fpiritual* power: juft as a power, *feated in the throne of Cæfar*, could only be interpreted of a *civil* power.

Nor fay, becaufe the context runs thus— " that he, AS GOD, fitteth in the temple of God, SHEWING himfelf that he IS GOD —that therefore it only means his claiming *divine honours*: a degree of blafphemy, very applicable to a *civil* power." This objection has clearly no force: becaufe his *fitting in the temple of God* was the very

---

° 2 Theff. ii, 4.

means

means (if we rightly apply this prophecy) by which the man of fin rofe to that abominable pre-eminence. It was by virtue of his *fpiritual,* that he affumed a *divine* character. So that the phrafe—*as God*—and that other—*fhewing himfelf that he is God*—fets before us, indeed, the extravagant height to which the man of fin afpired, and to which he afcended; but, no way invalidates the conclufion from his fitting in the temple of God—that he was a *fpiritual power.* Rather, we fee the propriety of this conclufion; becaufe the text, thus underftood, fuggefts the *way* in which the man of fin accomplifhed his blafphemous purpofe: His *fuccefs* arofe, from his *ftation* in the temple. On the other hand, a power *fitting in the throne of Cæfar,* might fit there *as God,* and might *fhew himfelf that he was God* (as many of the Roman Emperors did:) So that the claufe—*fitting in the temple of God*—has evidently no peculiar

liar

liar fitnefs, as applied to the ufurpation of divine honours by a *civil tyrant*; whereas we fee it has that fitnefs, when applied to a *fpiritual* tyrant. The context therefore proves nothing againft the interpretation, here propofed and defended.

But, what is this *temple of God?* The temple at Jerufalem, it will be faid ; the only temple, fo called, then fubfifting in the world ᴾ. Admit this to be the literal fenfe of the words. Yet ye remember fo much of what hath been faid concerning the prophetic ftyle, as not to think it ftrange, that the literal fenfe fhould involve .in it another, a *myftical* meaning. And this, without any uncertainty whatfoever. For fo, the term, *Jew*, means a *Chriftian*; the term, *David*, means *Chrift*;

ᴾ See Grotius, on the place : who applies this prophecy to Caius Cæfar, and thinks it was fulfilled when that Emperor commanded his ftatue to be placed in the temple of Jerufalem. A ftrange conjecture ! which many writers, and very lately an excellent prelate has well confuted. Bifhop Newton's *Diff. on the Prophecies,* Vol. ii. p. 375.

the

SERM.
XI.

the *incense* of the temple-fervice, means
the *prayers* of Chriftians; plainly and con-
feffedly fo, in numberlefs inftances. Agreeably to this analogical ufe of Jewifh terms,
in the ftyle of the prophets, *the temple of
God*, nay *the temple of Jerufalem* [q] (if that
had been the expreffion) muft, in all reafon,
be interpreted of the *Chriftian church*, and
could not, in the prophetic language, be
interpreted otherwife. When, therefore,
Antichrift is faid to *fit in the temple of God*,
it is the fame thing as if it had been faid of
him, *That he fitteth*, or ruleth, *in the church
of Chrift.* Now, fubftitute thefe words—
the church of Chrift—in the room of thofe
other words—*the temple of God*; and fee,
if St. Paul, fuppofing his purpofe had been
to exprefs a fpiritual power in oppofition to

[q] *Hierofolyma* in fcriptis prophetarum occurrit ut
emblema alterius cujufdam *Hierofolymæ*, myfticè fic
dicendæ; quæ *Hierofolyma* non poteft effe urbs quædam
in montibus Zione & Acra conftructa, qualis fuit anti-
qua illa; fed oportet effe *rem fpiritualem*, in quâ attri-
buta antiquæ Hierofolymæ *myfticè* demonftrentur.
VITRINGA, *Apocalypf. Exp. & Illuftr.* p. 762.

a civil;

a civil; fee, I fay, if St. Paul could have conveyed that purpofe more plainly.

Still, we have another, and, if poffible, a more decifive teftimony in the *Revelations*. For, among the different views, which St. John gives us of Antichrift, in fo many diftinct vifions, one is fet before us in the following manner—*And I beheld another beaft coming up out of the earth, and he had two horns like a lamb, and he fpake as a Dragon*[r]. Now, if we had known nothing more of thefe fymbols, than what the obvious qualities of the animals themfelves fuggefted to us, we could only have inferred, that this ruling power (for that is the idea conveyed by the term, *Beaft)* would put on the appearance of a gentle and pacific adminiftration: I fay, the *appearance*; for what its *real* character was to be, is clearly enough expreffed in what follows, that this lamb-like beaft *fpake as a Dragon*. But, when we further reflect,

---

[r] Rev. xiii. 11.

that

that *horns*, in the prophetic ftyle, are the emblems of *power*, and that a *Lamb* is the peculiar, the *appropriated* fymbol of Chrift, *the lamb of God, which taketh away the fin of the world*, and is conftantly fo employed throughout this whole prophecy of the Revelations, we muft, of neceffity, conclude that *a beaft with the horns of a lamb* can only be a ftate or perfon, pretending to fuch powers, as Chrift exercifed, and his Reliligion authorifeth; that is, powers, *not of this world*, but purely fpiritual.

The other fymbol of a *Dragon*, confirms this conclufion. For a *Dragon*, in the prophecies, is the known fymbol of the old Roman Government in its pagan, perfecuting ftate. When, therefore, it is faid that the beaft *fpake as a Dragon*, the meaning is, That Antichrift fhould affume the higheft tone of civil authority in promoting his tyrannous purpofes, though he

' John i. 29.

cloked

cloked his fierce pretenfions under the meek femblance of a fpiritual character. Taken together, thefe two fymbols fpeak as plainly, as fymbolic terms can fpeak, That Antichrift was to be a *religious perfon,* acting in the fpirit of a *fecular tyrant.* So exactly is he characterifed by the poet Mantuan, addreffing himfelf to one of the Popes—

Enfe potens *gemino,* cujus veftigia adorant
Cæfar et aurato veftiti murice reges.

On the whole, I leave it to be confidered, whether, when the prophecies pronounce of Antichrift, that he fhould be, a power *diverfe* from all others—that he fhould *fit in the temple of God*—and that he fhould have *the horns of a lamb*—I leave it, I fay, to your confideration, whether it be not plain that this extraordinary power, a Roman power, and refiding at Rome, was to be a *Chriftian and Ecclefiaftical,* and not a *Pagan and Civil* power.

IV.

IV. Another obvious character of Anti-christ, or rather, *complication* of characters, is that triple brand, impreſſed upon him, of a *tyrannical, intolerant, and idolatrous,* power.

The prophets hold him up to us, as *reigning,* or exerciſing an oppreſſive and ſupereminent dominion, *over the kings of the earth,* that is, of the weſtern empire [t] ; as *making war with the lamb, and the ſaints who receive not his mark in their foreheads* [u], that is, perſecuting good and conſcientious Chriſtians, who refuſe to wear the badge of Antichriſt, and to ſerve under him; and as another *Babylon, the mother of harlots and abominations of the earth* [x], that is, as polluted himſelf with the groſſeſt idolatry, and as corrupting the nations with the ſame prophane worſhip.

[t] Dan. vii. 8. 20. Rev. xvii. 1. 16, 17.
[u] Dan. vii. 21. Rev. xvii. 14. xiii. 7. 16.
[x] Rev. xvii. 5.

But

But thefe marks, it will be faid, have been found upon fo many powers, which have appeared in the world, that they cannot be given as the *diftinctive* marks of *one*, that is, of the Papal Power: Nay, the Bifhop of Meaux goes further, and attempts to fhew, by a very refined argument, that the very *terms* of *whoredom* and *fornication*, in which the *laft* of thefe marks, I mean, IDOLATRY, is fet forth by the prophet in the *book of Revelations*, make it impoffible for us to apply that mark to Rome Chriftian.

Let us fee, then, *firft*, what force there is in the criticifm of this learned Prelate.

That *whoredom*, or *fornication*, in the language of fcripture, means *idolatry*, is agreed on all hands, and cannot be difputed: Whether the figurative ufe of this term arofe from obferving, how conftantly that pollution attended idolatrous worfhip, or how fitly a communication with falfe gods may be compared with that unlawful commerce: Whatever be the ground of the analogy, it is clear to a demonftration

B b   that

that *whoredom* is but another name for *ido-latry*, which, under this idea, is very frequently charged upon the Jews by the antient prophets.

Sometimes, however, (without doubt, to aggravate the charge) the idolatry of the Jews is confidered in the light of *adultery*, that is, of infidelity to the God of Ifrael; to whom, as to her proper Lord and *Huf-band*, the Jewifh nation had, by exprefs ftipulation, and in the moft folemn manner, contracted herfelf.

But, notwithftanding this promifcuous application of the terms, *fornication*, and *adultery*, to the idolatry of the Jews in the antient prophecies, it hath been remarked by the Bifhop of Meaux, "That Babylon, or Rome, in the Revelations, is conftantly and uniformly fpoken of, as a *whore*, and not as an *adulterefs :* whence he concludes, that this charge is brought againft Pagan Rome only, and not Chriftian Rome. For, why, he afks, is fo much care taken not to impute

impute *adultery* to idolatrous Rome, if it
had been a Chriſtian city? when its pol-
luting itſelf with this crime, contrary to
the moſt expreſs engagements, which
Chriſtians take upon themſelves, of fideli-
ty to the only true God, might juſtly deſerve, and, in propriety, may ſeem to require, this opprobrious charge, rather than
that other lighter one of *fornication*;
whereas, if Pagan Rome be here meant,
its idolatry could only be ſet forth under
the idea of *fornication*, and not of *adultery* ?."

? Le ſaint apôtre a bien pris garde de ne pas nommer
la proſtituée, dont il parle, une adultere, μοιχάδα,
μοιχαλίδα, mais une femme publique—ſans jamais
avoir employé le mot d'*adultere*; tant il étoit attentif a
éviter l'idée d'une epouſe infidelle.—Loin de marquer
la Proſtituée, comme une *Eglize corrumpuë*, nous avons
montré clairement qu'il a pris des idées toutes contrai-
res à celles-là, puis qu'au lieu de produire une *Jeruſa-
lem infidelle*, ou du moins une *Samarie*, autrefois partie
du peuple ſaint, comme il auroit fait s'il avoit voulu
nous repréſenter une egliſe corrompuë, il nous propoſe
une *Babylone*, qui jamais n'a eté nommée dans l'alliance de Dieu. Nous avons auſſi remarqué qu'il n'avoit
jamais donné à la Proſtituée le titre d'épouſe infidelle

SERM.
XI.

Now, although, as I obferved, the ido-latrous Jews are frequently treated by their prophets, as *fornicators,* as well as *adulterers,* nay, are much more frequently [z] re-prefented under the *former* idea, than the *latter* ; and although it be therefore true, that *fornication* is not neceffarily, and exclu-fively, to be underftood of Pagan idolatry,

ou repudiée ; mais que par tout il s'étoit fervi du terme de *fornication,* et de tous ceux qui revenoient au même fens.   Je fçais que ces mots fe confondent quelquefois avec celui d'*adultere,* mais *le fort du raifonnement confifte en ce que de propos deliberé* Saint Jean *evite toûjours ce dernier mot* qui marqueroit *la foi violée, le marriage fouillé, et l'alliance rompuë,* &c.—*L'Apocalyfe avec une Explication ; par Meffire Jaques Benigne Boffuet, Eveque de Meaux.* PREF. 26, 29.   AVERTISEMENT, *p.* 321—323. *Par.* 1690, 12°.

[z] The reafon I take to be, That *fornication,* that is, vague luft, and general proftitution, ferved beft to ex-prefs the unbridled and indifcriminate paffion of the Jews for the dæmon-worfhip of their neighbours : Whereas the crime of *adultery,* though of a blacker dye, and, in that view, more proper to expofe the malignity of their offence, does not convey the fame ideas of uni-verfal pollution, being ufually committed, *becaufe* it is fo criminal, with more diftinction and reftraint.

but

but may well be applied to Chriſtian idolaters, as it was to the Jewiſh ; yet the force
of the learned objector's argument will not
be obviated by this obſervation only. For
the ſtreſs of it lies in this, " That the idolatry of Rome in the Revelations is *every*
where, that is, purpoſely, termed *fornica-*
tion (to inſinuate to us, that the charge is
directed againſt a Pagan City, and not a
Chriſtian Church), and *no where*, that is,
purpoſely again, called *adultery*."

The objection is extremely ingenious ;
and, ſo far as I know, hath been, hitherto,
unanſwered. Yet, if any good reaſon can
be aſſigned why the prophet ſhould thus
ſtudiouſly prefer the term, *fornication*, to
that of *adultery*, in deſcribing the idolatry
of Chriſtian Rome, notwithſtanding thoſe
terms be uſed indifferently by the Jewiſh
prophets, when they reprove the idolatry
of their own countrymen, the Biſhop of
Meaux would himſelf acknowledge, that
his objection falls to the ground.

B b 3 Now

Now fuch a reafon offers itfelf to us in the EMBLEM, under which St. John chufes to reprefent his idolatrous fociety. This emblem is, *Babylon*; a Pagan idolatrous city; to which the idea of *fornication* may be colourably, and hath, in fact, been, applied [a], in order to exprefs the tranfgreffion of the law of nature, in its idolatrous worfhip: But to fuch a city, *adultery*, could in no proper fenfe, be applied; becaufe, it had never entered into any clofe engagement, or *marriage-contract*, as it were, with the God of heaven.

This being admitted, we fee the reafon, why Rome Chriftian is taxed as a *whore* fimply, and not as an adulterefs. For what had been improperly faid of the *type*, cannot, on the principles of decorum, be transferred to the *anti-type*. If Babylon be only a *harlot*, fhe is a harlot ftill, and nothing more, when fhe ftands for Rome, whether Pagan, or Chriftian. The concinnity of the figure, and the juft corre-

[a] Ifaiah xxiii. 16, 17. Nahum iii. 4.

fpondence

fpondence of the thing fignified to the fign,
demands the obfervance of this rule;
which cannot be violated without manifeft abfurdity and confufion.

" But why then, it is afked, was fuch
an emblem employed ? Why was not Jerufalem, or Samaria (of which *adultery*
might be predicated) rather chofen, than
Babylon, for the type, or reprefentation
of *idolatrous Chriftian Rome ?*"

The reafon, again, is obvious. It was,
becaufe Babylon was the *firft* of all idolatrous cities; and the *fitteft* [b] to emble-
matize the enormous guilt, or to fet in
full light the extenfive influence, of idolatrous Rome. For each, in its turn,
was *the mother of harlots and abominations of
the earth*; the *former* corrupting the *heathen*

---

[b] *—for it is the land of graven images, and they are mad
upon their idols.* Jer. l. 38. Again: *Babylon hath been a
golden cup in the Lord's hand, that made all the earth
drunken : the nations have drunken of her wine, therefore the
nations are mad.* Jer. li. 7. Compare *Rev.* xvii —*the inhabitants of the earth have been made drunk with the wine
of her fornication.*

B b 4   world

world with her fornication, and the latter, the *Christian.*

When therefore for this, or the like reason, Babylon was made the emblem of Christian Rome, the prophet was obliged to retain the idea of fornication, only, and not to interpofe that of adultery, through the whole tenour of his application.

It may, further, be worth obferving, that *pagan* idolatry is, for the moft part, expofed by the antient prophets under the notion of LYES, or LYING VANITIES^c; and very rarely, I think in no more than one or two fhort paffages, under that of *fornication.* For vague luft was fo generally practifed in the heathen world, and the law of nature, condemning that vice, fo little known, or refpected by it, that the metaphor would not have conveyed to a Pagan idolater the atrocious nature of his crime. The Mofaic Law, on the other hand, interdicting fornication in the fevereft

^c Mr. Mede. Works, *p.* 49.

terms,

terms, and requiring that *there should be no whore of the daughters of Israel* [d], the guilt of idolatry was very forcibly, as well as naturally, reprefented to a Jew, under that idea.

Accordingly, we find, that the prophets every where, and in whole pages, employ this figure, when they addrefs themfelves to Jewifh idolaters. Whence it may feem that, although there be fufficient authorities to juftify the prophet St. John in con-fidering his emblematic Babylon under the idea of a *harlot*, yet he would not have profecuted even this inferior charge of *fornication* fo far as he has done, and in fo many parts of his prophecy, if his purpofe had not been to apply it to a *believing*, and not a Pagan city. If the myftical Babylon be *Chriftian* Rome, we fee the force and propriety of this reprefentation; which had clearly been lefs apt, if Pagan Rome, ac-

[d] Deut. xxiii. 17.

cording

cording to the Bishop of Meaux, had been
intended by the prophet.

We see then, in both ways, why Rome
is not an *adulteress* in the Revelations; and
why she is so emphatically, a *harlot.*
The type employed forbad the *former*
charge, though the anti-type be *Rome
Christian:* The *latter* charge had not been
so much laboured, if the anti-type had been
Rome Pagan.

Thus, the edge of this acute objection
is entirely taken off, and the execution, it
was to make on the Protestant system, prevented.

To return, now, to the consideration of
our *three* marks. These marks, it is said,
agree to so many other powers, besides that
of the Papacy, that they cannot be made the
peculiar, distinctive characters of Christian
Rome. And, without doubt, considered
merely in themselves, they cannot. But,
having already understood that the power,
thus stigmatized, is a power seated in the

seven-

seven-hilled city, and that too, an *ecclesiasti-cal* power, one sees clearly that, if the pro-phecies have hitherto received their ac-complishment in any degree, these marks can only be sought in Papal Rome, and must be the proper, exclusive characters of that power. I say, *one sees this*; but, it must be owned, not without amazement, That a species of government, calling it-self Christian, and professing to model itself on the example of the *Lamb*, on the pure and simple principles of the Gospel, should yet be all over stained with those specific vices, which Christianity most abhors—the utmost pride of secular domination—the most relentless zeal against the rights of conscience—and, what is still more incre-dible, the most blasphemous idolatry. The accumulated infamy of these crimes struck the prophet, St. John, so forcibly, that, on the sight of this portentous monster, exhibited to him in the vision, *he wondered,*

as

as himſelf expreſſes it, *with great admiration*ᵉ.

But, ſtrange as this viſion appeared to
the ſacred *prophet*, the Papal hiſtory is
found to realize all the wonders of it : And
backward, as *we* may be to interpret this
viſion of a church, profeſſedly Chriſtian,
that church herſelf is ſo little ſcandalized
at the imputation of theſe crimes, that
ſhe is ready to avow them all; the *two firſt*,
directly and openly ; and the *laſt*, when ſet
in a certain light, and explained in her
own manner. In ſhort, ſhe prides herſelf
in the *extent of her ſway*ᶠ, and the *fire of*

ᵉ Rev. xvii. 6. ἰθαύμασα Θαῦμα μέγα.

ᶠ Not held of the civil power, or acknowledged to
be ſo held, but uſurped upon it, and inſolently directed againſt it; as is well known from eccleſiaſtical
hiſtory. *The Pope is not Antichriſt: God forbid!* (ſays
the good Abbé Fleury, with a zeal becoming a member
of the Papal communion.) *But neither is he impeccable, nor
has he an abſolute authority in the church over all things both
temporal and ſpiritual—Le pape n'eſt pas l'Antichriſt ; à
Dieu ne plaiſe ; mais il n'eſt pas impeccable, ni monarque*

her

her zeal[g], and only quibbles with us about the meaning of the term, *idolatry.*

---

absolu dans l'eglise pour le temporel et pour le spirituel [4eme *disc. sur l'hist. ecclesiastique,* p. 173. *Par.* 1747, 12°.]

The Pope, he says, *is not an absolute monarch in the church over all things temporal and spiritual:* That is, he *ought not* to arrogate to himself the power of an absolute monarch ; for that the pope assumes to be such a monarch, and, in fact, exercised this supreme monarchical power in the church, through many ages, the learned and candid writer had indisputably shewn, in the discourse, whence these words are quoted. But now this *monarchical sovereignty in all things temporal, as well as spiritual,* is certainly one prophetical note or character, by which the person or power, styled antichristian, is distinguished. Let the Pope, then, be what he will, we are warranted by M. Fleury himself to conclude, that he hath, at least, this mark of antichrist.

[g] In the *persecution of heretics* ; which M. Bossuet regards as so little dishonourable to his communion, that he thinks it *a point not to be called in question*—calls the use of the sword in matters of religion, *an undoubted right*—and concludes, that *there is no illusion more dangerous than to consider* TOLERATION, *as a mark of the true Church*—*l'exercice de la puissance du glaive dans les matieres de la religion & de la conscience ; chose, qui ne peût être revoquée en doute*—*le droit est certain*—*il n'y a point d'illusion plus dangereuse que de donner* LA SOUF-FRANCE *pour un caractere de vraye Eglise.* Hist. des Var. l. x. p. 51. Par. 1740, 12°.

To

To cut the matter fhort, then, and to keep clear of thofe endlefs debates concerning the worfhip of *Images,* of the *Crofs,* and of the *Hoft* in the celebration of the Mafs; debates, which a dextrous fophift may find means to carry on with a fhew of argument, and with fome degree of plaufibility; To fet afide, I fay, all thefe topics, let it be obferved, at once, That *idolatry,* in the fcriptural fenfe of the word, is of *two forts,*

Thus, this great doctor of the catholic Church, towards the clofe of the laft century. And juft now, another eminent writer of that communion very roundly defends the *murder* of the Bohemian martyrs at Conftance, and (what is more provoking ftill) the *fraud and ill-faith,* through which the pious and tender-hearted *Fathers* of that council rufhed to the perpetration of it. *M. Crevier, Hift. de l'Univerfité de Paris,* t. iii. l. vi. *p.* 435, *&c.* Par. 1761, 12°.—Can it be worth while to fpend words in fixing this charge of *intolerance* on the church of Rome, when her ableft advocates, as we fee, even in our days, openly triumph in it? But, then, hath fhe forgotten who it was that the prophet *faw, drunken with the blood of the faints, and with the blood of the martyrs of Jefus—Rev.* xvii. 6? Alas, no: But fhe wonders, by what figure of fpeech *heretics* are called *Saints;* and *rebels to the Pope, Martyrs of Jefus.*

and

and confifts either, 1. in giving the honour
due to the one true God, as maker and
governour of the world, to any other fuppofed, though fubordinate god; Or, 2, in
giving the honour due to Chrift, as the
fole mediator between God and Man, to
any other fuppofed, though fubordinate,
mediator. The *former*, is the idolatry
forbidden by the Jewifh law, and by the
law of Nature: The *latter*, is Chriftian
idolatry, properly fo called, and is the abo-
mination, prohibited and condemned, in fo
fevere terms, by the law of the Gofpel.

Now, whether the *former* fpecies of idolatry be chargeable on the church of Rome
or not ; and whether the *crime* of that fpecies, may not be incurred by honouring
the true object of worfhip, through the medium of fome fenfible image: Whatever, I
fay, be determined on thefe two points
(which, for the prefent, fhall be fet afide)
The *other* fpecies of idolatry is, without all
doubt, chargeable on any Chriftian church
that fhall adopt or acknowledge, in its
religious

SERM.
XI.

religious addreſſes, another mediator, beſides Chriſt Jeſus.

But the church of Rome (I do not ſay,
in the private writings of her divines, but)
in the ſolemn forms of her ritual, *publickly
profeſſes*, and, by her canons and councils,
authoritatively enjoyns, the worſhip of ſaints
and angels, under the idea of mediators
and interceſſors : not indeed in excluſion
of Chriſt, as *one*, or, if you will, as *chief*
mediator, but in manifeſt defiance of his
claim to be, the *ſole* mediator. This
charge is truly and juſtly brought againſt
that Church, as it now ſtands, and hath
ſtood, for many ages ; and cannot, by any
ſubterfuge whatſoever, be evaded[h].   And

[h] See Vitringa *Apocalypſ. Exp. p.* 603, and the au-
thors cited by him : But, above all, ſee Mr. Mede's ex-
quiſite and unanſwerable diſcourſe, entitled, *The Apoſtacy
of the latter times.*

'Tis true, the Biſhop of Meaux is pleaſed to divert
himſelf with one part of this diſcourſe; I mean, that
part, which contains [ch. xvi. and xvii.] the learned
writer's interpretation of Daniel's prophecy, concerning
the Gods *Mahuzzim.*   He finds ſomething pleaſant in
this idea, or rather in this hard word, which he re-
peats ſo often, and in ſuch a way, as if he thought the

there-

therefore, to the other characters of *Pride*
and *Intolerance*, which she takes to herself
with much complacency, she muft, now,

very found of *Mahuzzim,* was enough to expofe the
comment and Commentator to contempt. *Hift. des
Var.* l. xiii. p. 260, 261. But, after all, the ingenious
Prelate would have done himfelf no difcredit by being
a little more ferious in difcuffing an interpretation,
which Sir Ifaac Newton adopts without fcruple [*Obf.
on the prophecies of Daniel, &c.* p. 192]; and which, in
mere refpect to the prophet, he fhould, at leaft, have
condefcended to replace by fome other and more reafonable interpretation. But it is the infirmity of this
lively man, to be jocular *out of feafon.* Thus, again,
he raillies Luther, for an affertion of his; delivered, it
feems, with fome affurance, and, in the form, as he
pretends, of a prediction, *That the Papal power would
fpeedily decline and come to nothing, in confequence of the
Reformation.* The event, he fays, has belied the prophet; the Pope ftill keeps his ground; and then (in an
unlucky parenthefis) laughs to think, *how many others,
befides Luther, will be dafhed to pieces againft this* STONE
—*bien d'autres, que Luther, fe briferont contre cette* PIERRE
[*Var.* l. xiii. p. 244]. Now, if the glory of faying a
good thing had not infatuated this Catholic Bifhop,
could he have helped ftarting at his own comparifon of
a *ftone,* as applied to Luther and the Reformation, when
it might fo naturally have put him in mind of that prophetical STONE, which fhall one day *become a great
mountain,* and *break in pieces a certain* IMAGE, *and ftand
for ever* [Dan. ii. 35, 44.]?

be

be content (whether she will or no) to have that of DÆMON-WORSHIP, or ANTICHRISTIAN IDOLATRY, fastened upon her.

Nor let the followers of that communion think to elude this charge, by saying, *That they only request the saints, as we commonly do any good man, to pray for them* [i], False, and disingenuous! *False*; because their breviaries and litanies shew, that they supplicate the saints to befriend them by their own inherent power, or to intercede for them to the throne of God by virtue of their own personal merits [k], in blasphemous derogation to the all-atoning and in-

---

[i] L'Eglise, en nous enseignant qu'il est utile de prier les Saints, nous enseigne à les prier dans ce même esprit de charité, & selon cèt ordre de société fraternelle qui nous porte à demander le secours de nos freres vivans sur la terre; & le Catechisme du Concile de Trente conclut de cette doctrine, que si la qualité de Mediateur, que l'ecriture donne à Jesus Christ recevoit quelque préjudice de l'intercession des Saints qui regnent avec Dieu, elle n'en recevroit pas moins de l'intercession des fideles qui vivent avec nous.

M. BOSSUET, *Exposition de la doctrine de l'Eglise Catholique*, p. 17, 18. *Paris*, 1671.

[k] Vitringa, *p.* 603, 604.

commu-

communicable interceffion of Jefus. *Dif-ingenuous*, too; becaufe they know very well, that the queftion is concerning un-feen and heavenly mediators only, not men like ourfelves, fuch as we live and converfe with on earth; whom we only admonifh of their duty, and to whom we only do ours, when we call upon them to exert an act of piety and common charity in praying for their fellow-chriftians. Our meaning is but that which the Apoftle well expreffes, when he would have us *confider one another, to provoke unto love and to good works*[1]; and not at all to fupplicate our Chriftian brethren as powerful interceffors, in whofe meritorious virtues we confide, and to whom, as poffeffing a proper intereft in the Almighty, by the worth of their own perfons, we commit our deareft concerns, The forgivenefs of our fins, and the falvation of our fouls.

" But this, it will be faid, is a very de-fective, and even unfair, account of the

[1] Heb. x. 24.

C c 2   matter.

matter. We do more than admoniſh our brethren of their duty, when we ſollicit their prayers for us. We invite them di-rectly, and formally, to *intercede* for us to the throne of Grace. We are allowed, nay encouraged, to lay a ſtreſs on their interceſſion; and, what is more, we are given to underſtand that ſuch inter-ceſſion, eſpecially if it be made by good men, will have weight and influence in heaven. What elſe is the meaning of the Apoſtle, when he aſſures us, *That the effectual fervent prayer of a righteous man availeth much.* James v. 16.? And, if the prayer of *a righteous man,* much more the prayer of glorified ſaints and angels."

I have put the argument, I think, in all its force, and (becauſe the advocates of the papal cauſe affect to think it unanſwerable) ſhall examine it, with care.

" We apply to good Chriſtians, or to thoſe we eſteem ſuch, to intercede for us by their prayers to heaven." We do ſo;
and

and are encouraged in this application, by the *example*, and by the *directions* of the Apostles. For I shall not take advantage of what some have conceived to be the meaning of St. James, in the place alledged, where he attributes so much to the prayer of a righteous man, That the prayer, there spoken of, is *the prayer of faith*, or a spiritual gift miraculously conferred on the first teachers of the Gospel, and confined to their ministry: I will not, I say, take advantage of this gloss; because, whatever foundation it may seem to have in the context of that epistle, I allow it to be clear from other places of the New Testament[m], That the duty of Christians is to pray, that is, to *intercede*, for each other.

But then I desire it may be observed,

1. What difference there is between desiring good men to pray for us, in the Gospel sense of that duty; and desiring Saints and Angels to pray for us, in the

[m] 1 Theff. v. 25. 1 Tim. ii. 1. and elsewhere, *passim*.

sense

fenfe of the papal rituals. We requeft thofe prayers, only as they fhall be offered up in the name, and through the merits, of the great, and properly fpeaking, fole interceffor; and we look for no effect from them, but on that condition. The Church of Rome addreffes herfelf to Saints and Angels, as *interceffors*, by, what we may call, their own right, by virtue of their own inherent fanctity: Or, rather, fhe applies to them directly, as to *Saviours*, for their proper and immediate help, and expects it from the fuppofed privilege of their rank, or merits, independently of their *prayers*, or, at leaft, of the *manner* in which thofe prayers fhall be prefented through the name of Jefus. The formal words of their Litanies fhew, that fuch is their meaning.

But they will fay, that this condition of interceding, or faving, through the merits of Chrift, is implied, though not expreffed. I reply then,

2. That,

2. That, admitting it to be fo, there is,
yet, the wideft difference between *praying*
to Saints and Angels to pray for us, though
in the Gofpel forms of interceffion ; and
merely *requefting* good men to pray for us,
in thofe forms.   The *latter* addrefs is made
in a way remote from all appearance of
idolatry, and free from the fufpicion of it :
The *former*, is preferred in the *place*, at
the *time*, with the *pofture*, in the *language*,
in fhort, with all the circumftances and
formalities of divine worfhip.

3. I obferve, that, when we afk the
prayers of men, we know that they hear
our addrefs to them : We cannot even fuppofe thus much of Saints and Angels,
without afcribing to them the incommunicable attributes of the Almighty.

Still, it may be infifted, That prayers,
whether offered up to God by men, or
glorified fpirits, are however to be confidered in the light of *Interceffions* ; and that
therefore, fo far as we combat the practice

C c 4   of

of faint-worſhip on that ground, Proteſtants, as well as Papiſts, when they
employ the prayers of others, are guilty
of idolatry.

This, in truth, is the hinge, on which
the queſtion turns: And, to ſhew the
difference of the two caſes, palpably and
clearly, I ſay,

Fourthly, and laſtly, That the Goſpel,
in permitting, or rather in commanding
us to aſk the prayers of each other, juſti-
fies this ſort of interceſſion, and abſolves
it from the blame and guilt of idolatry.
It gives a ſanction to this mode of medi-
ating with God by his Saints, on earth;
and does not regard it as a practice that
interferes with the mediatorial office of
Jeſus, in heaven.

The ſame Goſpel, on the contrary, (I
inquire not, for what reaſons) ſays not a
word, from which we can infer, that any
ſuch addreſs is directed, or permitted, to be
made to Angels or Spirits. It even con-
demns

demns all addresses of this kind, under
the opprobrious name of unauthorized, or
WILL-WORSHIP[n]. Though we be allowed, then, to have good men, in some
sense, for our mediators or intercessors on
earth, we are not allowed to have any
mediator or intercessor in the tabernacle of
heaven, but Jesus, the great high priest
of Christians, only. This last sort of intercession, by Angels and glorified Saints,
is against the spirit and letter of our religion. It is a practice, which, not being
enjoined, is forbidden; which, being dif-
allowed, is reprobated. In a word, It
entrenches on the incommunicable honour
and prerogatives of the great, the appointed, the sole-Mediator in heaven, seated
at God's right hand, *who ever liveth to
make intercession for us*[o]. It sets up new
mediators, without, and against his leave:
It is, then, un-christian, and *idolatrous*.

[n] Coloss. ii. 18,   [o] Heb. vii. 25.

Thus

Thus at length, I suppose, it appears indisputably, That we are neither unreasonable, nor uncharitable, in charging IDOLATRY, as well as the other two antichristian vices of *pride*, and *intolerance*, to the account of papal Rome.

V. The last prophetic mark of Antichrist, which I shall have time to point out to you, and what perhaps you may esteem the most material of all, is, *The* TIME, *in which that power is said to make its appearance in the world.*

It hath been already observed [P], that the *chronology* of the prophecies is, for the most part, not defined with that exactness, which we expect in historical compositions. It is commonly expressed in terms that may be interpreted with some latitude; or, when the date is more precisely delivered, we are still at a loss, in some respect or other, before the event, in what manner to form our calculation. However, the expression is not so loose and

[P] Page 276—279, and *p.* 309.

vague,

vague, but that we may clearly apprehend *about* what time the predicted event will come to pass.

Thus, for instance, the season of Christ's *coming into the world* was fixed by such circumstances as these—that it should be before the total dissolution of the Jewish state—or while the second temple was yet standing: And, when it was determinately foretold to be after the expiration of *seventy weeks, from the going forth of the commandment to return and to build Jerusalem,* still, besides the prophetic and somewhat obscure sense of the word *weeks,* we cannot beforehand calculate exactly *when* these weeks commence⁹, or in what term they

⁹ " Whatsoever time of Messiah's appearing Almighty
" God pointed out by Daniel's 70 Weeks, yet I be-
" lieve not that any Jew, before the event, could in-
" fallibly design the time without some latitude ; be-
" cause they could not know infallibly where to pitch
" the head of their accounts, untill the event discover-
" ed it: yet in some latitude they might." *Mede,*
Works, p. 757.

And so in other instances. " I do not believe that
" the Jews themselves could certainly tell from which
are

are to be accomplifhed. Yet, notwithftanding thefe uncertainties, the Jews faw
very clearly, and, from them, the reft of
the world conceived an expectation, that
the perfon predicted was to appear in that
age, or *about* that time, in which he did
appear, and which, from the tenour of the
prophecies, they had computed would be
the time of his appearance.

In like manner, the feafon of Antichrift's
appearance in the world is left to be
collected from general intimations; and,
when the duration of his tyranny is limited to *twelve hundred and fixty days*,
befides that the expreffion, as before, is
ænigmatical, we have no means of fixing
the commencement of that period fo precifely, but that fome doubts may arife
about it, till the accomplifhment of the
prophecy fhall give light and certainty to

" of their *three captivities* to begin that reckoning of
" LXX years, whofe end fhould bring their return from
" Babylon, until the event affured them thereof."
Mede, Works, p. 662.

the

the computation. Yet ftill, as in the former cafe, we have fuch *data* to proceed upon in calculating the reign of Antichrift, as may let us fee *about* what time it was to be expected.

Thus much being premifed, I have now only to remind you of what the prophets exprefly declare concerning the rife of Antichrift. The eldeft of thefe, the prophet Daniel, fays it was to be in the time of the *fourth* kingdom, that is, of the Roman; which, for the convenience of the prophetic calculations, is confidered as fubfifting, though in a new form, under the ten kings, among whom it was to be divided. He further tells us, that Antichrift was to arife from *among*, and *after*, the ten kings; that is, we are to look for him *then*, (and not before) when the Roman empire has undergone that change of government [r].

Next, St. Paul, it feems, had told the Theffalonians; what it was that, for a

[r] Dan. vii.

time,

time, prevented the appearance of Anti-chrift: But that information hath not been tranfmitted to us. However, he fays to them—*Ye know* WHAT *with-holdeth that he might be revealed in his time:* and further adds, HE, *who now letteth, will let, until he be taken out of the way*[s].

Now, by putting thefe paffages together, and by comparing them with the predic-tions of Daniel, not we of thefe later times only, before whom *the man of fin* is fup-pofed to be evidently difplayed, but the early fathers of the church, long before the events happened to which thefe pro-phetic notices could be applied, clearly faw, or at leaft generally conjectured, that the impediment, here mentioned, was the then fubfifting power of the Cæfa-rean government; which, they faid, was firft to be taken away, and then Antichrift would be revealed[t].

---

[s] 2 Theff. ii. 6, 7.
[t] P. 220—222. But fee efpecially Mede's Works, p. 657.

Laftly,

Laſtly, the Apoſtle St. John not only confirms the prophecies of Daniel, that Antichriſt ſhould ariſe out of the ten kings, who were to have the weſtern empire ſhared out among them, but adds this remarkable circumſtance, That he ſhould RIDE the ten kings ᵘ; which implies, that he ſhould *co-exiſt* with them: And it further appears, that he was to receive his whole power from them, and was finally to be deſtroyed by them.

Now, turn to the hiſtory of the *fourth* kingdom, and ſee how it correſponds to theſe prophecies. Obſerve, when the weſtern empire under its Cæſarean head, was taken away; how it was, afterwards, diſmembered by the northern nations; by what degrees it fell at length, into *ten*, that is, *many* diſtinct, independent kingdoms; at what time this partition was made, or rather fully ſettled and completed. From this time, and not before,

ᵘ Rev. xvii. 7.

you

SERM.
XI.

_____

you are to look for Antichrist, now gradually rearing himself up among the ten
kings; and, at length, in a condition, by
the power, which they gave to him, to
ride, that is, to direct and govern them.
From this time, again, compute the 1260
years, the predicted period of his government; and, keeping your eye all along
on the ecclesiastical and civil state of our
western world (the predicted theatre of
all these transactions) see, if you can help
concluding, I do not say at what precise
time, but *about* what time, Antichrist appeared; see, if the *commencement* of his
reign be not so far determined as that you
may be certain of its being long since past;
and see, if very much, at least, of that
allotted *period*, through which his dominion was to continue, according to the
prophecies, be not, by the evident attesta-
tion of history, now run out.

To DRAW, then, what hath been said
on the several marks of Antichrist, to a
point.

point. Confider, within *what part* of the world, he was to appear; in *what seat* or throne, he was to be eftablifhed; of *what kind*, his fovereignty was to be; with *what attributes*, he was to be invefted; in *what feafon*, or *about what time*, and for *how long a time*, he was to reign and profper: Confider thefe FIVE obvious characters of Antichrift, which the prophets have diftinctly fet forth, and which, from them, I have fucceffively held up to you: And, then, compare them with the correfpondent characters, which you find infcribed, by the pen of authentic hiftory, on a certain power, fprung up in the Weft; feated in the city of Rome; calling himfelf the Vicar of Chrift; yet *full of names of blafphemy*, that is, ftigmatized with thofe crimes, which Chriftianity, as fuch, holds moft opprobrious, the crimes of tyrannic dominion, of perfecution, and even Idolatry; and laftly, now fubfifting in the

D d   world,

world, though with evident fymptoms of decay, after a long reign, whofe rife and progrefs can be traced, and whofe duration, hitherto, is uncontradicted by any prophecy: Put, I fay, all thefe correfpondent marks together, and fee if they do not furnifh, if not an abfolute demonftration, yet a high degree of probability, that apoftate papal Rome is the very Antichrift foretold.

At leaft, you will admit that thefe correfpondencies are fignal enough to merit your attention, and even to juftify your pains in looking further into fo curious and interefting a fubject. Ye will fay to yourfelves, That the prophecies concerning Antichrift deferve at leaft to be confidered with care, fince in fo many ftriking particulars, they appear, on the face of them, to have been completed.

This

This *conclusion*, it is presumed, is a rea- S E R M.
sonable one : And the end of this dif-   XI.
course will be answered, if ye are, at
length, prevailed upon to *draw* this conclusion.

S E R M O N XII.

Uses of this Inquiry into the Prophecies.

Rev. xxii. 7.

Behold, I come quickly: Bleſſed is he that keepeth the ſayings of the Prophecy of this book.

SERM.
XII.

BEFORE we engage in a work of time and difficulty, we naturally aſk, " Cui bono, to what conſiderable end and purpoſe, are our labours to be referred?"

Although

Although it may, then, be prefumed, that enough hath been faid on the prophecies to excite a reafonable defire of looking further into them, and even to produce a general perfuafion, that they have been, or may be, underftood; yet, it may quicken your attention to this argument, and fupport your induftry in the profecution of it, to fet before you the USES, which may refult from a full and final conviction (if fuch fhould be the iffue of your inquiries), That thefe prophecies are not intelligible only, but have, in many inftances, been rightly applied, and clearly fulfilled.

Thefe USES are very many. I fhall collect, only, *two or three* of the more important, for your confideration.

Though every period of prophecy be inftructive, that which takes in the great events and revolutions, which have come to pafs in the *Chriftian Church*, is, for obvious reafons, more efpecially interefting to us, who live in thefe latter ages of the world.

Of the numerous predictions, contained in either Teſtament, which, it is preſumed, reſpect theſe events, the moſt conſiderable by far, becauſe the moſt minute and circumſtantial, are thoſe of St. John in the *Revelations*; which treat profeſſedly of ſuch things as were to befall *the ſervants of Jeſus* [a], from the prophet's own days, down to that awful period, when all the myſterious councils of God, in regard to the Chriſtian diſpenſation, ſhall be finally ſhut up in the day of judgement. To theſe predictions, then, a more particular attention is due, the rather becauſe they have been fulfilling from the time of their delivery, — *behold, I come quickly* — and, above all, becauſe a *bleſſing* is pronounced on thoſe, who *keep*, that is, who obſerve, who ſtudy and contemplate, *the ſayings of this book.*

[a] Rev. i. 1.

Affuredly,

Affuredly, then, this ftudy will be rewarded with fignal benefits. And one fees
immediately:

I. In the firft place, that no fmall benefit
muft arife to thofe, who admit the completion of thefe prophecies, fo far, I mean,
as the tenour of the book makes it probable that they have been completed, *from the
awful fenfe, which this conviction muft needs
give them of the Chriftian difpenfation itfelf.*

That this difpenfation, ufhered in by fo
long a train of prophecies, fhould ftill be
attended by others, through all the ftages
and periods of it; that fecular empires
fhould rife and fall, unnoticed, as it were,
by the fpirit of God, while the kingdom
of his Son is fo peculiarly diftinguifhed,
and its whole hiftory, in a manner, anti-
cipated, by the moft exprefs predictions:
that Jefus fhould be, as he fays of himfelf,
*the alpha and omega, the beginning and the
end*[b], of all God's religious difpenfations

[b] Rev. ii. 8. xxi. 6.

Dd 4   to

to mankind: that his *firſt coming*, or perſonal appearance in the fleſh, ſhould be
ſignified from the foundation of the world,
and from time to time more explicitly declared in a variety of ſucceſſive prophecies,
till the great event, at length, fulfilled
them all: and that, together with this
event (the foundation of others, ſtill more
illuſtrious) his *ſecond coming*, in the future
and gradual manifeſtations of his power
(for they were to be *gradual*) ſhould be
diſtinctly marked out, and duely accompliſhed, in the fortunes of the Chriſtian
church, or of that kingdom, which he
came to erect in the world; while this
ſubject, and no other, engaged the ultimate attention of all the prophets: There
is, I ſay, in this ſcheme of things, ſomething ſo aſtoniſhingly vaſt, ſomething ſo
much above and beyond the attention that
was ever known to be paid to any other
perſon or thing in the compaſs of univerſal hiſtory, as muſt ſtrike an awe into the
hearts

hearts of all men, who confider Chriftianity in this point of view; and muft compel the moft negligent to confefs, or fufpect at leaft, That *fuch* a difpenfation is a matter of no light moment, but, indeed, the moft important in the eyes of providence, and the moft interefting to mankind, that can be conceived, or expreffed.

If, then, there be reafon, to *admit* the completion of fuch prophecies, refpecting fuch a fubject, in any confiderable number of inftances, within that fpace of time which is already elapfed; and, therefore, to *expect* that the remaining prophecies will, in like manner, be fulfilled, The conclufion is, that the difpenfation of God through Chrift is of the laft confequence to the inhabitants of this world; And the obvious *ufe* of this conclufion will be, that it further obliges all ferious men who have thus far profited by a ftudy of the facred oracles, to put that falutary queftion to

them-

themfelves—*How fhall we efcape, if we neglect fo great falvation* [c] ?

Connected with *this* ufe of prophecy,

II. A *fecond* is, That it fets before us, not the importance only, but the *truth* of Chriftianity, in the ftrongeft light.

So many illuftrious events falling in, one after another, juft as the word of prophecy foretold they fhould, muft afford the moft convincing proof, That our Religion is, as it claims to be, of divine inftitution : a *proof,* the more convincing, becaufe it is continually growing upon us ; and, the farther we are removed from the fource of our religion, the clearer is the evidence of its truth. Other proofs are fuppofed to be, and, in fome degree, per-haps, are, weakened by a length of time. But this, from prophecy, as if to make amends for their defects, hath the peculiar privilege of ftrengthening by age itfelf: till hereafter, as we prefume, the

[c] Heb. ii. 3.

accumu-

accumulated force of fo much evidence S E R M. fhall overpower all the fcruples of infi- XII. delity; and bring about, at length, that general converfion both of Jew and Gentile, which the facred oracles have fo exprefly foretold.

In both thefe ways, then, by impreff-ing on the mind the moft affecting fenfe of Chriftianity; that is, by giving us, *firft,* the moft *awful view of its pretenfions,* and *then,* by producing the *firmeft conviction of its truth,* the word of prophecy hath an evident tendency, in proportion as we fee its accomplifhment, to promote the great ends, for which it was given, till *the earth fhall be filled with the knowledge of the Lord,* and *all the inhabitants of the world fhall learn righteoufnefs* [d].

Thefe ufes are general, and concern *all* men : The

III. *Next,* I fhall mention, is more efpe-cially addreffed to *thinking* and inquifitive men.

[d] Hab. ii. 14. If. xxvi. 9.

When

When the view of things, exhibited under the two preceding articles, has raif- ed our admiration, to the utmoft, of the divine councils in contriving, preparing, and at length executing fo vaft a fcheme, as that of Chriftianity, for the benefit of mankind; we are led to expect that the *effect* will correfpond to the *means* employ- ed, and that a ftriking change will, at length, be brought about in the condition of the moral world.

But, in furveying the hiftory of this new religion, the theme of fo many pro- phecies, and the great, the favourite ob- ject, if I may fo fpeak, of divine provi- dence, " fome are not a little fcandalized to obferve that nothing hath come to pafs in any degree equivalent to fuch an ex- pence of forethought and contrivance; that, for a feafon, indeed, virtue and piety feemed to triumph, in the exemplary lives of the firft converts to this religion, and in the overthrow of Pagan idolatry ; but that

this

this golden age was foon over; and that, now, for more than fourteen hundred years, the paffions of men have kept their ufual train, or rather have expatiated with more licence and fury in the Chriftian world, than in the Pagan; that *idolatry*, in all its forms, has revived in the bofom of Chriftianity; and, as to *private morals*, that this Religion has even made men worfe than it found them, or, at beft, of corrupt fenfualifts, has only made them intolerant and vindictive bigots; that, in a word, the *kingdom of heaven*, as it is called, has, hitherto, neither ferved to the glory of God, nor to the good of mankind; at leaft, to neither of thefe ends, in the *degree*, that might have been expected from fuch high pretenfions."

The colouring of this picture, we will fay, is too ftrong: but the outline, at leaft, is fairly given. The corruptions of the Chriftian world have been notorious and great; and though they are indeed

the

the corruptions of men calling themselves Chriftians, and not the vices of Chriftianity, yet he who the moft difpaffionately contemplates fo fad a fcene, can hardly reconcile appearances to what muft have been his natural expectations.

Here, then, the prophecies of this book I mean, of the Apocalypfe, come in to our relief. This book contains a detailed account of what would befall mankind under this laft and fo much magnified difpenfation. It foretells all that hiftory has recorded. It fets before us the corrupt ftate of the Chriftian world in almoft as ftrong a light, as that in which our indignant fpeculatift himfelf has placed it. But it, likewife, opens better things to our view. It fhews, that the *end* of this difpenfation is to promote virtue and happinefs; and that this end fhall finally, but through many and long obftructions, be accomplifhed. It reprefents the caufe of righteoufnefs, as ftill maintaining itfelf in all

the

the conflicts, to which it is expofed; as gradually gaining ground, and prevailing, through the fecret aid of divine providence, over all oppofition, till it obtains a firm and permanent eftablifhment; till *the Saints reign* (not in a fanatical, but in the fober and evangelical fenfe of that word, *reign*) *in the earth*ᵉ; till *the Lord God omnipotent reigneth*ᶠ.

So far, then, as thefe prophecies appear to have been completed, they reconcile us to that difordered fcene, which hath hitherto been prefented to us; and give repofe to the anxious mind, in the affured hope of better things to come. The worft, that has *happened,* was forefeen; and the beft, that we *conceive,* will hereafter come to pafs. Thus, the reafonable expectations of men are anfwered, and the honour of God's government abundantly vindicated.

IV. The *laft* ufe, I fhall fuggeft to you, is that which immediately refults from

ᵉ Rev. v. 10.　　ᶠ Rev. xix. 6.

the

the study of the Apocalyptic prophecies *concerning Antichrist*; I mean, *The support, that is hereby given to Protestantism against all the cavils and pretensions of its adver-saries.*

. For, if these prophecies are rightly ap-plied to papal Rome, and have, in part, been signally accomplished in the history of that church, it is beyond all doubt, that our communion with it is dangerous; nay, that our separation from it is a matter of strict duty. *Come out of her, my people, that ye be not partakers of her sins, and that ye receive not of her plagues*[g] — are plain and decisive words, and, if allowed to be spoken of that church, bring the con-troversy between the Protestant and Papal Christians to a short issue.

I know, the advocates of Rome pretend, that, not a sense of duty, but a *spirit of revenge* operates in the minds of Protest-ants, when they affect to lay so great a

[g] Rev. xviii. 6.

stress

ſtreſs on the Apocalyptic prophecies. " *Re-*
ward her, even as ſhe rewarded you [h] "—is,
they ſay, another of their favourite texts,
by which they take themſelves to be as
much obliged, as by that which they ſo
commonly alledge for quitting her communion.   It is not, therefore, to cover themſelves from the imputation of ſchiſm, but
to authorize the vengeance, they meditate
againſt us, that we are ſtunned with the
cry of Antichriſt and Babylon [i]."

To this charge, I can only reply, That,
if any Proteſtant writers have put that ſenſe
on the words—*reward her, as ſhe rewarded
you*—they muſt anſwer for their own temerity and indiſcretion.   They, who underſtand themſelves, and the language of
prophecy, diſclaim the odious imputation.
They ſay, That they neither admit the
lawfulneſs of perſecution in any caſe, on
the account of religion, nor have the leaſt

[h] Rev. xviii. 4.
[i] M. de Meaux : *L'Apocalypſe avec une explication.
Avertiſement aux Proteſtants,* p. 303, &c. Par. 1690.

E e   thought

thought of inftigating the Chriftian world
to any fanguinary attempts againft the
Papacy. What the *event* may be in the
councils of Providence, is another confideration : But they neither avow, nor ap-
prove thofe principles, which tend to produce it. They, further, infift, That the
two paffages under confideration, though,
both of them, expreffed in the *imperative*
form, require a very different conftruction :
That the language of prophecy *feems* very
often to authorife what it only foretells ;
and to command that which it barely per-
mits: that, therefore, the fenfe of fuch
paffages is to be determined by the circumftances of the cafe ; that, where obedience
is lawful, there the *preceptive* form may be
admitted ; but, where it is not, there
nothing more is intended than the certainty of the *event:* That this diftinction
is to be made in the prefent cafe ; for that
Chriftianity doth not allow vindictive re-
taliations, or *holy wars,* for the fake of
religion,

, religion, and that offenfive arms taken up in the caufe of God (how confidently foever fome, have juftified their zeal by the autho- rity of the Jewifh Law, ill-applied) are abominable and *antichriftian :* Whence we rightly conclude, that—*reward her, as fhe rewarded you*—are words not to be taken injunctively ; while thofe other words— *come out of her, my people*—expreffing no- thing but what it was previoufly our duty to do, are very clearly to be fo taken.

Laftly; We fay, that the context in the two places alledged, juftifies this diftinction. *Come out of her, my people.* Why? *That ye be not partakers of her fins, and that ye receive not of her plagues.* The reafon is juft, and fatisfactory. *Reward her.* Why? No reafon is affigned, or could be affigned confiftently with the fpirit of the Chriftian religion : It only follows, *as fhe has re- warded you*—words, which exprefs only the *meafure,* and the *equitable grounds* of

E e 2   the

the allotted punifhment, not the *duty* of Chriftians to inflict it.

I return, then, from the confutation of this cavil (the moft plaufible, however, as well as invidious, which the wit of Rome has ftarted on this fubject) to the conclu-fion, before laid down, That the comple-tion of the Apocalyptic prophecies in the Papal apoftafy, if feen and confeffed, affords an unanfwerable defence and vindication of the Proteftant churches.

This conclufion, that THE POPE IS ANTICHRIST, and that other, that THE SCRIPTURE IS THE SOLE RULE OF CHRISTIAN FAITH, were the *two* great principles, on which the Reformation was originally founded, How the *firft* of thefe principles came to be DISGRACED *among ourfelves*, I have fhewn in another dif-courfe [k]. It may now be worth while to obferve, in one word, through what fa tal mifmanagement the *latter* principle was even *generally* DISAVOWED and DESERTED.

[k] Sermon VIII.

When

When the Reformers had thrown off all
refpect for the Papal chair, and were for
regulating the faith of Chriftians by the
facred fcriptures, it ftill remained a queftion, *On what grounds, thofe fcriptures fhould
be interpreted.* The voice of the church,
fpeaking by her fchoolmen, and modern
doctors, was univerfally, and without
much ceremony, rejected. But the Fathers of the primitive church were ftill in
great repute among Proteftants themfelves;
who dreaded nothing fo much as the imputation of novelty, which they faw would
be faftened on their opinions, and who,
befides, thought it too prefuming to truft
entirely to the dictates of what was called
the private fpirit. The church of Rome
availed herfelf with dexterity, of this prejudice, and of the diftrefs to which the
Proteftant party was reduced by it. The
authority of thefe antient and venerable
interpreters was founded high by the Catholic writers; and the clamour was fo

E e 3 great

great and fo popular, that the Proteftants knew not how, confiftently with their own principles, or even in mere decency, to decline the appeal which was thus confidently made to that tribunal. The Reformers, too, piqued themfelves on their fuperior fkill in antient literature; and were afhamed to have it thought that their adverfaries could have any advantage againft them in a difpute, which was to be carried on in that quarter. Other confiderations had, perhaps, their weight with particular churches : But, for thefe reafons, chiefly, all of them forwardly clofed in with the propofal of trying their caufe at the bar of the antient church : And, thus, fhifting their ground, maintained henceforth, not that the fcriptures were the fole rule of faith, but the fcriptures, *as interpreted by the primitive fathers.*

When the ftate of the queftion was thus changed, it was eafy to fee what would be the iffue of fo much indifcretion. The difpute

pute was not only carried on in a dark and remote fcene, into which the people could not follow their learned champions; but was rendered infinitely tedious, and, indeed, interminable. For thofe early writings, now to be confidered as of the higheft authority, were voluminous in themfelves; and, what was worfe, were compofed in fo loofe, fo declamatory, and often in fo hyperbolical a ftrain, that no certain fenfe could be affixed to their doctrines, and any thing, or every thing, might, with fome plaufibility, be proved from them.

The inconvenience was fenfibly felt by the Proteftant world. And, after a prodigious wafte of induftry and erudition, a learned foreigner [J], at length, fhewed the inutility and the folly of purfuing the conteft any further. In a well-confidered difcourfe, *On the ufe of the Fathers,* he clearly evinced, that their authority was

[J] M. Daillé.

E e 4 much

much lefs, than was generally fuppofed,
in *all* points of religious controverfy ; and
that their judgement was efpecially in-
competent in *thofe* points, which were agitated by the two parties.   He evinced this
conclufion by a variety of unanfwerable
arguments; and chiefly by fhewing that
the matters in debate were, for the
moft part, fuch as had never entered
into the heads of thofe old writers, being,
indeed, of much later growth, and having
firft fprung up in the barbarous ages.
They could not, therefore, decide on
queftions, which they had no occafion to
confider, and had, in fact, never confidered ; however their carelefs or figurative expreffion might be made to look that way,
by the dextrous management of the contro-
verfialifts.

This difcovery had great effects.   It
opened the eyes of the more candid and
intelligent inquirers: And our incomparable Chillingworth,   with fome others [m],

[m] Lord Falkland, Lord Digby, Dr. Jer. Taylor, &c.

took

took the advantage of it to set the contro-
versy with the church of Rome, once more,
on its proper foot; and to establish, for
ever, the old principle, THAT THE BIBLE,
and that only, (interpreted by our best
reason) IS THE RELIGION OF PROTEST-
ANTS.

Thus, ONE of the two pillars, on which
the Protestant cause had been establish-
ed, was happily restored. And, though
Mr. Mede, about the same time, succeeded
as well in his attempts to replace the
OTHER, yet, through many concurring
prejudices, the merit of that service hath
not, hitherto, been so generally acknowledged. Whether *the Pope be the Antichrist
of the prophets,* is still by some Protestants
made a question. Yet, it seems as if it
would not continue very long to be so:
And it may not be too much to expect,
that this institution will, hereafter, conti-
bute to put an end to the dispute.

The Reformation will, then, be secured
against the two invidious charges of SCHISM
and

and HERESY (for *neither* of which is there
any ground, if *the Pope be Antichrift*, and
if *the fole Rule of faith to a Chriftian be the
canonical fcriptures*) and will, thus, ftand
immoveably on its antient and proper
foundations.

In faying this, I do not, however, mean
to affert, that the Reformation has no fupport, but in this principle—*that the Pope
is Antichrift.* There are various other confiderations, which are decifive in the controverfy between us and the Papifts. So
that, if the prophecies fhould, after all,
be found to fuit any other perfon or power,
better than the Roman Pontif, we fhall
only have one argument the lefs to urge
againft his pretenfions, and the Proteftant
caufe, in the mean time, ftands fecure.
But, on the fuppofition that the prophecies
are rightly, and muft be exclufively, applied to the church of Rome (of which
every man will judge for himfelf, from the
evidence hereafter to be laid before him)

on

on this fuppofition, I fay, it muft be allowed that the fhorteft and beft defence
of the Proteftant caufe is that which is
taken from the authority of thofe prophecies, becaufe they exprefsly enjoin a feparation from that fociety, to which they are
applied.

Ye perceive, then, in all views, the
utility of ftudying this prophecy of the
Revelations, provided there be reafon to
admit the completion of it in the hiftory
of the Chriftian Church, and particularly
in the hiftory of Papal Rome. The *importance* and the *truth* of Chriftianity will
be feen in their full light—The *wifdom* of
the divine councils, in *permitting the Apoftafy to take place for a time,* will be acknowledged—And the *honour* of our common
Proteftant profeffion will be effectually
maintained.

CON-

CONCLUSION.

SERM.
XII.
————

THIS LECTURE is now brought down to that point, from which, poffibly, ye expected me to fet out. But, in the entrance on an argument, new to many perfons, and mifunderftood by moft, it feemed expedient to take a wide compafs. The true *fcriptural idea* of the fubject, was to be opened, at large [n]; the *general argument* from prophecy, enforced [o]; the *method* of the prophetic fyftem deduced, and further illuftrated in a view of the prophecies more immediately refpecting the Chriftian church [p]; Of *thefe* prophecies, thofe concerning *Antichrift, or the apoftafy of Papal Rome*, were to be cleared of all prejudices and objections [q]; and the *principles*, on which the *Apocalyptic* prophecies, in particular, are to be explained, propofed and juftified [r]: It was, further, neceffary to

[n] Serm. I. II. III. [o] Serm. IV.
[p] Serm. V. VI. [q] Serm. VII. VIII. [r] Serm. IX. X,

befpeak

befpeak your attention to the *argument* from the Apocalyptic prophecies, efpecially, concerning Antichrift, by fhewing the feveral prefumptions there are of its *force* ; and by fetting before you the *ufes*, to which this whole inquiry may be applied.

This preliminary courfe, then, though it has been tedious, will not be thought improper, if it may ferve, in any degree, to prepare and facilitate the execution of the main defign, which is, *To interpret and apply particular prophecies*: A work, of labour indeed; but not unpleafant in itfelf; and (if carried on with that diligence and fobriety, which are, in reafon, to be fuppofed) capable, I think, of affording to fair and attentive minds the fulleft fatiffaction.

The SEASON, I know, may be thought unfavourable to fuch an attempt. For the main ftrefs muft be laid on prophecies, about which Chriftians themfelves are not

* Serm. XI.   ʈ Serm. XII.

agreed,

SERM.
XII.

agreed, at a time when the number of thofe perfons is fuppofed to be very great, and increafing every day, who are not eafily brought to acknowledge the reality of *any* prophecies.

This *laft* would be an unwelcome confideration, if the fact were certain; I mean, if the prefent ftate of religion were altogether fuch as fome, perhaps, wifh, and as others too eafily apprehend, it to be. But I hope, and believe, it is not; the truth of the cafe, fo far as I am able to form a judgement of it, being no more than this. A few fafhionable men make a noife in the world; and this clamour, being echoed on all fides from the fhallow circles of their admirers, mifleads the unwary into an opinion, that the irreligious fpirit is univerfal and uncontrolable. Whereas, the good and wife, are modeft and referved: having no doubt themfelves concerning the foundation of their faith, they pay but little regard to the cavils, which empty or corrupt men throw out againft it:

They

They either treat thofe cavils with a filent contempt; or, they lament in fecret the libertinifm of the age, without taking any vigorous meafures to check and oppofe it. Befides, they rarely come into what is called, *free company*; and they are too well employed, and at the fame time too well informed, to hearken after every idle publication, on the fide of irreligion.

For thefe, and the like reafons, the number of true believers is overlooked; or thought to be lefs confiderable than, in fact, it is, and would prefently be known to be, if a juft eftimate were taken of them.

Let me then, under this perfuafion, exprefs myfelf in the fpirit, and almoft in the words, of an antient apologift [n]—" Let " no man too haftily defpair of the caufe,

[n] Verum non eft defperandum. Fortaffe, *non canimus furdis.* Nec enim tam in malo ftatu res eft, ut defint fanæ mentes, quibus et veritas placeat, et monftratum fibi rectum iter et videant et fequantur.
Lactant. Div. Inft. l. v. *p.* 417. *ed. Sparke.*

" we

" we are now pleading. When we ſtand
" up in its defence, there are thoſe who
" will lend an ear to us. For, whatever
" the vain, or the vicious may pretend,
" the prophetic writings are not fallen ſo
" low in the eſteem of mankind, but that
" there are numberleſs perſons of good ſenſe
" and ſerious diſpoſitions, who wiſh to ſee
" the truth of the Goſpel confirmed by
" them ; and are ready to embrace that
" truth, when fairly ſet before them, and
" ſupported by the clear evidence of hiſto-
" rical teſtimony and well-interpreted
" ſcripture."

Such is the language, which I am not
afraid to hold to the deſponding party
among us. But ſhould my confidence, or
my candour, tranſport me too far, ſhould
even *their* apprehenſions be ever ſo well
founded, the zeal of thoſe, who preach
the Goſpel, is not to abate, but to exert
itſelf with new vigour under ſo diſcourag-
ing a profpect. If there be a way left to
ſtrike conviction into the hearts of unbelievers,

lievers, it muft, probably, be, by preffing
this great point of prophetic infpiration,
and by turning their attention on a *miracle*,
now wrought, or ready to be wrought
before their eyes. Or, let the event be
what it will, our duty is to illuftrate the
word of prophecy, and to enforce it; to
withftand the torrent of infidelity with
what fuccefs we may, and, if it fhould
prevail over all our efforts, to make full
proof, at leaft, of our fincerity and good
will.

In the mean time, it becomes all *others*
to retain and cultivate in themfelves a refpect for the prophetic writings; which
either are, or, for any thing that has yet
appeared, may be divine. To treat them,
without the fulleft conviction of their
falfhood, with neglect and fcorn, is plainly indecent, and may be highly criminal
and dangerous.

Jofephus tells us, that, in the laft dreadful ruin of his unhappy country-men, it

F f   was

was familiar with them, *to make a jeſt of divine things, and to deride, as ſo many ſenſe-leſs tales and juggling impoſtures, the ſacred oracles of their prophets* [w]; though they were then fulfilling before their eyes, and even upon themſelves.

But the caſe, perhaps, is different ; and *we* have no concern, in the prophecies concerning Papal Rome.

What! Have WE no concern in thoſe prophecies (ſuppoſing, I mean, that they are prophecies, at all, and, that there is reaſon for applying them to the church of Papal Rome) WE, who have but juſt been delivered from the more than Egyptian bondage, which they predict; and are, therefore, bound by every tye of intereſt, of gratitude, and of charity, to aſſert to ourſelves, and to communicate to others, as far as we are able, the bleſſings of *that*

---

[w] Ἐγελᾶτο δὲ τὰ θεῖα, κ᾽ τὰς τῶν προφήλῶν θεσμὰς, ὥσπερ ἀγυρίικὰς λογοποιίας, ἐχλεύαζον·

Fl. Joſeph. B. J. l. iv. 6.

liberty,

*liberty, wherewith Chriſt has made us
free* *. Have WE no concern in the ſeveral
uſes, mentioned in this diſcourſe ; and in
many others, which I have not mentioned ; it being well known, that *all inſpired
ſcripture* (of which prophecy is ſo eminent
a part) *is profitable for doctrine, for reproof,
for correction, for inſtruction in righteouſ-
neſs* *?

Or, ſuppoſing that we had no *direct* concern in theſe prophecies, and ſuppoſing,
farther, that the divine authority of them
was even *problematical* ; ſtill it may deſerve
to be conſidered, I mean, by men the moſt
libertine, who have not yet convinced themſelves, by an exact and critical inquiry, of
their utter falſhood and inſignificancy ; I
ſay, it merits the reflexion of all ſuch,
That the *contempt* of the prophecies, under
theſe circumſtances, has a natural tendency
to corrupt the temper and harden the heart.
And is there no room to queſtion, whe-

---

* Gal. v. 1.   * 2 Tim. iii. 16.

F f 2   ther

ther this conduct, plainly an *immoral* conduct, be adviseable or safe?

Let us then, on a principle of *self-love*,
if not of piety, *keep the sayings of this book*,
concerning THE MAN OF SIN. From
many appearances, the appointed time for
the full completion of them may not be
very remote. And it becomes our prudence to take heed that we be not found
in the number of those, to whom that
awful question is proposed — *How is it,
that ye do not discern the signs of this time?*

Nay, there are prophecies, which, in
that case, may concern us more nearly,
than we think. St. Paul applied ONE of
these, to the unbelieving Jews; of whose
mockery, and of whose fate, ye have
heared what their own historian witness-
eth: And, if *we* equal their obdurate
spirit, *that* prophecy may clearly be *applied*, and no man can say, that it was not
intended to be applied, to *ourselves*.

                              Beware

Beware therefore (to fum up all in the S E R M. tremendous words of the Apoſtle[z]) *Beware, left that come upon you, which is fpoken by the Prophets:* BEHOLD, YE DESPISERS, AND WONDER AND PERISH; FOR I WORK A WORK IN YOUR DAYS, A WORK, WHICH YE SHALL IN NO WISE UNDERSTAND, THOUGH A MAN DECLARE IT UNTO YOU.

SERM. XII.

[z] Acts xiii. 40, 41.

THE END.